"Despite its remarkable claims, including new re[...] yet heard of the New Apostolic Reformation (NAR). Christians need to know about this movement and its extreme claims. In their fair and eminently readable book Geivett and Pivec inform us all of the history, founders, beliefs, and goals of NAR. The authors make it clear that NAR is not to be confused with mainstream Pentecostals and charismatics. Rather, the NAR movement is a phenomenon of very distinctive characteristics. Geivett and Pivec expose the movement's dubious theological foundations and quirky understanding of Scripture, and warn of the harm to the church's witness it has caused and will likely continue to cause. All who care for the health of the church need to read this book."

—**Craig A. Evans,** Payzant Distinguished Professor of New Testament,
Acadia Divinity College, Canada

"Geivett and Pivec have done the global church a great service in writing this book! While affirming the proper place of divinely wrought signs and wonders in addition to the gift of prophecy in our day, they expose a good deal of questionable practices and flawed theology found within the New Apostolic Reformation. The book is biblically sound—as well as thoughtful, even-handed, and charitable."

—**Paul Copan,** Professor and Pledger Family Chair of Philosophy and Ethics,
Palm Beach Atlantic University

"*A New Apostolic Reformation?* is a well-written survey of the apostolic movements that have recently exploded around the world. It offers balanced biblical and historical insights that will be very helpful for scholars and laypersons alike. The authors draw very important distinctions between the teachings of the historic Pentecostal churches and the newer independent charismatic views of such leaders as C. Peter Wagner and others."

—**Vinson Synan,** Dean Emeritus, Regent University School of Divinity

"This is a thorough study and objective view of the New Apostolic Reformation. It is a necessary read for both traditional Pentecostals and those participating in NAR. We have needed this material for a long time."

—**Gary R. Allen,** Former Executive Editor, *Enrichment Journal;*
General Council of the Assemblies of God

"This is an important book, a one-stop shop for an explanation and biblical assessment of the so-called New Apostolic Reformation. Anyone interested in this global movement, whether sympathetic or critical, should read it. With their careful elucidation of NAR views and even-handed critique, Geivett and Pivec have pushed the discussion forward at a high level. This book provides a much-needed service to the church!"

—**James S. Spiegel,** Professor of Philosophy and Religion, Taylor University

"Every movement that claims to be of the Holy Spirit should welcome scrutiny. Geivett and Pivec are exemplary critics in their respectful tone and portrayal of those with whom they disagree. Advocates of the so-called New Apostolic Reformation are invited to reconsider if and how their beliefs and practices are aligned with Scripture even as those looking to better understand this global phenomenon more will come away much more informed and be ready to draw their own conclusions."

—**Amos Yong,** Professor of Theology and Mission;
Director of the Center for Missiological Research, Fuller Theological Seminary

"Leaders of apostolic networks hold a range of views, but some teachings of particular figures should be a matter of significant concern, not only to cessationists or even charismatics, but even to many who affirm or identify with apostolic movements in other ways, and to some of the figures' fellow apostles. This critique invites all of us, wherever we stand on that spectrum, and whether we agree with every detail or criticism, to recognize and challenge these errors. Serious errors exposed here include Manifested Sons doctrine, dominionism, extrabiblical 'inspired' doctrines that exalt individuals, inappropriate fixation on esoteric information about evil spirits, and certain 'apostles' calling people out of other denominations or movements to submit to their 'coverings.'"

—**Craig Keener,** Professor of New Testament, Asbury Theological Seminary

"Geivett and Pivec have produced an eye-opening exposé of a rapidly growing phenomenon. The New Apostolic Reformation is increasing its numbers at an alarming rate, and is something that must be addressed by the church today. The authors have offered a carefully documented, balanced, and fair treatment of the NAR. Their penetrating analysis of the claims of NAR is biblically and logically powerful, and at times even brilliant. If you're not yet familiar with this movement, you need to be—and you need to read this book!"

—**Daniel B. Wallace,** Professor of New Testament Studies,
Dallas Theological Seminary

"The authors have taken up the Herculean task of providing a panoramic view of a little-known movement and subjecting it to a biblical critique. They contend that at the heart of the NAR is a move to usher in a new church government in which designated apostles lead in tandem with prophets to reform church structures. This in turn will impact the secular order as the kingdom of God is brought to earth through programs designed by the apostles and prophets, such as training in the 'five-fold ministries' and the 'Seven Mountain Mandate.' Weaving together information from a wide array of primary sources published by various leaders, the authors provide a much-needed profile of the NAR, although admitting this general description is not a one size-fits-all. Much of their attention has been devoted to filtering select NAR beliefs through the prism of their biblical examination. The basic premises of apostolic church government (by those holding the offices of apostles and prophets) and empowered by 'miracle-working power' (believed to be 'activated' by the leaders) were judged to be in error. The authors' detailed assessment provides a significant introduction to a global movement, offering food for reflection and a base from which to continue the pursuit of a better understanding of NAR's growth and its impact on future Christianity."

—**Margaret M. Poloma,** Professor of Sociology Emeritus, The University of Akron

"The authors clearly, systematically describe the movement's origins and outworkings, and they offer a thoughtful, balanced, and biblical counterpoint to its many errors and excesses. Their work is desperately needed and long overdue."

—**Paul Carden,** Executive Director, The Centers for Apologetics Research (CFAR)

"I thank Geivett and Pivec for this meticulously footnoted book on the New Apostolic Reformation. They will be praised by some and vilified by others for writing it, but one will not, or should not, deny that they have done their homework in a careful and professional manner. Here is a plea to compare claims with Scripture in a civil manner, a practice I wholeheartedly commend for all Christians regardless of their theological positions. The apostle Paul commended the Bereans for checking to see if what he was teaching complemented or contradicted the Scripture. If the apostle to the Gentiles commended this action from his hearers in the first century, one would hope that leaders of the NAR movement would see this as a biblical and prudent response to their message in the twenty-first century."

—**Karl I. Payne,** Pastor of Leadership Development and Discipleship Training, Antioch Bible Church, Redmond, Washington; Chaplain, Seattle Seahawks

A NEW APOSTOLIC REFORMATION?

A Biblical Response to a Worldwide Movement

R. Douglas Geivett and Holly Pivec

LEXHAM PRESS

A New Apostolic Reformation? A Biblical Response to a Worldwide Movement
© 2014 by R. Douglas Geivett and Holly Pivec

Lexham Press, 1313 Commercial St., Bellingham, WA 98225
LexhamPress.com

First edition by Weaver Book Company

Print ISBN 9781683591740
Digital ISBN 9781683591757

Cover art: Mark Dobratz
Cover design: Frank Gutbrod
Editorial, design, and production:
    { In a Word } www.inawordbooks.com
    /edited by Rick Matt/

To the Church, the Bride of Christ

Contents

Preface

Frequently, I (Holly) am asked, "What spurred your interest in researching the New Apostolic Reformation movement?"

In 2003, I was managing editor of *Biola Magazine* at Biola University. In that capacity, I would receive correspondence from the magazine's readers. One day, a particular e-mail message piqued my interest. The message was from a former Biola student. She was concerned about a new religious movement of alleged apostles and prophets that had become influential in her city. She contacted the university hoping to find someone with a book responding to this movement's teachings. Since I had not heard of the movement she described, I could not have imagined then that, more than a decade later, I would be writing that book, along with my coauthor, Dr. Doug Geivett.

But my launch into researching the New Apostolic Reformation (NAR, pronounced NAHR) began that day with a Google search. I wanted to see if I could find any information about the movement she described. Was I surprised! My simple search yielded webpage after webpage of information, including sites for large organizations founded by NAR apostles and prophets, for NAR churches and conferences, and for countless books by or about NAR leaders. It was obvious that NAR was large and influential. How had I never heard of it?

After my initial foraging, I began to see signs of NAR's influence all around me, signs I had previously overlooked because I didn't have a framework for noticing or interpreting them. I realized I had friends who attended NAR churches. I discovered that prayer rallies held in stadiums in my city were sponsored by NAR organizations. And I recognized books on store shelves that were written by NAR apostles and prophets. Though I hadn't encountered NAR in my conservative evangelical circles, clearly many other people had.

Today, it is hard for me to fathom a time when I knew nothing about this movement. Hardly a day passes when I don't see its influence around me—whether I'm driving by a NAR church or spotting a NAR book at a friend's house. And that is not taking into account the correspondence I receive from all over the world from readers of my blog as they share their own experiences with this movement.

We wrote this book with two major goals in mind: first, to give people an idea of the sheer size and reach of NAR; and, second, to systematize NAR's key teachings and practices and evaluate them on the basis of Scripture and careful reasoning. Our other book on this subject, titled *God's Super-Apostles: Encountering the Worldwide Prophets and Apostles Movement*, is a basic introduction to NAR. In addition to being brief and non-technical, it also contains stories of individuals' personal experiences with this movement and practical advice for responding to its teachings.

Most of our research focuses on the views of NAR leaders from the United States because US apostles and prophets have produced a vast amount of literature. These leaders also exert great influence worldwide through their apostolic networks. An evaluation of their teachings, which can be documented on the basis of their writings, is a natural place to begin. We endeavored to conduct such evaluation by using the best sources—that is, the literature produced by the movement's most influential and widely recognized leaders. Whenever possible, we have used books to document key NAR teachings. However, due to NAR leaders' extensive use of the Internet to disseminate their teachings, we have also found it necessary to cite material from websites and blogs.

We wish to warn readers about a possible confusion: Some critics have linked NAR with mainstream Pentecostalism and charismatics. We do not do this. In fact, it's our contention that NAR deviates from classical Pentecostal and charismatic teachings. This movement has emerged out of independent charismatic churches and thus has gained a foothold in many of those churches in varying degrees. But we do not argue for cessationism, the view that the miraculous gifts listed in 1 Corinthians 12 are no longer active in the church. Whether the miraculous gifts are ongoing or not has no bearing on the arguments of our book.

To assist us in our goal of presenting a fair and balanced treatment of NAR, we developed the following set of criteria. We have used these criteria to filter our claims and to moderate the tone of our book.

1. We assume that leading NAR figures are believers and genuine disciples of Jesus, and that their intention is to do the will of God in their lives and in the world.
2. We believe that the Bible sets forth guidelines for church governance and cultural engagement.
3. We acknowledge that the Scriptures are not specific about all details concerning church governance and cultural engagement. Thus,

there is room for divergent expressions of the church's presence in the world.

4. However, we think that certain broad parameters, revealed in Scripture and practiced in the historical orthodox church, set limits on the kind of flexibility and creativity that are permissible.

5. In our judgment, the NAR perspective crosses these boundaries, and it does so in part because of flawed theology rooted in a flawed understanding of Scripture.

6. It is natural and proper for believers to publish their respective positions and air out their disagreements.

7. Critical analysis of any theological perspective must be charitable and gracious, even if resolute and confident. As with any other Christian activity done for the sake of Christ and his church, the work of critical assessment should exhibit the full range of moral and intellectual virtues, insofar as this is possible for manifestly fallible believers. We do not generally insist on a particular theological perspective among several that have been historically and broadly considered viable. For example, we evaluate the eschatological theology of NAR, noting its contribution to what is unique about the NAR perspective, but we do not insist on a particular option among the chief alternatives prominent in the history of the orthodox Christian faith and to a reasonable degree defensible from Scripture. This point can best be captured, perhaps, by noting that our book is not confessional in the sense of advocating for a particular confessional stance among long-standing alternatives. But our effort to resist undue advocacy does not preclude exposition of and argument for specific theological claims.

8. An implication is that our perspective is itself fallible, and probably mistaken at points. This is true despite our best efforts to interpret and apply the Scriptures accurately and wisely.

9. Critical assessment should resort chiefly to the Scriptures, held in common with NAR leaders to be the authoritative Word of God.

10. We are not psychologists or sociologists, and we do not attempt to explain NAR in terms that require special expertise in sociology or any other disciplines outside our own.

11. This means that our analysis is informed by our own disciplines in biblical studies, theology, Christian philosophy, and logic, as well as

our experience in church ministries of preaching and discipleship, and in personal faith in Jesus.

12. We allow that Christian experience has a legitimate role in forming our theological understanding, biblical interpretation, and spiritual practice. Theological perspectives that do not lay such heavy stress on personal and corporate experience, as with the kind that is so pronounced within NAR, may and should nevertheless appeal in responsible fashion to the lessons of experience.

13. We consider it an important part of any Christian leader's vocation to serve the church. A believer with the gifts of teaching and discernment is responsible for alerting the church to risky theology and practices that issue from it. But this must be done in an exemplary manner for the good of the whole body of Christ, including those with whom there is disagreement. Any assessment of another position must be even-handed and should not be needlessly sensationalist or provocative.

14. We are especially cautious about passing judgment on the character or intentions of those whose work we critique.

15. We emphasize that not all people affiliated with this movement hold to all the same beliefs. Because one leader in this movement promotes a particular teaching does not necessarily mean that all other leaders we have identified in this book also promote that particular teaching.

There's a reason for being explicit and candid about these guidelines. They undergird our desire to establish and maintain a cordial spirit of theological reflection and ministerial practice. We write with calm assurance that knowledge of God's truth is possible and that wisdom is attainable. An alarmist reaction to competing views is a disservice to the church. Dallas Willard says it well: "It is not knowledge, but nervous uncertainty, that makes people dogmatic, close-minded, and hostile—which spokespeople for Christ must never be."[1] We have no desire to be dogmatic or closed-minded, much less hostile. Where we disagree with claims made by NAR leaders, we offer evidence that can be examined and tested by anyone who truly desires to know God's truth and do God's will. And we welcome the opportunity to consider evidence that we have erred in anything we have written.

---

[1] Dallas Willard, *Knowing Christ Today: Why We Can Trust Spiritual Knowledge* (New York: HarperCollins, 2009), 201.

Acknowledgments

We wish to express appreciation to the many individuals who helped us, in various ways, to research, write, and produce this book. Of course, their assistance in no way implies that they fully agree with our conclusions. Several did contribute to our research for sure: Todd Johnson, Vinson Synan, Daniel Wallace, Patrick Johnstone, Gary Allen, Paul Carden, Rachel Tabachnick, Kevin Lewis, Clint Arnold, Robert Saucy, Gary McIntosh, Kenneth Berding, Frank Chan, Doug Birdsall, Gerry Breshears, Anton Hein, and Jackie Alnor. Others read the manuscript and made many helpful suggestions: Paul Copan, James Spiegel, Karl Payne, Peter Everett, Doug Wubbena, David Limbaugh, Edmound Teo, Alan Hultberg, and Craig Dorsheimer. Ron Rhodes and Norman Geisler encouraged us to press on.

We express heartfelt thanks to Jim Weaver at Weaver Book Company for seeing the value of this work and bringing his inspiration and expertise to bear on it. Emily Varner brought her marketing know-how and enthusiasm to our project and was a joy to work with, as was Alexander Bukovietski and his skilled production team, including our copyeditor, Rick Matt. We owe a special debt of gratitude to Mark Dobratz, the cover artist, and to Frank Gutbrod, the cover designer. A special thanks to John Muether and David Veldkamp for creating the indexes.

Holly would like to thank Doug Geivett for his partnership in this project. She also thanks the members of her church family at Bethel Church in Fairbanks, Alaska, for their support, including the pastors and their wives, Sherina Anderson, Cheryl Sackett, and her small group. Holly is grateful to her own supportive family, including her late father, Herb, who was one of her biggest encouragers. Her deepest gratitude is to her husband, Adam, for his patience, encouragement, and insightful critique of her thinking and writing.

Doug is grateful to Holly for the privilege of collaborating. Her insight, compassion, and writing skill have made their partnership in this project truly gratifying.

Abbreviations

ACPE	Apostolic Council of Prophetic Elders
AG	Assemblies of God
HIM	Harvest International Ministry
ICAL	International Coalition of Apostolic Leaders
IHOP	International House of Prayer
NAR	New Apostolic Reformation
YWAM	Youth With a Mission

1

What Is the New Apostolic Reformation?

> We are now living in the midst of one of the most epochal chang-
> es in the structure of the Church that has ever been recorded.
> I like to call it the "Second Apostolic Age."
>
> —C. Peter Wagner, *Apostles Today:*
> *Biblical Government for Biblical Power*

Many Christians in the United States go to their traditional churches every Sunday morning unaware of the existence of a reformation that has been underway since the 1980s—a religious movement that has radically transformed other churches throughout their city and the world. The movement is called the New Apostolic Reformation (NAR).[1] It's *apostolic* because its leaders claim they're restoring the lost office of apostle to the church—an office endowed with astonishing authority, miraculous powers, and divine strategies for establishing God's kingdom on earth. It's a *reformation* because proponents say the movement will completely change the way church is done, and its effects will be as great—or even greater than—the sixteenth-century Protestant Reformation.[2]

The biggest innovation of NAR is the belief that apostles, working together with prophets, must take over governance of the church—taking the reins from the pastors, elders, and denominational leaders—so that God's end-time plans can be fulfilled and Christ can return.[3] Churches that do not

---

[1]   It is also sometimes called the apostolic-prophetic movement. Throughout this book, we will use the acronym NAR (pronounced NAHR) as shorthand to refer to the New Apostolic Reformation.

[2]   C. Peter Wagner, *Changing Church* (Ventura, CA: Regal Books, 2004), 10.

[3]   Many NAR leaders, though not all, see the restoration of apostles as eschatologically significant. David Devenish does not make such claims, but rather simply sees "the need for the restoration of New Testament patterns of church life, in which the work of the apostle should arguably be a part." David Devenish, *Fathering*

submit to the authority of these present-day apostles and prophets will sit on the sidelines as mere spectators.

These are astounding claims. Belief in present-day prophets and apostles who are seen to be on a par with the Old Testament prophets and Christ's apostles was virtually unknown in Protestant Christianity until the 1980s and 1990s when the New Apostolic Reformation emerged.[4] NAR leaders say apostles and prophets were suppressed in the early centuries of Christianity, leaving the church powerless to complete the Great Commission and advance God's kingdom. But that's changing. In 2001, the NAR claims, the church entered what proponents refer to as the Second Apostolic Age. "For the first time this side of the initial few centuries of the Church, a critical mass of the Body of Christ once again recognizes the contemporary gifts and offices of apostle and prophet,"[5] declares NAR spokesman C. Peter Wagner, a former professor of church growth at Fuller Theological Seminary in Pasadena, California, and former presiding apostle over the International Coalition of Apostolic Leaders (ICAL), the world's largest network of apostles with about four hundred members.[6] With the biblical government of the church in place again, the apostles and prophets can raise up God's end-time army. This army will be invincible. Its troops will work miracles, prophesy, and help the apostles cast out high-ranking super-demons that presently rule over cities and nations. The NAR will also cash in on the "Great End-Time Transfer of Wealth," a divinely orchestrated redistribution of the world's wealth from the wicked to the righteous. The result of these awe-inspiring activities will be a global revival. More than a billion souls will be saved—more than at any other time in world history.

Leaders, Motivating Mission: Restoring the Role of the Apostle in Today's Church (Milton Keynes, UK: Authentic Media Limited, 2011), Kindle edition, chapter 1.

[4]   The Roman Catholic Church does not refer to its leaders as apostles or prophets. But the church does hold to a doctrine of apostolic succession, in which the teaching and pastoral authority of the bishops is held to be derived from Christ's original apostles. This longstanding doctrine bears no relation to NAR.

[5]   C. Peter Wagner, *Dominion! How Kingdom Action Can Change the World* (Grand Rapids: Chosen Books, 2008), 22.

[6]   "Connecting Apostles for Kingdom Advancement," Oslokirken, November 17, 2012; accessed February 20, 2014, http://www.oslochurch.org/maler/article/article/131282. In 2013, the International Coalition of Apostles was renamed the International Coalition of Apostolic Leaders.

Some prominent leaders in this movement claim that their followers will overcome sickness and death and execute God's judgments on earth by prophetically calling down the plagues described in the book of Revelation. And some teach that any Christians who oppose this movement are under the control of a powerful demon known as the spirit of religion.[7] Though these teachings will sound radical to Christians, they're sweeping through churches in the United States and throughout the world.

Yet not all churches that are part of this movement look the same. As with any other large, multi-faceted movement, participants in NAR hold to a spectrum of beliefs, accepting some NAR teachings and being unaware of or rejecting others. Indeed, many people taking part in NAR don't even realize it is a movement, let alone embrace all the radical teachings surrounding it. Furthermore, not all NAR leaders work together or agree on everything.

Since NAR is not an organization or denomination there is no official listing of NAR beliefs, leaders, or churches. But the one thing all participants in NAR share in common, in our view, is the controversial belief in the present-day *offices* of apostle and prophet. And as you'll see, those in the NAR have established numerous organizations and developed intentional networks with one another.

Not New Teachings

Though called the *New* Apostolic Reformation, the movement's teachings are not really new. Fringe groups attempting to restore the offices of apostle and prophet have been around for a long time. These have included the Irvingites of the 1830s and the Apostolic Church of the early 1900s. Apostles and prophets also surfaced in the African Independent Churches movement, which began around 1900.[8] Today, the Jehovah's Witnesses and Mormons (more technically the Church of Jesus Christ of Latter Day Saints)

---

[7] Wagner, *Changing Church*, 18–21.

[8] Wagner states that NAR's "deepest roots" are found in the African Independent Church Movement, which began around 1900. He believes other "significant connections" can be found in the Chinese House-Church movement, beginning around 1976, and the Latin American grassroots churches, which, he says, became prominent around 1980. See C. Peter Wagner, "The Doc Responds," *Ministry Today*, accessed December 19, 2013, http://ministrytodaymag.com/index.php/ministry-today-archives/152-fivefold-ministries/10011-the-doc-responds#sthash.WuwTab-NB.dpuf.

claim God continues to give them revelation through present-day apostles and/or prophets.

The most noteworthy attempt to restore apostles and prophets in North America, prior to NAR, was the post-World War II Latter Rain movement, also called the New Order of the Latter Rain.[9] The Latter Rain movement sprang out of a revival that broke out at a Pentecostal Bible school in 1948 in North Battleford, Saskatchewan, Canada. This revival quickly spread to the United States and elsewhere around the world. Thousands flocked to North Battleford to take part in the enthusiasm. Leaders in the movement—including William Branham, Franklin Hall, and George Warnock—taught the "manifested sons of God" doctrine, which held that people who received the new apostolic and prophetic revelations could attain a degree of immortality in this life, which would then empower them to usher in God's kingdom. Wagner writes, "The leaders of those movements [Latter Rain and similar movements] had great expectations that what they had started would reform the entire Church in their generation. But it didn't happen."[10]

The movement was summarily denounced by the leadership of the Pentecostal denominations. On September 13, 1949, the General Council of the Assemblies of God in the United States passed a resolution that led to the demise of the Latter Rain cause. The minutes of the council meeting noted that the motion was adopted after only a brief debate and by "an overwhelming majority" of members. It states:

> RESOLVED, That we disapprove of those extreme teachings and practices, which being unfounded Scripturally, serve only to break fellowship of like precious faith and tend to confusion and division among the members of the Body of Christ, and be it hereby known that this 23rd General Council disapproves of the so-called "New Order of the Latter Rain," to wit: . . .
>
> 2. The erroneous teaching that the Church is built on the foundation of present-day apostles and prophets.[11]

---

[9] The name Latter Rain is taken from language in Joel 2:23, where a reference to God sending "the latter rain" is seen as a symbolic prediction of an end-time revival led by the Holy Spirit.

[10] C. Peter Wagner, *Apostles Today: Biblical Government for Biblical Power* (Ventura, CA: Regal Books, 2006), 13.

[11] See the entry under "The New Order of the Latter Rain" in *Minutes of the Twenty-third General Council of the Assemblies of God, Convened at Seattle,*

Other Pentecostal denominations followed suit. Latter Rain teachings were relegated to the sidelines.

But these teachings resurfaced in the 1980s when many independent charismatic churches began to embrace the idea of present-day prophets. These churches were transfixed by the stories of men like Bob Jones, who claimed that when he was seven years old and walking on a dirt road in Arkansas, the archangel Gabriel appeared to him on a white horse and blew a double silver trumpet in his face. The angel also threw down an old bull skin mantle at Jones's feet, which Jones returned and picked up many years later—accepting the mantle of a "seer prophet."[12] Jones was part of a group that became known as the Kansas City Prophets, along with Paul Cain and John Paul Jackson. These men all became influential in a church called the Kansas City Fellowship in Kansas City, Missouri, pastored by Mike Bickle. The Kansas City Prophets were also given prominent platforms within the early Vineyard movement, under its founder John Wimber.[13]

But the Kansas City Prophets came under heavy fire after a 233-page report was released in 1990 by a local charismatic pastor named Ernest Gruen. Gruen claimed to document aberrant teachings of these prophets, and his report—which was circulated widely—had significant reverberations in the young prophetic movement.[14] Following the report, Wimber found Bickle's

---

Washington, September 9–14, 1949: With Constitution and Bylaws, Revised (Springfield, MO: General Council of the Assemblies of God, 1949), 26. Available online from Flower Pentecostal Heritage Center, accessed September 1, 2014, http://ifphc. org/DigitalPublications/USA/Assemblies%20of%20God%20USA/Minutes%20 General%20Council/Unregistered/1949/FPHC/1949.pdf.

[12] Jennifer LeClaire, "Prophet Bob Jones Passes Away," *Charisma News.* February 14, 2014; accessed June 15, 2014, http://www.charismanews.com/us/42794-prophet-bob-jones-passes-away.

[13] Bill Jackson, *The Quest for the Radical Middle: A History of the Vineyard* (Cape Town, South Africa: Vineyard International Publishing, 1999), Kindle edition, chapter 12.

[14] Gruen, *Documentation of the Aberrant Practices and Teachings of Kansas City Fellowship (Grace Ministries)* (Shawnee, KS: Full Faith Church of Love, 1990); available online from Banner Ministries, accessed June 29, 2014, http://www.banner.org. uk/kcp/Abberent%20Practises.pdf . A report circulated on the Internet that Gruen later retracted his document, yet Gruen denied this report. See Gruen, *Thoughts*

church guilty of making errors in its oversight of the prophets, including failure to provide adequate accountability for their prophecies. The church was also faulted for allowing some of these prophets to establish doctrine based on their prophetic words.[15] Later, at a Vineyard pastor's conference in 1995, Wimber apologized for leading the Vineyard into the prophetic movement.[16] And Bickle—who went on to found the International House of Prayer (IHOP) in Kansas City, Missouri—acknowledged that, during this time, he made "many mistakes."[17]

Yet Bickle and others associated with the Kansas City Prophets went on to become leaders in what is now known as NAR. And in the 1990s, a number of independent charismatic churches started to form into networks under similar apostles. By 2001, such a significant number of churches accepted or approved apostles that Wagner felt confident marking it as the beginning of the "Second Apostolic Age."[18]

During these early years of the movement, Wagner coined the name "New Apostolic Reformation."[19] This name took hold and is now used widely as a general term for the movement examined in this book. However, while this designation suggests a largely new development, Wagner and many other NAR leaders freely admit that their key teachings are similar to those that defined the Latter Rain movement and had largely been repudiated. They think that the problem with the Latter Rain movement was not its key teachings, but rather denominational leaders who rejected those teachings

---

and Ponderings, blog post for February 2, 2008; accessed May 5, 2014, http://apollos. wordpress.com/2008/02/02/ernie-gruen/.

[15] Jackson, *Quest for the Radical Middle*, chapter 13. During the controversy surrounding Gruen's report, Wimber announced that the Kansas City Fellowship was going to become part of the Association of Vineyard Churches and come under Wimber's oversight. Bickle's church withdrew from the association in 1996. Jackson, *Quest for the Radical Middle*, chapter 19.

[16] Ibid.

[17] Mike Bickle, *Growing in the Prophetic: A Practical, Biblical Guide to Dreams, Visions, and Spiritual Gifts*, rev. ed. (Lake Mary, FL: Charisma House, 2008), 10; available online at Mike Bickle.org, http://mikebickle.org/books.

[18] Wagner, *Changing Church*, 12.

[19] C. Peter Wagner, *Wrestling with Alligators, Prophets and Theologians: Lessons from a Lifetime in the Church—A Memoir* (Ventura, CA: Regal Books, 2010), 213.

out of a desire to protect the *status quo*; that is, the problem was linked to the leaders' doctrine of democratic church government.[20] Wagner expresses warm regard for the leaders of the Latter Rain movement. He writes: "Let's also take off our hats to the Christian leaders of 50 years ago! They were true pioneers who began to shape the new wineskins that we are blessed with today in the Body of Christ."[21]

Not all NAR leaders link themselves to the Latter Rain movement. Bickle, for example, distances himself from Latter Rain teachings in a statement on the IHOP website that appears under the heading "The Latter Rain."

> We affirm that the Church will experience the greatest outpouring of the Spirit in history before Jesus returns (Joel 2:28–32). This outpouring will result in a great ingathering of souls and a renewing of the Church so that believers will walk in godliness as declared in the Sermon on the Mount (Matt. 5:1–7:28). We affirm the presence of the fivefold ministry for the equipping of the saints (Eph. 4:11–13).
>
> We deny the distinctive doctrines that go beyond Scripture that are often associated with the Latter Rain theology that was popularized in the 1950s.
>
> Explanation: Some have wrongly identified our ministry today with the false teachings that were popularized by some in the Latter Rain movement. At no time in the past did we have any relationship with this movement.[22]

Understandably, website visitors reading this statement will be confused, since IHOP does appear to embrace key Latter Rain teachings, including the restoration of the offices of apostle and prophet.[23]

---

[20] Wagner, *Changing Church*, 30.

[21] Wagner, *Apostles Today*, 14.

[22] Ernest Gruen and Mike Bickle, "Affirmations and Denials: Ernie Gruen and Mike Bickle's Joint Statement from 1993," May 16, 1993; available online from International House of Prayer, accessed June 18, 2014, http://www.ihopkc.org/about/affirmations-and-denials.

[23] That Bickle's belief is "consistent with the restorationist thesis that began in the Latter Rain" has been noted by other researchers. See Jackson, *Quest for the Radical Middle*, chapter 11.

THE FUTURE OF NAR

The short life of the Latter Rain movement raises the question: Will NAR also fizzle out or will it last?

It appears that it will last, in spite of continuing opposition from Pentecostal denominations. NAR already has outdistanced the Latter Rain movement, and it shows no signs of decline. Whereas the Latter Rain revival lasted only a few years, NAR has been around for more than thirty years—since the 1980s, when the office of prophet began to be restored. NAR teachings have gained enough momentum for an entire generation of young people to be raised in churches that promote them. For these people, NAR teachings are at the heart of Christianity.

NAR has gained so much momentum that its community now has its own Bible version, The Passion Translation, produced by the apostle Brian Simmons of Stairway Ministries (Wichita, Kansas).[24] Simmons claims that Christ visited him and commissioned him personally to make this new translation of the Bible, which has been endorsed by leading apostles and prophets and received enthusiastically by their followers.[25] Now they can support NAR teachings by pointing to chapter and verse, further strengthening the impression that NAR enjoys explicit biblical support.

Other signs that NAR will be an enduring presence in global Christianity include the massive size of the movement and its growing political influence. In chapter 2 we examine these two indicators.

SUMMARY

NAR has led a reformation among churches worldwide by restoring the governing offices of apostle and prophet. NAR is not the first movement to attempt the restoration of apostles and prophets. But unlike previous and short-lived movements, NAR has proved to be remarkably enduring and influential, as our next chapter will show.

---

[24]   The Passion Translation is published by 5 Fold Media, www.5foldmedia.com.

[25]   Brian Simmons, "Song of Solomon, Part 1," from *Passion for Jesus Conference*, YouTube video, 51:29, posted by "HealingWaters," February 19, 2012; accessed June 18, 2014, https://www.youtube.com/watch?v=H8pmNZnlzIA.

2

Massive Size and Growing Political Influence

> It is important to know up front that this is a massive movement,
> recognized widely by sociologists of religion, by church histori-
> ans and by other scholars as well.
>
> —C. Peter Wagner, *Dominion! How Kingdom Action Can*
> *Change the World*

Signs that NAR is here to stay include the massive size of the movement
and its growing political influence. We now examine these two indicators
in some detail.

A MASSIVE MOVEMENT

Unlike the Latter Rain movement, which was concentrated in revival hot
spots and so had only a limited number of participants, NAR is worldwide
in scope, with millions of participants. A movement of such size is not going
away soon. NAR accounts for much of the phenomenal growth of Christianity taking place in the Global South—Africa, Asia, and Latin America.
It's part of the fastest-growing segment of non-Catholic Christianity worldwide, a segment researchers call the Independent, or Postdenominational
segment, with more than 369 million participants.[1] Only the Protestant segment is slightly larger. At its current rate of growth, researchers expect that
NAR/Independent churches will soon overtake even the Protestants.

Leaders of many of the world's largest and fastest-growing churches promote present-day apostles and prophets, including E. A. Adeboye of Redeemed Christian Church of God in Nigeria (more than five million people)
and Embassy of the Blessed Kingdom of God for All Nations in Ukraine
(twenty thousand people). Redeemed Christian Church of God in Nigeria
is so large that its pastor, E. A. Adeboye—thought to be a prophet by his
followers—was named one of the fifty most powerful people in the world by

---

[1] Todd M. Johnson and Kenneth R. Ross, eds., *Atlas of Global Christianity* (Edinburgh: Edinburgh University Press, 2009), 78–79.

Newsweek magazine.[2] And César Castellanos, pastor of the largest church in South America—International Charismatic Mission in Bogotá, Columbia (250,000 members)—was named one of five apostles now "transforming their nations for Christ" by *Ministry Today* magazine.[3] Pastor David Yonggi Cho, the founder of Yoido Full Gospel Church in South Korea (one million people), endorsed an influential book promoting present-day apostles, declaring "God is restoring the powerful ministry of the apostle to His end-time Church."[4]

In the United States, NAR churches can be found in almost every city and town, from Santa Rosa Beach, Florida, to North Pole, Alaska. These churches are not always identifiable by their formal statements of faith, since their statements are frequently indistinguishable from those of more traditional churches. But they often can be identified by their use of the term *fivefold ministry*, which, as used in NAR, refers to the belief that God has given the church five continuing governmental offices: apostle, prophet, evangelist, pastor, and teacher.[5]

Many of these NAR churches are part of self-identified apostolic networks of churches and ministries that have banded together under the leadership of a single apostle or group of apostles. One very large apostolic network that claims to encompass more than 20,000 churches in 50 nations is called

[2]   Lisa Miller, "The *Newsweek* 50: E. A. Adeboye," *Newsweek*, December 19, 2008; accessed December 20, 2013, http://www.newsweek.com/newsweek-50-e-adeboye-83039.

[3]   Matthew Green, "Apostles among Us," *Ministry Today* (Nov./Dec. 2004); accessed February 20, 2014, http://ministrytodaymag.com/index.php/ministry-today-archives/163-fivefold-ministries-focus/9982-apostles-among-us.

[4]   David Cannistraci, *Apostles and the Emerging Apostolic Movement: A Biblical Look at Apostleship and How God is Using it to Bless His Church Today* (Ventura, CA: Renew Books, 1996).

[5]   We note that the term *fivefold ministry* is used outside of NAR—often by Pentecostal Christians—to refer to the belief that God has given some people the "spiritual gifts" (not church offices) of apostle, prophet, evangelist, pastor, and teacher. In addition, some people who identify with the missional church movement, such as Alan Hirsch, advocate a type of fivefold ministry. But Hirsch states that he does not share the NAR ideology and agenda. See Alan Hirsch, Letter to the editor, *Books and Culture* (September/October 2012), accessed December 20, 2013, http://www.booksandculture.com/articles/2012/sepoct/letters-so12.html.

Harvest International Ministry (HIM), operating under the leadership of the apostle Ché Ahn, senior pastor of HRock Church in Pasadena, California. Other influential apostolic networks include the Apostolic Network of Global Awakening (under the apostle Randy Clark) and MorningStar Fellowship of Churches (under the apostle Rick Joyner). Many churches, however, have joined much smaller networks, some consisting of perhaps a dozen churches.

In addition to NAR churches that are governed directly by apostles and prophets, a substantial number of churches in the Pentecostal denominations (such as the Assemblies of God, the Foursquare Church, and the International Pentecostal Holiness Church) and independent charismatic churches[6] have been influenced, in varying degrees, by these same apostles and prophets. Though the Assemblies of God and other Pentecostal denominations officially disassociate themselves from key NAR teachings, many of their churches—which have considerable freedom to govern themselves—have in fact embraced those teachings. This can be seen in their promotion of NAR teachings from the pulpit and their frequent invitation of NAR apostles and prophets to speak in their churches. Pentecostal churches are free to remain in their denominations while also formally associating with apostolic networks. HIM, a NAR organization, offers three levels of association with its apostolic network, including a level known as HIM Friends for churches and ministries that are affiliated with denominations.

People from many Pentecostal and independent charismatic churches attend NAR revivals (like the 2008 Lakeland Revival, in Lakeland, Florida, led by the prophet Todd Bentley), buy NAR books (like the bestselling *Final Quest*, authored by apostle and prophet Rick Joyner), and watch GOD TV (the first NAR television network, broadcast by satellite throughout the world). And what is learned through these and other channels is shared in Sunday school classes and Bible studies. At one independent charismatic megachurch—New Life Church in Colorado Springs, Colorado—NAR teachings are promoted through smaller group studies based on the teaching materials of NAR apostles and prophets like Bill Johnson, Randy Clark, and Doug Addison.[7] In these ways, apostles and prophets have entered through the back doors of many churches that don't formally embrace them.

------

[6] Independent charismatic churches are "independent" in that they do not hold formal membership in any denomination.

[7] "Prophetic Evangelism: Radical Faith for Miracles, Salvation, Daytime," class taught by Virginia Stehlik at New Life Church, Colorado Springs, Colorado, May 22,

NAR teachings have also reached into churches typically seen as outside the Pentecostal-charismatic stream of Christianity. For example, an article in *Perspectives: A Journal of Reformed Thought* reports a "prevalence" of NAR beliefs in new church starts of the Reformed Church in America (RCA) and that NAR apostles hold "key" leadership positions in the denomination. The article also states, "Pamphlets filled with NAR theology and resources were distributed at a major RCA conclave. At one time, nearly all the church multiplication resources on the RCA website were from Wagner and his followers. Although many of these resources have since been taken down, NAR influence on the RCA church multiplication webpage is still unmistakable."[8]

But NAR has been most influential within Pentecostal and charismatic churches. Evidence of this is the appointment of NAR apostles and prophets—including Bill Johnson and Cindy Jacobs—to the leadership of Empowered 21, an initiative focused on shaping the future of the Pentecostal-charismatic movement.

Counting all Pentecostal, Charismatic, and Neocharismatic Christians,[9] the total number of people in the United States who likely have come into significant contact with NAR teachings totals over 66 million.[10] Of these people, Neocharismatics—those attending charismatic churches that are

---

2013–August 27, 2014; accessed June 6, 2014. http://www.newlifechurch.org/group.jsp?ID=550.

[8] Steve *Mathonnet-VanderWell*, "The RCA and the NAR," *Perspectives: A Journal of Reformed Thought* (August/September 2012); accessed February 20, 2014, http://www.rca.org/perspectives-as-we-see-it-the-rca-and-nar.

[9] "Pentecostal" Christians, as defined by the World Christian Database, are church members affiliated with a classical Pentecostal denomination, such as the Assemblies of God. "Charismatic" Christians are baptized members affiliated with non-Pentecostal, mainline denominations who have had "the experience of being filled with the Holy Spirit." And "Neocharismatic" Christians are part of the Pentecostal/Charismatic Renewal, but are not affiliated with any denomination. Instead, they see themselves as "Independent," "Postdenominationalist" and "Neo-Apostolic." See Todd M. Johnson, ed., *World Christian Database* (Leiden/Boston: Brill, 2007), accessed September 1, 2014, www.worldchristiandatabase.org.

[10] Ibid., accessed December 15, 2013. This number includes all "Christian Renewalists" (Pentecostal, Charismatic, and Neocharismatic Christians) in the United States.

not affiliated with any denominations and who have been influenced the most by NAR—total close to 36 million.[11] And of the Neocharismatics, an estimated three million attend NAR churches that are a part of apostolic networks and overtly embrace the NAR vision.[12]

A Growing Political Force

The Latter Rain movement—so short-lived and quickly marginalized—had no significant impact on the surrounding culture. But NAR apostles and prophets have built up extensive databases of followers through their self-styled apostolic networks and prayer networks. And, because of their perceived spiritual authority, these leaders exert considerable influence on the local and national voting practices of their followers. They publish voter prayer guides and distribute them through their networks. One example is a guide—published by the United States Reformation Prayer Network (US-RPN) under prophet Cindy Jacobs—that opposed California labor unions before the 2012 election.[13] NAR leaders have thus emerged as a political force. And secular organizations have sounded an alarm.

Before explaining the concerns of these secular organizations, we want to be clear about our reasons for doing so. By drawing attention to these sources, we do not necessarily mean to imply agreement with their portrayals of NAR. We offer our own evaluation of the movement's teachings in this book. Also, we should note that we did not depend solely on these secular sources for understanding the views of NAR leaders, but instead went directly to the writings of the NAR leaders themselves—the best source for understanding their views. Nevertheless, our purpose in citing these other sources is to show how NAR is perceived by them to be a significant force, rather than merely a fringe movement. And while we don't share the same

---

[11]   Ibid.

[12]   Todd Johnson of the Center for the Study of Global Christianity at Gordon-Conwell Theological Seminary provided this estimate in a personal communication with one of the authors. Johnson said that, in addition to those three million people who attend NAR churches, there likely are more people whose churches are not part of apostolic networks yet are sympathetic to the NAR vision.

[13]   Rachel Tabachnick, "New Apostolic Prayer Guide Attacks California Labor Unions, Prepares for Election 2012," Talk to Action, March 2012; accessed December 17, 2013, http://www.talk2action.org/story/2012/3/1/13944/32151.

general outlook as the secularist critics, we do note that some of them have been careful to document their allegations.

NAR first caught attention during the 2012 US presidential election. Media outlets observed that NAR leaders helped organize a high-profile prayer-and-fasting event featuring Texas governor Rick Perry, who was expected to run for president. The event, called The Response, was billed as broadly representing the views of evangelicals. And many evangelicals took part, unaware of NAR leadership in organizing this event.

Yet not everyone was unaware. Several major media organizations—including CNN, MSNBC, National Public Radio, Voice of America, and *Time* magazine—reported on the NAR organizers behind the event, including the apostle Doug Stringer, of Somebody Cares International, and the prophet Lou Engle and other senior staff members from IHOP. These media featured exposés on NAR in the lead-up to the election. And liberal pundits hosted by these media cautioned about the growing influence of a Christian dominionist agenda on American policy.

A liberal blog called *Talk to Action*—which reports on what it calls "the rise of the dominionist movement in the Unites States" and "encroaching theocracy"—also produced a YouTube mini-documentary titled "Sarah Palin's Crazy Church." The video, which went viral before YouTube pulled it,[14] alleged NAR ties to Wasilla Assembly of God Church in Alaska, the long-time church of Alaska's then governor Sarah Palin. The video traced links between Palin's former church and MorningStar Ministries, founded by Rick Joyner, an outspoken dominionist. Though not shown in the video, Joyner has prophesied that God is raising up an "elite Delta force," that is, a "spiritual special forces" unit made up of apostles and prophets who are presently being prepared in various places throughout the world to advance God's earthly kingdom.[15]

And the *Business Insider* observed that NAR leaders, in their quest for political influence, have managed to enter the circles of prominent evangelicals. The article states: "As mainstream evangelical influence wanes, however, the New Apostolic Reformation is gaining broader acceptance among

---

[14]   *Talk to Action* features a link to the video on Vimeo.com. See Bruce Wilson, "YouTube Censors Viral Video Documentary on Palin's Churches," *Talk to Action*, September 13, 2008; accessed February 24, 2014.

[15]   Rick Joyner, *The Apostolic Ministry* (Wilkesboro, NC: MorningStar Publications, 2004), 168–184.

conservative Christians. The Response, whose endorsers also include more mainstream fundamentalists, is evidence of the New Apostles' emerging influence—and of its leaders growing appetite for political power."[16]

The *Business Insider* article also reported that the prophet Lou Engle "prayed over" former House Speaker Newt Gingrich at a 2009 Virginia rally called "Rediscovering God in America." The article's author could not have known then that in 2012, Gingrich would appear to form an even closer association with another NAR leader, Dutch Sheets, whom Gingrich appointed to sit on his Faith Leaders Coalition.[17]

Besides The Response, other high-profile events featuring apostles and prophets alongside leaders of the Religious Right included:

- A forty-day prayer and fasting initiative for Christians called Pray and Act, held prior to the 2010 mid-term election.
- The Awakening, an annual conference sponsored by the Freedom Federation, which brings together Christians with shared moral values to "fight for the soul of America."
- The Call assemblies of Christian young adults—focused on prayer, worship, and fasting—held in major cities throughout the United States, the first of which, held on September 2, 2000, at the National Mall in Washington, DC, reportedly drew 400,000 people.
- The Day of Prayer for the Peace of Jerusalem, an initiative held on the first Sunday of every October—claiming hundreds of thousands of participants—co-chaired by Jack Hayford, pastor emeritus of The Church on the Way in Van Nuys, California, and Robert Stearns, founder of Eagles' Wings in Clarence, New York.

In addition to NAR leaders—including Cindy Jacobs, Ché Ahn, Mike Bickle, Lou Engle, and Rick Joyner—many notable individuals, some even with national influence at the governmental level, have participated in these

---

[16] Grace Wyler, "Meet the Radical Evangelical Army Behind Rick Perry," *Business Insider,* July 21, 2011; accessed December 17, 2013, http://www.businessinsider.com/rick-perry-the-evangelicals-behind-the-response-2011-7-21?op=1#ixzz2nlgGO600.

[17] Brian Tashman, "Newt Gingrich Names 'Apostle' Dutch Sheets to His Faith Leaders Coalition," Right Wing Watch, January 26, 2012; accessed December 17, 2013, http://www.rightwingwatch.org/content/newt-gingrich-names-apostle-dutch-sheets-his-faith-leaders-coalition.

events. By identifying such individuals, we're not suggesting that they all share in the outlook of NAR leaders. On the contrary, we emphasize that many of them are friends and allies in Christian ministry who would likely disagree with some of the express tenets and practices of NAR. Nevertheless, their participation in events alongside NAR leaders demonstrates how influential some NAR leaders have become—they naturally welcome the perception that common cause on some issues indicates that they are in the mainstream among evangelicals and other prominent leaders who have not affirmed NAR tenets. Prominent figures who have participated in NAR events include:

- David Barton of WallBuilders[18]
- Sam Brownback, former US Senator of Kansas[19]
- Charles Colson of Prison Fellowship[20]
- James Dobson of Focus on the Family[21]
- Steve Douglass of Campus Crusade for Christ[22]
- Father Joseph Fessio of Ignatius Press[23]
- Maggie Gallagher of the National Organization for Marriage[24]
- Jim Garlow of Renewing American Leadership[25]

---

[18] Kevin Shorter, "Call to Pray and Act by Chuck Colson and Jim Garlow," *Prayer Coach*, September 20, 2010; accessed June 6, 2014, http://prayer-coach. com/2010/09/20/call-to-pray-and-act-by-chuck-colson-and-jim-garlow/.

[19] "The Call Nashville: Senator Brownback," YouTube video, 7:58, posted by "XSTATICMOM," July 18, 2007; accessed February 24, 2014, http://www.youtube. com/watch?v=is0KfyriSfA.

[20] Shorter, "Call to Pray and Act."

[21] "The Call San Diego: Dr. James Dobson," YouTube video, 4:37, posted by "kdarpa," November 3, 2008; accessed June 6, 2014, https://www.youtube.com/watch?v=7NuwK18b6KI.

[22] Scott Tompkins, "California Event Mobilizes New Missions Partners," *Resonate News*, accessed June 6, 2014, http://www.resonatenews.com/home/news-headlines/331; "Video: Steve Douglas [*sic*], 'Join the Movement,'" Call2All, May 1, 2011; accessed June 6, 2014, http://www.call2all.org/Articles/1000103667/call2all/About/E_zine_Archive/2011_Archive/0501_Video_Steve.aspx#.U5IpHSghXNt.

[23] Shorter, "Call to Pray and Act."

[24] Ibid.

[25] Ibid.

- Mike Huckabee, former governor of Arkansas and Republican presidential candidate[26]
- Andrea Lafferty of the Traditional Values Coalition[27]
- Richard Land of the Southern Baptist Convention's Ethics and Religious Liberty Commission[28]
- Bishop Richard Malone, eleventh Bishop of Portland, Maine[29]
- Penny Nance of Concerned Women for America[30]
- Tony Perkins of the Family Research Council[31]
- Rick Scarborough of Vision America[32]
- Alan Sears of the Alliance Defense Fund[33]
- Tim Wildmon of the American Family Association[34]

Another sign of NAR's emerging political influence is the creation of the Freedom Federation in 2009. This coalition of "faith-based and policy organizations" is an eclectic mixture of mainstream organizations—like Concerned Women for America, the National Hispanic Christian Leadership Conference, the Traditional Values Coalition, the Family Research Council Action, and the American Association of Christian Counselors—together with overtly NAR organizations, such as Generals International, The Call, Harvest International Ministry, and MorningStar Ministries.[35]

---

[26]   Ibid.

[27]   "The Awakening Schedule: April 15–16, 2010," Freedom Federation, accessed June 6, 2014, http://freedomfederation.org/content/schedule.

[28]   "The Awakening 2012 Speakers, Page 2" Freedom Federation, accessed June 6, 2014, http://freedomfederation.org//content/awakening_2012_speakers2.

[29]   Shorter, "Call to Pray and Act."

[30]   Ibid.

[31]   Ibid.

[32]   "The Awakening 2012 Speakers," Freedom Federation, accessed June 6, 2014, http://freedomfederation.org/content/awakening_2012_speakers.

[33]   Shorter, "Call to Pray and Act."

[34]   Ibid.

[35]   See the pages "About the Freedom Federation" and "Members" on the website of the Freedom Federation, accessed February 25, 2014, http://freedomfederation.org.

The Oak Initiative, led by NAR apostle Rick Joyner, is another politically active organization, founded in 2009, that has been monitored closely by NAR's secular critics. This initiative seeks to bring about a spiritual awakening in America by mobilizing Christian leaders to work in every level of government. Its website claims that, within months of its founding, the organization had developed a presence in all fifty states and more than fifty nations, with new chapters forming rapidly.[36]

Among the past leadership of the Oak Initiative is Samuel Rodriguez, the head of the National Hispanic Christian Leadership Conference, who helped found the initiative, served as its vice president, and served on its board until stepping down in 2011. One NAR critic speculated that Rodriguez's resignation may have been "damage control" to distance himself from a NAR extremist agenda.[37] This may or may not be the reason for Rodriguez's resignation, but such speculation does reflect the perception that NAR is controversial and something to be troubled about.

Critics of NAR are also concerned about the growing political influence of NAR leaders outside of the United States. A blogger for *The Huffington Post* reported that, in Uganda, the prophet Lou Engle publicly promoted anti-homosexuality legislation—the so-called Kill the Gays bill that called for tougher sanctions against homosexuality.[38]

SUMMARY

Two signs that NAR will be an enduring presence in global Christianity are the massive size of the movement and its growing political influence in the United States and beyond. In the next chapter we look at specific efforts that NAR leaders have made in order to mainstream NAR.

---

[36] "Our Purpose," The Oak Initiative, accessed February 25, 2014, http://www.theoakinitiative.org/our-purpose#.UwzvqoV6V8o.

[37] Rachel Tabachnick, "Oak Initiative Confirms Resignation of Co-Founder and Vice President Samuel Rodriguez," *Talk to Action*, September 21, 2011; accessed December 17, 2013, http://www.talk2action.org/story/2011/9/21/01935/7353.

[38] Waymon Hudson, "American Evangelical Lou Engle Promotes 'Kill the Gays' Bill at Sunday's Rally in Uganda," *The Huffington Post*, May 4, 2010; accessed December 11, 2012, http://www.huffingtonpost.com/waymon-hudson/american-evangelical-lou_b_560819.html.

3

Mainstreaming the New Apostolic Reformation

> We are not talking about something on the fringes, but about a
> dynamic movement at the very heart of 21st-century Christianity.
>
> —C. Peter Wagner, *Dominion! How Kingdom Action Can*
> *Change the World*

NAR leaders have begun to mainstream their movement within the larger
Christian world in a number of specific ways. These efforts include:

- partnering with Christian media,
- using the Internet to disseminate NAR teachings,
- making inroads into academia,
- increasing their network with influential evangelicals, and
- focusing on training youth.

NAR AND CHRISTIAN MEDIA

NAR leaders have become a significant voice by partnering with Christian media. For example, Charisma Media, a Pentecostal-charismatic publishing empire, has actively promoted NAR teachings through its large book
publishing company, Charisma House, and its flagship publication, *Charisma* magazine. The magazine regularly features articles by and about NAR
apostles and prophets and even publishes their prophecies. Both the magazine's publisher, Stephen Strang, and its former editor in chief, J. Lee Grady,[1]
are previous apostles in the International Coalition of Apostolic Leaders.[2]

Charisma Media also helped promote NAR teachings when it—and one
of its publications, *Ministries Today* magazine—convened a consultation

---

[1]   Grady is now a contributing editor for the magazine.

[2]   See the 2007 membership list in the collection maintained by Talk to Action,
"International Coalition of Apostles Membership Lists," *Talk to Action,* September 3,
2011; accessed June 6, 2014, http://www.talk2action.org/story/2011/9/3/9571/00192.

held in Orlando, Florida, January 6–7, 2004, to explore issues related to the "fivefold ministry."[3] This event drew more than fifty high-profile charismatic, Pentecostal, and NAR leaders, including Jack Hayford (the event moderator), Ted Haggard, R. T. Kendall, Reinhard Bonnke, Myles Munroe, C. Peter Wagner, Rod Parsley, and Joyce Meyer.[4] At the end of the symposium, the leaders produced a document called the "Orlando Statement." While the document focused on issues of ministry accountability and morality in the Pentecostal-charismatic movement, it also affirmed the validity of the present-day offices of apostle and prophet and the use of those titles.[5] Hayford called the document a "watershed moment," stating that, "The significance of this statement is in the scope of the global visibility and voice representing virtually every sector of North America's charismatic/Pentecostal fellowship."[6]

Destiny Image Publishers is a NAR company started in 1983 in response to visions that founder Don Nori said God gave to him, showing him the need for a company that would "publish the prophets."[7] Destiny Image has since become a major producer of books written by NAR apostles, prophets, and teachers, including Bill Hamon, Bill Johnson, Ché Ahn, James Goll, and Jonathan Welton. In addition, NAR apostles and prophets have even managed to have their books published by mainstream evangelical publishers, including Rick Joyner's *Shadows of Things to Come* and Héctor Torres's *The Restoration of the Apostles and Prophets* (both published by Thomas Nelson) and Cindy Jacobs' *The Reformation Manifesto* (published by Bethany House). Thus multiple books written by NAR leaders can be found on the shelves of Christian bookstores as well as those of national chains like

---

[3]   The consultation was convened when Charisma Media was named Strang Communications and *Ministry Today* magazine was named *Ministries Today*.

[4]   Matt Green, "Leaders Tackle Tough Integrity Issues," *Charisma* (n.d.), accessed June 6, 2014, http://www.charismamag.com/spirit/devotionals/daily-break throughs?view=article&id=1180:leaders-tackle-tough-integrity-issues&catid=154.

[5]   "Orlando Statement," *Ministries Today* (March/April 2004): 63.

[6]   Jack Hayford, "A Watershed Moment," *Ministry Today*, n.d.; originally published in *Ministries Today* (March/April 2004); accessed February 20, 2014, http://ministrytodaymag.com/index.php/ministry-today-archives/155-special-report/8629-a-watershed-moment#sthash.GYsTEGTT.dpuf.

[7]   "How It All Began," Destiny Image, accessed February 25, 2014, http://www.destinyimage.com/about-us.

Barnes and Noble. Some of these books are bestsellers and have even made it to the shelves of Sam's Club, such as the tenth anniversary edition of *When Heaven Invades Earth,* by Bill Johnson (Destiny Image Publishers).

Two major Christian networks, Trinity Broadcasting Network and Daystar, air programs featuring apostles and prophets. Examples include Kim Clement's *Secrets of the Prophetic* and Sid Roth's *It's Supernatural.* One of the youngest and fastest-growing networks, GOD TV, is the first NAR network, produced by self-described apostolic prophetic ministers Rory and Wendy Alec.[8] In addition to NAR shows like *God Knows* and *Extreme Prophetic,* GOD TV boasts that it "airs more live programming from revival hotspots across the globe than any other broadcaster."[9] Those hotspots have included Lakeland, Florida—the location of the prophet Todd Bentley's 2008 revival— and Kansas City, Missouri—home to IHOP, which experienced an eleven-month "spiritual awakening" from November 11, 2009, to October 9, 2010.[10]

NAR AND THE INTERNET

The Internet has proven especially valuable for the dissemination of NAR teachings. Whereas formerly, people had to buy expensive plane tickets or drive thousands of miles to attend NAR revivals, now they can follow apostles on Twitter or friend their favorite prophet on Facebook. In the parlance of the times, NAR has gone viral.

Through technology, apostles and prophets can now broadcast their prophetic words instantaneously to their followers around the world. The Identity Network is a clearinghouse for NAR prophetic words, regularly e-mailing prophetic messages alongside advertisements for NAR products and conferences to more than 154,000 subscribers. A similar organization, called The Elijah List, has more than 135,000 subscribers.[11] The Elijah List

---

[8] "Biography [of Rory and Wendy Alec]," GOD TV, accessed February 19, 2014, http://www.god.tv/rory_and_wendy/biography.

[9] Ibid.

[10] Charisse Van Horn, "IHOP Revival Stirs Controversy, Cult or Genuine Move of God (Videos)," *Examiner.com,* April 20, 2011; accessed February 17, 2014, http://www.examiner.com/article/ihop-revival-stirs-controversy-cult-or-genuine-move-of-god-videos.

[11] These figures were obtained from the organizations' websites.

also launched *Prophetic TV*, an Internet television show that streams interviews with prophets like Kim Clement, Chuck Pierce, Graham Cooke, and Patricia King. And Elijah Streams Internet radio is the Pandora of the NAR world, playing "the best mix of prophetic and mainstream worship 24/7."[12]

One of the first revivals to be driven by the Internet was the prophet Todd Bentley's 2008 healing revival in Lakeland, Florida. In addition to the estimated 3,000 to 10,000 people who attended the revival on location each night, thousands more watched online. Forty-five days into the revival, the webstream had received more than one million hits.[13]

Since then, another revival that was broadcast by webstream took place at the IHOP headquarters in Kansas City, Missouri—an organization aimed at young adults. The revival began November 11, 2009, when the "Holy Spirit moved" in a Bible class that lasted more than fifteen hours.[14] Word spread quickly, and 2,000 people from the Kansas City area gathered spontaneously in an auditorium, where they had experiences of physical and emotional healings. About 1,600 people continued to meet at the auditorium each night, and many more watched the live webcast, including entire churches and groups of students from universities such as Georgia Institute of Technology, Wheaton College, and the University of California-Berkeley.[15] The organization received more than 6,000 testimonies of physical and emotional healings from Internet viewers around the world.[16]

---

[12]   Elijah Streams Facebook page, accessed February 20, 2014, https://www.facebook.com/ElijahStreams/info. An emerging musical genre, "prophetic music"—also known as "soaking songs"—features lyrics and sounds that purportedly come directly from the throne room of heaven, launching listeners into ecstatic encounters with God and experiences of physical and emotional healing.

[13]   Carey McMullen, "Florida Outpouring: Internet Draws Thousands to Lakeland Revival," *The Ledger.com,* May 18, 2008; accessed February 20, 2014, http://www.theledger.com/article/20080518/NEWS/805180341.

[14]   Craig von Buseck, "Revival Breaks Out at Kansas City IHOP: Spread Via Web," *Church Watch,* November 25, 2009; accessed August 15, 2014. http://blogs.cbn.com/ChurchWatch/archive/2009/11/25/revival-breaks-out-at-kansas-city-ihop-spreads-via-web.aspx.

[15]   Ibid.

[16]   "Special Message from IHOP-KC," International House of Prayer Northwest, October 12, 2010; accessed February 20, 2014, http://

NAR and Academia

NAR has made inroads into academia, in large part through the efforts of Peter Wagner, a professor of church growth at Fuller Theological Seminary, where he taught for thirty years (1971–2001).[17] During his tenure at Fuller, Wagner taught a course on NAR.[18] He also organized the National Symposium on the Postdenominational Church, held May 21–23, 1996, on Fuller's campus, and drawing about five hundred church leaders, church growth experts, and denominational leaders. This event introduced the idea of present-day apostles and prophets to the evangelical academic community.

In addition, NAR has formed its own educational institutions, which are producing graduates to provide ongoing leadership for the burgeoning movement. In 1998, Wagner founded the Wagner Leadership Institute to train leaders specifically for NAR. Wagner claims that traditional seminaries offer a curriculum that is largely theoretical—such as courses in theology and biblical languages—and have not provided adequate training for relevant ministry. In contrast, the Wagner Leadership Institute positions itself as providing training that has direct, practical application to ministry.[19] Courses offered by the Institute in traditional classrooms and online have included:

- Apostles and Apostolic Ministry, taught by C. Peter Wagner
- Basic Training for the Prophetic Ministry, taught by Kris Vallotton

---

internationalhouseofprayernorthwest.org/special-message-from-ihop-kc.

[17]   Wagner became influential among evangelicals in 1979, with the publication of his bestselling book *Your Spiritual Gifts Can Help Your Church Grow* (Regal). The book has since been updated and reprinted several times, with a fifteenth anniversary edition in 1994 and additional reprints in 2005 and 2012.

[18]   C. Peter Wagner, "The New Apostolic Reformation," *Renewal Journal* (April 12, 2012), accessed June 6, 2014, https://renewaljournal.wordpress.com/2012/04/12/the-new-apostolic-reformation-byc-peter-wagner/. This article was originally published as chapter 14 of *The Transforming Power of Revival: Prophetic Strategies into the Twenty-first Century*, edited by Harold Caballeros and Mel Winger (N.p.: Peniel, 1998).

[19]   C. Peter Wagner, "Are Seminaries Making the Grade?," *Ministry Today*, posted August 31, 2000; accessed June 6, 2014, http://ministrytodaymag.com/index.php/ministry-leadership/higher-education/536-are-seminaries-making-the-grade.

- The Power of Apostolic-Prophetic Alignment Seminar, taught by Chuck Pierce, Doris Wagner, and Barbara Yoder
- Strategy and Protocol for Dominion I and II, taught by Jim Chosa
- The Seven Mountain Mandate, taught by Johnny Enlow
- Advanced Spiritual Warfare, taught by Kim Daniels, Riva Timms, and Kimble Knight
- Walking in the Supernatural, taught by Bill Johnson
- School of Signs and Wonders, taught by Brian Thomson
- Dream Interpretation, by Barbie Breathitt
- Walking in Prophetic Revelation, by David and Jeanie Richardson
- Prophetic Evangelism, taught by Ché Ahn and Stacey Campbell
- Discovering Your Destiny Through the Fivefold Ministry Gifts, taught by Mark Tubbs
- Living in the Miraculous, taught by Aiko Hormann

One notable person who has acted as the dean of the Wagner Leadership Institute in Colorado Springs, Colorado, is Jack Deere, a former associate professor at Dallas Theological Seminary in Dallas, Texas, and author of the bestselling book *Surprised by the Voice of God* (Zondervan).[20] In 2010, the eighty-year-old Wagner passed his institute's baton of leadership to Ché Ahn, the international chancellor for the Wagner Leadership Institute. Wagner continues to act as the chancellor emeritus.

Now headquartered in Pasadena, California, the Institute's reach extends well beyond the city, with regional training centers and satellite programs in sixteen locations in the United States and international training centers and extensions in Australia, Bolivia, Brazil, Canada, China, Hong Kong, Indonesia, Malaysia, Nicaragua, Rwanda, Singapore, South Korea, and United Kingdom.

NAR AND INFLUENTIAL EVANGELICALS

Unlike Latter Rain leaders, whose teachings were widely and strongly denounced, NAR leaders have enjoyed growing influence among mainstream evangelicals. Some NAR leaders who are influential in broader evangelicalism include Mike Bickle (IHOP), Lou Engle (The Call), and Bill Johnson (Bethel Church in Redding, California).

---

[20]   Ibid.

Bickle's influence is growing to such an extent that conferences sponsored or co-sponsored by IHOP have featured well-known evangelicals, including the late philosopher Dallas Willard,[21] apologist Josh McDowell,[22] and Bible teacher Francis Chan. And when Bill Johnson spoke at the Voice of the Apostles 2013 conference in Orlando, Florida—sponsored by Global Awakening—his presentation was opened by popular Christian rock band Third Day.[23]

Of course, simply because Willard, McDowell, Chan, or the members of Third Day accepted an invitation to appear at a conference does not mean that they share in the outlook of these NAR leaders. In fact, it is noteworthy that, at one of the conferences, Chan took his speaking opportunity to admonish his NAR audience to study Scripture in order to detect unscriptural teaching.[24] Nevertheless, these evangelical leaders' participation in IHOP events testifies to the broadening influence NAR leaders have achieved within mainstream evangelicalism.

NAR leaders have also received a big credibility boost from another mainstream leader. Jack Hayford, one of America's best-known pastors and the fourth president of the International Church of the Foursquare Gospel, has endorsed NAR books, like *Understanding the Fivefold Ministry*, edited by Matthew Green, to which he wrote the foreword. Hayford speaks at NAR conferences, such as the 2010 Annual International Leadership Conference, sponsored by HIM, a large apostolic network. Hayford was one of four featured speakers at the conference, including apostles and prophets Ché Ahn, Peter Wagner, and Cindy Jacobs.[25] Hayford was also a featured speaker at

---

[21] "Transform World Vision 2020," *Transform World Newsletter*, February 14, 2013, accessed June 6, 2014, http://www.transform-world.net/newsletters/2013/PrayerHost.docx.

[22] Ibid.

[23] "Voice of the Apostles 2013: Third Day," Sched, accessed June 6, 2014, http://voiceoftheapostles2013.sched.org/artist/thirdday#.U5JJzCghXNs.

[24] Francis Chan, "Francis Chan Speaking at IHOP-KC's Onething 2013," YouTube video, 1:02:26, posted by "BeautyforAshes 613," December 31, 2013; accessed September 2, 2014, https://www.youtube.com/watch?v=yMy4hDMOMj4.

[25] "HIM Annual International Leadership Conference," Facebook page, accessed June 6, 2014, https://m2.facebook.com/events/118728981474114?_rdr.

the Voice of the Apostles 2013 conference, alongside Randy Clark, Ché Ahn, Heidi Baker, Bill Johnson, Reinhard Bonnke, and Larry Randolph.[26]

NAR AND YOUTH

The Latter Rain revival fizzled out before the teachings could be passed on to a new generation. But NAR leaders have focused intentionally and strategically on reaching the younger generations with their teachings, forming camps, clubs, and curricula designed for children. This focus on children is noteworthy: many prophecies have been given about the important role children will play in the end time.

Indeed, God is raising up what NAR leaders call a Samuel Generation— that is, a company of children to lead his end-time army, according to apostles and prophets Rick Joyner,[27] Bill Hamon,[28] and Catherine Brown.[29] These prophets teach that the current generation of children will likely make up the last generation of the church. So they must be trained for their pivotal role in ushering in God's kingdom. This training includes teaching children to develop miraculous powers. Joyner has said, "Young children will cast out demons, heal the sick, raise the dead, and divert raging floods with a word. Some will actually take dominion over entire hospitals and mental institutions, healing every patient in them by laying hands on the buildings."[30]

Part of this training was depicted in a 2006 documentary titled *Jesus Camp*. It featured children attending the Families on Fire Summer Camp in

---

[26] "Voice of the Apostles Conference – Orlando, Florida, August 12–16, 2013," Global Celebration website, accessed June 6, 2014, http://www.globalcelebration. com/news/370/16/Voice-of-Apostles-Conference

[27] Rick Joyner, *The Apostolic Ministry* (Wilkesboro, NC: MorningStar Publications, 2004), 168–172.

[28] "Bill Hamon Prophecy," Kids in Ministry International, accessed February 20, 2014, http://kidsinministry.org/bill-hamon-prophecy.

[29] "Catherine Brown Prophecy," Kids in Ministry International, December 30, 2004; accessed February 20, 2014, http://kidsinministry.org/catherine-brown-prophecy.

[30] Rick Joyner, "On Women and Children," Kids in Ministry International, accessed February 20, 2014, http://kidsinministry.org/rick-joyner, excerpt taken from Rick Joyner, *The Harvest* (New Kensington, PA: Whitaker House, 1997), 34.

Devil's Lake, North Dakota. Controversy was sparked by scenes of campers wearing military fatigues and green face paint as they trained for spiritual war. The media backlash was directed at the camp's anti-evolution, anti-homosexuality, and anti-abortion teachings, with some critics drawing parallels to terrorist training camps. But while the documentary portrayed the camp as an evangelical camp with a rightwing agenda, it missed the camp's ties to NAR. The camp's founder, Becky Fischer, energetically promotes NAR teachings through her organization, Kids in Ministry International in Mandan, North Dakota, which describes itself as an "apostolic, prophetic ministry focused on equipping and training a generation of boys and girls to walk in the supernatural power of God."[31] The organization's website, at one time, featured profiles of "Pee Wee Prophets" and it continues to devote a page of links to "What the Prophets Are Saying about Kids."[32]

To help children develop miraculous gifts, like healing people and prophesying, Kids in Ministry International started PowerClubs in 2006—"held in churches, backyards, schools, slums, ghettos, and homes," according to the organization's website. As of January 2013, the organization reported that nearly 2,000 PowerClubs were attended by over 35,000 children in eighteen nations.[33]

And IHOP offers a weeklong Signs and Wonders camp for children ages six through twelve, directed by Lenny and Tracy LaGuardia. The camp is held on the Kansas City campus, as well as in other states. It is described as a "summer boot camp to train kids in prayer and spiritual authority."[34] The "vision is to see one million children radically committed to Jesus, experiencing the power of the Holy Spirit, and moving in signs and wonders."[35]

---

[31] Kids in Ministry International Facebook page, accessed June 6, 2014, https://www.facebook.com/kidsinministry/info.

[32] "What the Prophets Are Saying About Kids," Kids in Ministry International, accessed February 20, 2014, https://kidsinministry.org/what-the-prophets-are-saying-about-kids.

[33] "What is a PowerClub?" Kids in Ministry International, accessed February 25, 2014, http://kidsinministry.org/what-is-a-powerclub.

[34] See the video on the webpage "Signs and Wonders Camp 1," International House of Prayer, accessed February 20, 2014.

[35] "Signs and Wonders Camp 1," International House of Prayer, accessed February 20, 2014, http://www.ihopkc.org/signsandwonders1.

During the camp, ill people from the local community are invited to have the children pray for their healing.

In addition to clubs and camps, Sunday school curricula have been created for churches to train children to work miracles. One such curriculum, called *Kids Carrying the Kingdom*, is designed for children ages six through eleven. It was developed by Kids in His Presence, a California-based organization co-founded by Mike Seth, the former children's director at Bethel Church in Redding, California. Kids in His Presence also sells another resource called *My Heart Is a Bucket*, designed for preschoolers.

But what does training children to work miracles look like in an actual church setting? An example is Bethel Church, where the children's classes have been described as "practice rooms for the supernatural."[36] The children talk with angels, interpret each other's dreams, and practice raising the "dead" by wrapping each other in toilet paper like mummies.[37]

Young children are not the only focus in this movement; so are teenagers and young adults. NAR prophets speak frequently about a coming youth "awakening." IHOP, for example, was founded by Bickle following prophetic words about youth given by the prophet Bob Jones. Jones claimed he received over one hundred prophetic revelations between 1975 and 1983 about a youth movement that would rise in Kansas City, Missouri—the home base for IHOP. Jones said God showed him that "this will be the end generation that is foreknown to inherit all things. Their children will attain a level of the Spirit that they themselves will not attain. Their children and grandchildren will possess the Spirit without measure for they are the best of all the generations that have ever been upon the face of the earth. They will move into the supernatural as never before."[38]

---

[36] C. Hope Flinchbaugh, "Ignite the Fire," Charisma, February 28, 2007; accessed February 20, 2014, http://www.charismamag.com/site-archives/146-covers/cover-story/2172-ignite-the-fire.

[37] Ibid. The Bethel Redding website features a video of the children's pastor, Seth Dahl, describing the supernatural activities in the Bethel Church children's classes. See "Children's Ministry," Bethel Redding, accessed February 20, 2014, http://bethelredding.com/ministries/children.

[38] Mike Bickle, "Session 2: Great Light, White Horse, Chariot, and Sands of Time," *Prophetic History*, International House of Prayer, [September 18, 2009?], accessed September 28, 2009, http://www.ihopkc.org/resources/files/2011/09/

Since Jones shared these prophetic words, IHOP has grown into an influential organization with programs aimed at young adults. IHOP operates a non-stop, around-the-clock Prayer Room and hosts conferences such as the annual Onething conference, which drew 25,000 attendees to Kansas City in December 2013. IHOP also operates the International House of Prayer University, which, as of January 2014, reported an enrollment of about 700 full-time students.

SUMMARY

NAR leaders have begun to mainstream their movement within the larger Christian world. Their efforts include partnering with Christian media, using the Internet to disseminate NAR teachings, making inroads into academia, increasing their intersection with influential evangelicals, and focusing on training youth.

In the next chapter we explain NAR teachings about the nature of an apostle.

PH02-_Friday_AM_Great_Light_White_Horse_Chariot_and_Sands_of_TimeMS. pdf. This source is no longer available on IHOP's website and has been replaced by a newer document detailing Bob Jones' prophecies about IHOP. In this newer document, some of the previous wording has been changed or omitted, including the wording of the Jones' prophecy that we cited. The newer document is Mike Bickle, "Session 2: Explosion of Light, the White Horse, and the Chariots," *Encountering Jesus: Visions, Revelations, and Angelic Activity from IHOP-KC's Prophetic History*, Transcript, MikeBickle.org, April 25, 2011; accessed September 2, 2014, http://www. mikebickle.org.edgesuite.net/MikeBickleVOD/2011/20110425_T_Explosion_of_ Light_the_White_Horse_and_the_Chariots_IPH02.pdf. Other researchers have accused IHOP of revising its "prophetic history" over the years and have said that such revision "speaks to the veracity and authenticity of Mike Bickle's ministry." See, for example, William Fawcett, "Mike Bickle: The White Horse Prophecy," *Beyond Grace*, August 24, 2011; accessed September 2, 2014, http://beyondgrace.blogspot. com/2011/08/mike-bickle-white-horse-prophecy.html.

4

NAR Apostles: The Generals

> Warfare is the number-one role of the apostle. Prophets will woo you with the Word of the Lord; teachers will educate you; pastors will help you through your problems and hurts; evangelists will get folks saved; but it is the apostle who will declare war on the enemy and lead the Church to war.
>
> —John Kelly and Paul Costa, *End-Time Warriors: A Prophetic Vision for the Church in the Last Days*

Imagine a war in which there are no generals. What would that look like? The troops would flounder and fire aimlessly, with no one to give them orders, devise a winning strategy, or lead them to battle. Without the generals' strategic leadership, the troops couldn't defeat the enemy and achieve victory. According to NAR leaders, that's exactly what the church, God's army, has experienced for the past 1,800 years. The church has been waging the greatest spiritual war of all time. But without apostles in command, it is powerless to conquer Satan and advance God's kingdom.

In NAR church government, apostles are often described as generals—strategizing, giving orders, and drawing up battle plans. These leaders use secret intelligence they receive from prophets to neutralize and disarm the enemy. And they have a massive arsenal of weapons—the ability to perform supernatural signs, wonders, and miracles—that can advance God's army and shock and awe its enemies into submission.

Presently most Protestant churches and ministries are not led by apostles. They're led by pastors, elders, and denominational administrators, who, in the NAR view, are mere foot soldiers, bereft of fresh revelation and supernatural firepower. When the foot soldiers finally step aside and let apostles take charge, the church will be an unstoppable force.

In this chapter we look at both a moderate view of present-day apostles and the revolutionary NAR view.

DEFINING APOSTLES

The term *apostle* is prominent in Christian ecclesiastical groups. But those who talk about apostles view them in very different ways. Roman Catholic, Eastern Orthodox, and Anglican Christians, for example, hold to a doctrine known as "apostolic succession" and believe that the authority of their church leaders—called bishops— stems from the original twelve apostles. Many Protestant denominations that disavow a church government based on apostolic succession employ the term *apostle* differently.

At one end of the spectrum are many Protestant Christians who believe that the original apostles—those appointed directly by Jesus, including the Twelve and Paul—founded the early church and that the active role of an apostle died with them. These original apostles' primary responsibilities were to establish the first churches and oversee the writing of Scripture. After faithfully fulfilling these responsibilities, the perpetuation of apostolic activity was no longer needed or provided for within the church.

Other Protestants apply the term *apostle* to an additional class of individuals, namely, the great missionaries who were first to take the gospel to foreign lands. For example, William Carey and Hudson Taylor have been referred to as apostles in this more restricted sense of the word. And individuals today who plant churches are also sometimes thought of as apostles. But these apostles are not considered to possess the authority of the original apostles. This particular understanding of apostles is not so common today.

In the middle of the spectrum are many classical Pentecostals and charismatics[1] who agree with the above definition of present-day apostles as pioneering missionaries and church planters. Yet they give these leaders added authority. These groups believe that apostles exist today who are authorized to perform miraculous signs to confirm the truth of the gospel they proclaim. These Pentecostals believe that many present-day individuals function, in some ways, as old-style apostles—preaching the gospel, planting

---

[1] Notice that we use the term *charismatics* (with a lowercase "c") to refer to people who are not part of a classical Pentecostal denomination, but do emphasize the miraculous gifts of the Holy Spirit, such as speaking in tongues, prophesying, and the working of miracles. These people can be found within mainline, non-Pentecostal denominations or in independent charismatic churches. This use of the word combines the definitions of *Charismatic* (uppercase "C") Christians and *Neocharismatic* Christians given in chapter 2, note 8.

churches, and performing miracles. But they don't see present-day apostles as equal in authority to the original twelve apostles or Paul, and they don't believe these leaders must govern the church. They also do not speak of any present-day *office* of apostle, as NAR leaders do. Rather, they affirm the present-day *ministry function* or *ministry gift* of apostle. That is, they believe that today's apostles have apostolic-type ministries, without holding a specially recognized official position in church government. Those who hold this Pentecostal view may refer to certain persons as Apostle William or Apostle Ann. But they don't mean to imply that these people have the same authority as Peter or Paul.

Far at the other end of the spectrum are NAR leaders who affirm the existence of apostles today and hold that these apostles have governing authority equal to the original apostles. On this permissive conception, apostles hold an official church office and wield unexcelled authority extending to workplaces, cities, and nations.

Before examining the NAR view of apostles, we take a closer look at the more moderate Pentecostal view. Contrasting the views will highlight the more spectacular NAR claims.

PENTECOSTAL VIEW:
THE PRESENT-DAY MINISTRY FUNCTION OF APOSTLE

For a comparatively moderate view of present-day apostles consider the Assemblies of God (AG), the world's largest Pentecostal denomination with some sixty-five million members and adherents. Leadership of the Assemblies of God does not recognize a present-day office of apostle. Adjectives like *deviant* and *problematic* are used in at least one of the denomination's official documents that assesses "the teaching that present-day offices of apostles and prophets should govern church ministry at all levels."[2] Another document states: "We look with grave concern on those who do not believe in congregational church government, who do not trust the maturity of local church bodies to govern themselves under Scripture and the Spirit.

---

2   "End-Time Revival—Spirit-Led and Spirit-Controlled: A Response Paper to Resolution 16," General Presbytery of the Assemblies of God, August 11, 2000, 2; accessed September 30, 2010, http://ag.org/top/Beliefs/Position_Papers/pp_downloads/pp_endtime_revival.pdf.

Such leaders prefer more authoritarian structures where their own word or decrees are unchallenged."[3]

At the same time, the AG governing body holds that many people in the church today fulfill the ongoing "ministry functions" of apostles. It allows for individual Assemblies of God churches to identify certain leaders as "apostles," provided they recognize that those leaders are not equal in authority to the original "foundational apostles."[4] It argues that the foundational apostles were commissioned directly by the risen Lord not only to preach the gospel, as present-day apostles do, but also to perform specific, unique roles in founding the church, including overseeing the writing of Scripture.[5]

A denominational document lists three groups of apostles identified in the New Testament:[6]

- The twelve disciples (including Matthias, who replaced Judas)
- The Twelve plus Paul, together with a larger group of an unknown number (1 Cor. 15:3–8)
- Others, such as Epaphroditus (Phil. 2:25) and the unnamed brothers Paul wrote about (2 Cor. 8:23)

The document states that the first two groups were often referred to in Scripture as "apostles of Jesus Christ" and were foundational apostles. It also says they possessed authority, which can be seen with "even a cursory reading of the New Testament."[7] Evidence of their authority was demonstrated in many ways. Ananias and Sapphira fall down dead when the apostle Peter confronts them about their sin of deception (Acts 5:1–11). Paul and Peter assert apostolic authority in letters they wrote to churches that they did not found (Rom. 1:1; 1 Peter 1:1). And Paul sternly admonishes another church to discipline a member of that church (1 Cor. 5:1–5). In short, "the pattern of evidence throughout the New Testament indicates their authority was

---

[3] "Apostles and Prophets," General Presbytery of the Assemblies of God, August 6, 2001, 11; accessed September 29, 2010, http://ag.org/top/Beliefs/Position_Papers/pp_downloads/pp_4195_apostles_prophets.pdf.

[4] Ibid., 10.

[5] Ibid.

[6] Ibid.

[7] Ibid., 6.

universal in doctrinal and ethical matters, binding in some sense upon all the churches."[8]

Unlike these "apostles of Jesus Christ," members of the third group of apostles were not commissioned directly by Christ, according to the AG document. These apostles were commissioned by early churches to fulfill specific roles and responsibilities on behalf of the churches. As a result, these "apostles of the churches" did not possess the same great authority as the foundational apostles. The Assemblies of God denomination affirms the continued function of this third category of apostle in the church today.

People today with "apostolic functions" don't have "unique revelatory and authoritative roles in establishing the church and producing the New Testament."[9] Rather, these people bring the gospel to unevangelized territories and plant churches. Still, they are expected to demonstrate several special marks of an apostle, including the performance of miracles together with preaching and teaching that are empowered by the Holy Spirit.

> The function of apostle occurs whenever the church of Jesus Christ is being established among the unevangelized. As Pentecostals, we fervently desire a generation of men and women who will function apostolically: to take the gospel with signs following to people at home and abroad who have not yet heard or understood that "God so loved the world that he gave his one and only Son, that whoever believes in him shall not perish but have eternal life" (John 3:16).[10]

The Assemblies of God view is summed up this way: "We affirm that there are, and ought to be, apostolic- and prophetic-type ministries in the Church, without individuals being identified as filling such an office."[11]

NAR VIEW: THE PRESENT-DAY OFFICE OF APOSTLE

Peter Wagner, a prominent NAR apostle, is clearly at odds with the Assemblies of God position. The denomination's talk about "apostolic-type ministries" is not accompanied by any present-day office of apostle. But this is akin to the denomination "having [its] cake and eating it too!" says

---

[8]   Ibid.

[9]   Ibid., 10.

[10]   Ibid.

[11]   "End-Time Revival," 3, accessed February 20, 2014.

Wagner. In his view, it's impossible for there to be apostolic-type ministries unless there are present-day apostles invested with the authority of a formal office. "How can you have a ministry and not have the ministers minister?"[12]

Though the aging Wagner has named successors for many of the organizations he has founded or led, his voice still is one of the most influential within NAR and will continue to be after he's gone.[13] He's authored six books on the topic of apostles. He was the presiding apostle over the International Coalition of Apostolic Leaders (ICAL) during its formative years, from 2001 to 2010. Wagner does the heavy lifting theologically for the movement. Many sources amplifying and supporting the NAR perspective depend for their status within NAR on his endorsement of them.[14]

Not all NAR leaders work directly with Wagner or even agree with all his teachings. Even so, there is significant overlap between the teachings of many NAR leaders and those of Wagner. To understand NAR, one must know Wagner's views.

To Wagner, there's no good reason to think that the office of apostle ever ceased. He acknowledges that most Protestant Christians, including the Assemblies of God, have long disagreed with his position.

> Most Christians would affirm that they believe in apostles because Jesus led a group of 12 of them. However, apostles are generally seen as figures of a bygone age, like Vikings, Roman Legions, Spanish conquistadors, or pioneers in covered wagons . . .

---

[12] C. Peter Wagner, *Apostles Today: Biblical Government for Biblical Power* (Ventura, CA: Regal Books, 2006), 64.

[13] C. Peter Wagner turned eighty on August 15, 2010. He handed over leadership of the Wagner Leadership Institute to Ché Ahn. He also appointed Chuck Pierce to take over his organization, called Global Harvest Ministries (which Pierce renamed Global Spheres), though Wagner continues to serves as Global Spheres' vice president and apostolic ambassador. And he appointed John P. Kelly to assume his role as presiding apostle (now called convening apostle) of the International Coalition of Apostolic Leaders.

[14] In this section, we have drawn extensively from material in Wagner's book *Apostles Today* (see note 12 above). This is Wagner's sixth and final book on the topic of apostles, according to his memoir. See C. Peter Wagner, *Wresting with Alligators, Prophets, and Theologians: Lessons from a Lifetime in the Church—A Memoir* (Ventura, CA: Regal Books, 2010), 301.

One reason why this kind of thinking is so prevalent is that this is what most of our church leaders were taught in seminary and Bible school. I know—I was one of them. The notion that there could be contemporary apostles never came up in the seminaries I attended, not even as a suggestion. We were taught that the original 12 apostles had a singular, one-of-a-kind mission that was completed by the time of their deaths, and that was that— the end of the brief life of apostles on Earth. Consequently, I graduated assuming that apostles did not continue long after the first hundred years or so of the church.[15]

Wagner believes that this long-standing attitude is changing. "True," he says, "many Christian leaders do not as yet believe that we now have legitimate apostles on the level of Peter or Paul or John, but a critical mass of the Church agrees that apostles are actually here."[16]

The Nature and Scope of an Apostle's Authority

Wagner thinks he understands why denominational leaders, like those of the Assemblies of God, oppose the office of apostle: they feel their democratic style of government is threatened by it.[17] And, of course, they're right.

Of all the changes involved with the emergence of the New Apostolic Reformation, the most radical of all is the following: *the recognition of the amount of spiritual authority delegated by the Holy Spirit to individuals* [Wagner's emphasis]. Previously, church authority, whether in local congregations or in denominational structures, invariably rested on groups, not on individuals. The groups were called church councils, sessions, vestries, presbyteries, conferences, synods, deacon boards, annual conventions, districts, cabinets, general councils, or what have you. With the exception of those leaders who stepped out of their traditional molds and founded whole new movements, individuals were not to be trusted to make final decisions.

However, this is not true of churches that find themselves as part of the New Apostolic Reformation.[18]

---

[15]   Wagner, *Apostles Today*, 6.

[16]   C. Peter Wagner, *Dominion! How Kingdom Action Can Change the World* (Grand Rapids: Chosen Books, 2008), 26.

[17]   C. Peter Wagner, *Changing Church* (Ventura, CA: Regal Books, 2004), 31.

[18]   C. Peter Wagner, *Church in the Workplace: How God's People Can Transform Society* (Ventura, CA: Regal Books), 2006, 25.

So how does that individual authority play out? In a NAR church, on the local level, the senior pastor calls the shots. The pastor is viewed as the *leader* of a church—not an *employee* of the church—and has final authority over the staff and budget.[19] He or she does not answer to the elders; rather, the elders serve and support the pastor. This CEO-type role for pastors is much different from many traditional churches where the pastors are treated as employees of the church.

But on the translocal level—involving all churches in an apostolic network—the apostle is in command. A benefit of this arrangement is "pain-free church government," says Wagner.[20]

Though denominational leaders may feel threatened by the extraordinary authority of contemporary apostles, this is no excuse for rejecting such authority, according to Wagner. The church's mission depends on continued apostolic authority. He writes: "When we do this [submit to apostles], the [church] government will be in place to receive the powerful outpouring of the Holy Spirit upon our cities, which will lead to social transformation on a worldwide scale."[21] In other words, without the authority of today's apostles, the church cannot fulfill its mission of transforming societies and advancing God's kingdom.

But what, more precisely, are apostles authorized to do? The answer is revealed in Wagner's definition of an apostle—a definition adopted by ICAL. [22]

---

[19]   Wagner, *Wrestling with Alligators, Prophets, and Theologians*, 207.

[20]   Wagner, *Dominion!*, 34.

[21]   Wagner, *Apostles Today*, 134.

[22]   Under Wagner's leadership, the International Coalition of Apostolic Leaders adopted a definition nearly identical to Wagner's. More recently the coalition website has featured two definitions of an apostle, Wagner's and a second called the "ICAL Definition of Apostle," with some changes made to Wagner's original definition. This second, revised definition reads: "An apostle is defined by ICAL as a Christian leader gifted, taught, commissioned, and sent by God with the authority to establish the foundational government of a church or business within an assigned sphere by hearing what the Holy Spirit is saying and one who sets things in order accordingly for the growth and maturity of the group or complex of groups (churches or businesses)." See "About ICAL," International Coalition of Apostolic Leaders, accessed December 26, 2013, http://www.coalitionofapostles.com/about-ica.

> An apostle is a Christian leader gifted, taught, commissioned and sent by God *with the authority to establish the foundational government of the Church* within an assigned sphere of ministry by hearing what the Spirit is saying to the churches and by setting things in order accordingly for the expansion of the Kingdom of God [our emphasis].[23]

So, apostles have God-given authority "to establish the foundational government of the church." What does that mean? Notice Wagner's definition.

> An apostle is a Christian leader gifted, taught, commissioned and sent by God with the authority to establish the foundational government of the Church within an assigned sphere of ministry *by hearing what the Spirit is saying to the churches and by setting things in order accordingly* for the expansion of the Kingdom of God [our emphasis].

NAR apostles establish the foundational government of the church, first, by "hearing what the Holy Spirit is saying to the churches." In other words, they receive new revelation from God. This new revelation is often referred to by NAR leaders as "present truth" or "new truths." Wagner says the new revelation can only be received by apostles and prophets.

> Whereas every believer can and should hear directly from the Holy Spirit, it is only the apostles, in proper relation to prophets, who hear what the Spirit is saying to the churches. Parents hear what the Spirit is saying to their families. CEOs hear what the Spirit is saying to their businesses. Teachers hear what the Spirit is saying to their classes. Pastors hear what the Spirit is saying to their church (singular). But apostles, along with prophets, are those who hear what the Spirit is saying to the churches (plural).[24]

Apostles either receive the revelation directly from God, or they receive it from prophets. Some apostles receive revelation that applies only to churches in their own apostolic networks. But other apostles—whom Wagner calls "broadband apostles"—receive revelation for the entire body of Christ.[25] Examples of revelation intended for the entire church include key NAR teachings, such as the revelation that God would restore apostles and prophets

---

[23]   Wagner, *Dominion!*, 31.

[24]   Wagner, *Apostles Today*, 81.

[25]   Wagner, *Dominion!*, 36–37.

to the church.[26] They also include the revelation that social transformation is "one of the highest items on God's current agenda for His people."[27] After the apostles receive new revelation, they must go about "setting things in order accordingly." This means that apostles must implement the revelation they receive in the churches and ministries that come under their authority. In short, Wagner describes the role of apostles like this: "Apostles take the word of the Lord from the prophets (and they also, of course, hear from God directly), they judge it, they interpret it, they strategize their procedures, and they assume leadership in implementing it."[28]

There is a chain of command in the church. Apostles, though they have been restored only lately, sit at the top. Prophets, pastors, evangelists, and all others submit to them. Prophets submit to apostles by providing them with new revelation, then stepping aside for apostles to interpret and implement it.[29] Pastors, the local authority of a church, submit to the translocal authority of an apostle when they voluntarily join an apostolic network. When a pastor submits to an apostle, by extension all the people in the pastor's congregation are under the proper "apostolic covering" (also called "spiritual covering"). Pastors must submit to apostles because they themselves don't have what it takes to lead the church in advancing God's kingdom. "The responsibility of pastors is to care for, nurture and comfort the flock. Very few pastors have either the gifts or the temperament to mobilize an army for war. Apostles, on the other hand, do."[30]

By joining an apostolic network, a pastor agrees to be subject to the authority of the apostle who rules over the network.[31] A pastor further agrees that his or her church will contribute financially to the apostolic network

---

[26]   Bill Hamon's biography says that, in 1983, he received revelation that God would raise up a great company of prophets to restore prophets and apostles to the church. See " Dr. Bill Hamon's Story," Christian International Ministries Network, accessed February 20, 2014, http://christianinternational.com/dr-bill-hamon.

[27]   Wagner, *Dominion!*, 37.

[28]   Wagner, *Dominion!*, 27.

[29]   Ibid., 27.

[30]   Ibid., 123.

[31]   C. Peter Wagner, *Churchquake! How the New Apostolic Reformation is Shaking Up the Church as We Know It* (Ventura, CA: Regal Books, 1999), 99, 122; *Changing Church*, 35.

For example, the apostolic network HIM expects churches to make a monthly donation and recommends that the donation be between 5 percent and 10 percent of their monthly gross income.[32]

In turn, the apostle over an apostolic network assumes spiritual authority over the pastor. Since a pastor joins the network voluntarily, he or she is free to leave at any time. But this rarely happens, according to Wagner. "Why? It is because apostolically oriented pastors feel that the apostle adds value to their life and ministry. They are convinced that they would not be able to reach their full destiny in serving God apart from the spiritual covering of the apostle."[33]

There's an even more pressing reason. Failure to submit to a NAR apostle is seen as failure to submit to God. As prophet-apostle Bill Hamon says, "It is almost impossible for individuals to humble themselves under God without humbling themselves in submission and relationship to Christ's delegated representatives of Him to His Church."[34]

If apostles sit at the top of church government, then how are they kept from abusing their authority? To whom are they accountable? Wagner allows that the issue of apostolic accountability is tricky. One attempt at providing accountability is the formation of apostolic networks, such as ICAL, where a group of apostles voluntarily submit themselves to the authority of an "overseeing apostle."[35] But Wagner admits, "The question remains: To whom is the overseeing apostle accountable?"[36] Wagner's hope is that overseeing apostles will voluntarily develop accountability relationships with other overseeing apostles. But this remains experimental. As he says, "On this one, the jury is still out."[37]

---

[32] "Ministry Assumptions," Harvest International Ministry, accessed February 20, 2014, http://harvestim.org/index.php?a=about&s=membership&ss=ministry-assumptions.

[33] Wagner, *Changing Church*, 36.

[34] Bill Hamon, *Apostles, Prophets, and the Coming Moves of God: God's End-Time Plans for His Church and Planet Earth* (Santa Rosa Beach, FL: Destiny Image Publishers, 1997), 153.

[35] Wagner, *Churchquake!*, 123.

[36] Ibid.

[37] Ibid.

The Source of an Apostle's Authority

Where do apostles get their authority? Directly from God, according to Wagner. They are chosen by God and are given the "spiritual gift" of being an apostle by him. Like any other spiritual gift, this is a gift of grace and is unearned. The office of apostle is another story. It is earned.[38]

Apostles earn their office—grounded in public recognition that they are apostles—first by demonstrating that they have the spiritual gift of apostleship. They must also demonstrate extraordinary character that is especially marked by holiness and humility.[39] Genuine apostles need never appoint themselves to the office because others will recognize them as apostles and confer on them the office of an apostle. This conferral often occurs during a formal commissioning ceremony led by other apostles, as well as prophets. An example is a ceremony held in 1999, when a group of NAR leaders from the New Apostolic Roundtable—including Chuck Pierce and Bill Hamon—prayed and prophesied over Wagner, anointed him with oil, and commissioned him an apostle.[40]

Once the office of apostle is conferred, it's appropriate for that individual to use the title of apostle. Indeed, use of the title may be essential for an apostle to get his or her job done, though other NAR leaders disagree with Wagner on this point.[41]

While apostles have the duty to demonstrate their gift, others have the duty to recognize it. And since an apostle's authority comes directly from God, failure to recognize a true apostle is a serious matter. Wagner writes: "On that point let me make a strong statement: *To the degree that the Corinthian believers did not recognize that the Lord had made Paul an apostle, they*

---

[38]   Wagner, *Apostles Today*, 25–26.

[39]   Ibid., 35–45.

[40]   Wagner, *Wrestling with Alligators, Prophets, and Theologians*, 210.

[41]   Wagner, *Apostles Today*, 59–70. In 2013, the Apostolic Council of the International Coalition of Apostles voted unanimously to rename the organization the International Coalition of Apostolic Leaders and stated a reason for the change as "we do not major on titles, we major on function." See "Why the Name Change?," European Coalition of Apostolic Leaders, November 16, 2013; accessed December 27, 2013, November 16, 2013. http://ecaleaders.eu/maler/convenors-blog/article/329181.

were out of the will of God [Wagner's emphasis]! That would have been a dangerous place to be!"[42]

To help Christians find the apostle or apostles in their own city, Wagner suggests they look for them in three likely "fishing pools":[43]

- *Workplace apostles*: The "movers and shakers" in a city who work in influential sectors of society, like government, business, education, media, and the arts.
- *Megachurch pastors*: The pastors of dynamically growing churches.
- *Parachurch leaders*: Those who lead effective ministries in a given city, especially those focused on social transformation.

Once the apostles in a region are identified, Christians must submit to them. Wagner says: "The people of God must encourage them, award them the office when appropriate, and submit gratefully to the authority of the apostle or apostles who are over whatever territorial sphere in which we find ourselves."[44]

Types of Apostles

Wagner holds that there are three broad categories of apostles.[45]

- *Vertical apostles:* These apostles lead organizations, such as apostolic networks, and provide direct "spiritual covering" (counsel and correction) for those in their networks.
- *Horizontal apostles*: These apostles lead groups of peers—such as all the pastors in a city or all the apostles in a nation—to work together to accomplish specific purposes.
- *Workplace apostles*: These apostles provide leadership for Christians working in different sectors of society (for example, real estate, government, health care, or the media).

Of these three categories, workplace apostles presently receive the most attention. Wagner and other NAR leaders now grasp the opportunity for influence these men and women may exert in the power structures of

---

42   Wagner, *Apostles Today*, 25.

43   Ibid., 134–36.

44   Ibid., 134.

45   Ibid., 85–101.

society.[46] They want to leverage the influence of leaders like these to advance God's kingdom.

In addition to the three broad categories of apostles, Wagner believes there are four subcategories within each of the vertical and horizontal apostle categories.[47] Those within the vertical category are:

- *Ecclesiastical apostles*: These apostles lead apostolic networks of churches and parachurch ministries; examples include Ché Ahn (Harvest International Ministry, based in Pasadena, California), Bill Hamon (Christian International Ministries, based in Santa Rosa Beach, Florida), and Naomi Dowdy (Global Leadership Network, based in Singapore).
- *Apostolic team members*: These apostles are part of a leadership team that supports an apostle in the governance of his or her ministry. They can be other apostles who minister under the ecclesiastical apostle. Having an apostolic team allows an apostolic network to grow much larger because a single apostle can't provide direct oversight of hundreds or thousands of churches—and direct oversight is seen as crucial to the health of the network.[48] For example, HIM—an apostolic network of more than 20,000 churches—is led by presiding apostle Ché Ahn but also has an apostolic team under Ahn's leadership made up of apostles Sam and Linda Caster, Brian and Candace Simmons, Charles and Anne Stock, Mark and Ann Tubbs, and Lance and Annabelle Wallnau.
- *Functional apostles*: These apostles lead individuals or groups working within a specialized area of ministry; an example is Jane Hansen (Aglow International, an organization for women based in Edmonds, Washington).
- *Congregational apostles*: These apostles lead large churches, such as pastors of megachurches.

The subcategories of horizontal apostles are:

- *Convening apostles*: These apostles call together peer-level leaders who minister in a specific field. Wagner has acted as the convening

---

46 Ibid., 103–17.

47 Ibid., 90–100.

48 Ibid., 92.

apostle over a number of groups, including ICAL, the ACPE, and the International Society of Deliverance Ministers.

- *Ambassadorial apostles*: These are itinerant apostles who catalyze apostolic movements in nations and various regions of the world through activities such as convening regional apostolic summits or assisting apostles in organizing their networks. John Kelly—before becoming the convening apostle of ICAL—served as the coalition's ambassadorial apostle.

- *Mobilizing apostles*: These apostles mobilize Christians for a specific cause or project. For example, Cindy Jacobs mobilizes Christians in prayer and spiritual warfare efforts to reform America back to its "biblical roots."

- *Territorial apostles*: These apostles provide leadership in specific regions, such as cities, states, and nations. For example, John Bene-fiel is seen as a territorial apostle in the state of Oklahoma. Doug Stringer has been seen as a territorial apostle in Houston, Texas.

Wagner also notes that apostles do not all fit into neat categories, and many apostles have more than one spiritual gift. Wagner, for example, sees himself as an "apostle-teacher."[49] And Bill Hamon sees himself as a "prophet-apostle."[50]

SUMMARY

Protestant Christians today define apostles in a variety of ways. Some think apostleship of any kind ceased after the church was founded. Others believe apostles exist today, but as missionaries and church planters. In the Pentecostal view, apostles are missionaries and church planters who also perform miraculous signs and wonders to confirm the truth of the gospel they proclaim. But NAR leaders hold that apostles are more than miracle-working missionaries and church planters; they are individuals with formal offices in church government and authority extending to workplaces, cities, and nations.

In the next chapter we take a closer look at NAR apostles.

---

[49]   Ibid., 100.

[50]   Ibid.

5

NAR Apostles: A Closer Look

> We are excited about the great movement God is leading to unite apostolic leaders worldwide! ICAL . . . is currently the largest known Christian society of God-ordained and man-recognized apostles in the world.
>
> —John P. Kelly, ICAL Convening Apostle
> *International Coalition of Apostolic Leaders website*

What exactly do NAR apostles do? Does their authority have any limits? And which arguments and Scriptures are assembled to support their existence? We now explore the answers to these questions.

THE FUNCTIONS OF NAR APOSTLES

Here is a list of the things that any apostle will do, according to Peter Wagner:[1]

- An apostle will receive revelation (directly and from prophets).
- An apostle will cast new vision for the church (based on the revelation the apostle has received).
- An apostle will govern within the church.
- An apostle will "birth" new ministries.
- An apostle will lead the church in spiritual warfare.
- An apostle will teach.
- An apostle will impart God's blessings in others (including spiritual gifts[2]).

---

[1]   C. Peter Wagner, *Apostles Today: Biblical Government for Biblical Power* (Ventura, CA: Regal Books, 2006), 28–34, 146–47.

[2]   Wagner describes the impartation in terms of "spiritual gifts" in his book *Spheres of Authority: Apostles in Today's Church* (Colorado Springs, CO: Wagner Publications, 2002), 32.

- An apostle will initiate and carry out projects by strategizing and fundraising.
- An apostle will complete projects by bringing them to desired conclusions.
- An apostle will equip others for ministry.
- An apostle will send out others who are equipped to fulfill their roles in expanding the kingdom of God.
- An apostle will raise up future leadership.

Here is a list of things that are true for many, but not all, apostles.[3] They will:

- have seen Jesus personally;
- perform supernatural manifestations, such as miraculous signs and wonders;
- expose heresy;
- plant new churches;
- appoint and oversee local church pastors;
- settle disputes in the church;
- impose church discipline, including excommunication;
- provide "spiritual covering" (counsel and correction) for other leaders;
- suffer physical persecution;
- attract and distribute financial resources within the network of churches;
- minister cross-culturally;
- fast frequently;[4]

---

[3] Wagner, *Apostles Today*, 30–33, 147. The book includes two lists of the things "many" apostles do. They contain some differences. Our list merges both Wagner's lists. Notice that Wagner says that some will disagree with his judgment that certain apostolic functions are optional. In contrast to Wagner, Rick Joyner believes that having seen Jesus literally and visibly is a non-negotiable characteristic of all apostles. See Joyner, *The Apostolic Ministry* (Wilkesboro, NC: MorningStar Publications, 2004), 78. Bill Hamon believes that all true apostles will perform signs, wonders, and miracles. See Hamon, *Apostles, Prophets, and the Coming Moves of God: God's End-Time Plans for His Church and Planet Earth* (Santa Rosa Beach, FL: Destiny Image Publishers, 1997), 32–34.

[4] Wagner does not describe the purposes of fasting, at least not in this book. He only notes that the apostle Paul fasted often, inappropriately citing 2 Corinthi-

- take back territory from the enemy and transfer it to the kingdom of God;[5]
- cast out demons; and
- break curses of witchcraft.[6]

Limits of an Apostle's Authority

Though apostles have extraordinary authority, they still have limitations, five of which we look at here.

First, apostles have limited spheres of authority. No one apostle has authority over the entire church. NAR leaders note that this marks a major difference between the authority of a NAR apostle and the alleged universality of the Roman Catholic papacy.[7] They explicitly deny the authority of the Pope and see his role as unbiblical. God gives apostles limited specific spheres of authority. Within their assigned spheres, their authority is

---

ans 11:27 as his source. See Wagner's book *Apostles Today*, 33. We say "inappropriately" because, in 2 Corinthians 11:27, Paul does not say that he intentionally fasted often. Rather, he says he went without food. If the statement is read in context, it is clear that his lack of food was involuntary and that hunger was one of many hardships he suffered as an apostle. He lists these hardships starting in verse 23; they include sleep deprivation, exposure to the elements, shipwreck, and severe beatings. So Wagner could as easily, and just as erroneously, have included shipwreck among apostolic functions!

[5] In his lists, Wagner does not specify what this involves or how it is accomplished.

[6] In his comments about this particular apostolic function, Wagner says only: "[The apostle] Paul broke the spirit of divination (witchcraft) in Philippi (see Acts 16:16–18) and directly confronted the occult sorcerer Elymas in Cyprus (see Acts 13:8–11)." See *Apostles Today*, 33.

[7] NAR apostles differ sharply with Roman Catholics, who insist on apostolic succession. See David Cannistraci, *Apostles and the Emerging Apostolic Movement: A Biblical Look at Apostleship and How God is Using it to Bless His Church Today* (Ventura, CA: Renew Books, 1996), 29. Cannistraci implies that apostolic succession is not justified because the teaching "relies more on extrabiblical church tradition than on the clear interpretation of Scripture."

tremendous. But outside their respective spheres, they have no more authority than any other member of the body of Christ.[8]

Nor does any so-called territorial apostle have exclusive jurisdiction in a
geographic region. Instead, multiple apostles may operate in one city at the
same time. In that case, individual apostles are assigned to different sub-
spheres within the city. For example, one apostle might operate within the
black community, another within the Hispanic community, and yet another
within the white community. Some apostles might operate in different parts
of the city, such as the northern part or the southern part. One apostle might
be assigned to youth. Or, among workplace apostles, some may operate in
real estate while others may work in media or education.[9]

None of this implies that present-day apostles have less authority than
the original apostles, according to Wagner. He believes that even the greatest
New Testament apostles had limited spheres of authority and did not function as apostles to the entire church. According to Wagner, the authority of
the apostle Paul was limited to certain regions—Corinth, Ephesus, Philippi,
and Galatia, for example. But Paul's sphere of apostolic authority did not
include Alexandria or Jerusalem or Rome.[10] Those cities were the turf of
other first-century apostles.

Second, apostles should never interfere with the affairs of local churches
in their apostolic networks, according to ICAL convening apostle, John Kelly.
Kelly admits that other NAR leaders disagree with him on this point. But he
believes that an apostle's authority is directly over pastors—not the people in
those pastors' churches. Kelly believes that the only time an apostle should
intervene directly in the affairs of a local church is if the pastor is engaged
in immoral behavior or is teaching heresy.[11] This teaching is in line with the
policy of HIM—one of the largest apostolic networks—which states on its
website that it "will not violate the autonomy of each local congregation."[12]

---

[8]   Wagner, *Apostles Today*, 76.

[9]   Ibid., 99, 132–33.

[10]   Ibid., 75.

[11]   John Kelly and Paul Costa, *End Time Warriors* (Ventura, CA: Regal Books,
1999), 114.

[12]   "Ministry Assumptions," Harvest International Ministry, accessed February
20, 2014, http://harvestim.org/index.php?a=about&s=membership&ss=ministry-
assumptions.

Third, apostles hear from God, but they generally do not hear from him as clearly or consistently as prophets do. They must team with prophets in their reception of revelation. Wagner says, "I would not want to move one step as an apostle without being properly aligned with prophets."[13] In practice, an apostle and a prophet will often "hitch" themselves together in ministry, much as Wagner has teamed with the prophet Chuck Pierce.

Fourth, present-day apostles cannot add new revelation to the canon of Scripture. On this point, most NAR leaders seem to agree. They acknowledge that the twelve apostles had a uniquely authoritative role when it came to writing Scripture.

Nevertheless, present-day apostles can receive new revelation that supplements Scripture so long as it doesn't contradict it. Wagner states: "*The one major rule* governing any new revelation from God is that it cannot contradict what has already been written in the Bible. It may supplement it, however."[14] Nevertheless, an apostle's revelation has great authority. Wagner writes: "While subsequent apostles, such as those recognized as apostles today, will never write holy Scripture, what they do hear from God should nevertheless be taken very seriously by the churches."[15]

Fifth, some NAR leaders teach that present-day apostles cannot have the "unique prominence" of Christ's original twelve apostles, who personally witnessed Christ's resurrection and ascension and were personally trained by him.[16] David Cannistraci writes: "Because they worked and lived directly with Jesus, they shall remain preeminent among the entire apostolic

---

[13] C. Peter Wagner, *Wrestling with Alligators, Prophets, and Theologians: Lessons from a Lifetime in the Church—A Memoir* (Ventura, CA: Regal Books, 2010), 216.

[14] C. Peter Wagner, "The New Apostolic Reformation Is Not a Cult," *Charisma News*, August 24, 2011; accessed June 6, 2014, http://www.charismanews.com/opinion/31851-the-new-apostolic-reformation-is-not-a-cult.

[15] C. Peter Wagner, *Church in the Workplace: How God's People Can Transform Society* (Ventura, CA: Regal Books), 2006, 28.

[16] Wagner, writing before he adopted NAR beliefs, said that the "original 12 apostles have a unique place in Christian history." He does not elaborate on what makes them "unique." In more recent books he doesn't seem to make any distinction between the Twelve and present-day apostles except that the Twelve could write Scripture. See Wagner, *Your Spiritual Gifts Can Help Your Church Grow*, 15th Anniversary Edition (Ventura, CA: Regal, 1994, c1979), 181.

company, and will possess a special prominence in the Kingdom that other New Testament apostles will not achieve" (see Matt. 19:28; Rev. 21:14).

Despite granting a prominence to the Twelve, NAR leaders frequently look to the authority and functions of the Twelve as examples of the authority and functions of present-day apostles. Thus, the place of prominence appears, in our opinion, to be more of an honorary designation than an authoritative one. The major exception made by NAR leaders is that present-day apostles don't have the authority to write Scripture, as did the Twelve. But it does appear that NAR leaders allow for new revelation that is treated on a par with Scripture—despite denials to the contrary. We argue for this later in this book. We also note that NAR leaders typically do not grant a place of prominence to the apostle Paul, while most Protestant Christians believe Paul's stature was equal to that of the Twelve.

ARGUMENTS AND SCRIPTURES USED TO SUPPORT NAR TEACHINGS ON APOSTLES

One major argument Wagner uses to support the present-day office of apostle is a pragmatic one. He notes that churches led by apostles are the fastest-growing churches in nearly every region of the world. Since growth of these churches is accelerating, they must have the "blessing of God" on them.[17] Numerical growth, then—according to Wagner, a widely recognized church growth expert—is a sign of God's blessing.

In contrast to apostle-led churches, Wagner observes that the old-line denominations in the United States, which aren't led by apostles—including Methodists, Lutherans, Episcopalians, and Presbyterians (but excluding Baptists)—began losing members in the late 1960s and 1970s.[18] And Pentecostal denominations in the United States—which "topped the growth charts" from the 1950s through the 1990s—also began to flatten out in the 1990s.[19] Wagner documents his discovery of this connection between fast-growing churches and their apostolic leadership in his 1999 book *Churchquake*: "In 1993, a pattern of divine blessing . . . began to be apparent to me. That was when I began my research . . . seeking to identify and describe

---

[17] C. Peter Wagner, *Churchquake! How the New Apostolic Reformation is Shaking Up the Church as We Know It* (Ventura, CA: Regal Books, 1999), 8–11.

[18] Ibid., 11.

[19] Ibid., 12.

the salient characteristics of what I began to call the New Apostolic Reformation."[20]

Wagner acknowledges that church growth trends don't in themselves validate the New Apostolic Reformation if its teachings cannot be supported by Scripture. Which Scriptures do NAR leaders point to in support of the present-day office of apostle? Here are the three main references. Though others are mentioned as well, Wagner considers these three to be the key supporting texts.[21]

Ephesians 4:11

The passage most cited by NAR leaders to assert both the present-day office apostle and the office of prophet is Ephesians 4:11: "And he gave the apostles, the prophets, the evangelists, the shepherds and teachers . . ."

On the NAR interpretation, Jesus, at his ascension, gave the church five ongoing governmental offices: apostle, prophet, evangelist, pastor, and teacher. This is where the term *fivefold ministry* comes from. These five offices are also commonly called ascension gifts.

A common Protestant understanding of this verse sees the first two groups in the list (apostles and prophets) as foundational and temporary.[22] And it sees the other three groups as ongoing. This understanding is promoted by contemporary cessationist scholars.[23] John MacArthur argues that this verse must be interpreted in light of an earlier verse in the book of Ephesians—Ephesians 2:20—which teaches that apostles and prophets "were limited to the foundation age of the church."[24]

But NAR leaders say there is no good reason to see only three of the five roles as ongoing. They often compare the present church to a hand that has

---

[20] Ibid., 11.

[21] Wagner, *Apostles Today*, 10–13.

[22] John Calvin saw the first three groups, including evangelists, as temporary. See his commentary on Ephesians 4:11 in *The Epistles of Paul the Apostle to the Galatians, Ephesians, Philippians, and Colossians*, Calvin's New Testament Commentaries 11, trans. T. H. L. Parker, ed. David W. Torrance and Thomas F. Torrance (Grand Rapids: Eerdmans, 1996), 179–80.

[23] John MacArthur, *Strange Fire: The Danger of Offending the Holy Spirit with Counterfeit Worship* (Nashville: Thomas Nelson, 2013), Kindle edition, 98–100.

[24] Ibid., 99–100.

only three fingers. According to the metaphor, the church today has limited influence because it does not yet exhibit appropriate regard for all five offices. When the majority of Christians accept all five present-day offices, the church will become God's powerful hand to advance his kingdom.

Wagner asserts that the continuation of all five offices is indicated by the word *until* in verse 13.[25] Verses 11–13 read:

> And he gave the apostles, the prophets, the evangelists, the shepherds and teachers, to equip the saints for the work of ministry, for building up the body of Christ, until we all attain to the unity of the faith and of the knowledge of the Son of God, to mature manhood, to the measure of the stature of the fullness of Christ . . .

Verse 13, Wagner claims, teaches that all five offices must continue for a specified length of time: "until we all [the church] attain to the unity of the faith and of the knowledge of the Son of God, to mature manhood, to the measure of the stature of the fullness of Christ." In other words, he believes that verse 13 teaches that all five offices are needed until the church attains maturity. Wagner writes, "Who in their right mind can claim that we have arrived at that point? The only reasonable conclusion is that we are still in need of all five offices."[26]

We note that NAR leaders are not alone in challenging the standard interpretation of Ephesians 4:11 cited above. That interpretation has also been challenged by more traditional commentators. Clinton Arnold, professor of New Testament and dean at Talbot School of Theology, reasons that there is no exegetical basis for drawing a line between the first two types of gifted leaders in the list (apostles and prophets) and the latter three (evangelists, pastors, and teachers). In contrast to Ephesians 2:20, in which Paul is "reflecting back on the beginnings of the church," in Ephesians 4:11 he addresses the church's "present and ongoing structure." Arnold adds: "Christ is continuing to give these leaders to the church for the equipping of the individual members and facilitating their growth to maturity."[27] Thus Arnold argues that Ephesians 4:11 supports the continuation of apostles through

---

[25]   Wagner, *Apostles Today*, 10–11, 13.

[26]   Ibid., 13.

[27]   Clinton E. Arnold, *Ephesians*, Zondervan Exegetical Commentary on the New Testament (Grand Rapids: Zondervan, 2010), 256.

church history. But, in contrast to Wagner, Arnold denies that these apostles have the same level of authority as the Twelve or Paul.[28]

Ephesians 2:20

Another verse cited by NAR leaders is Ephesians 2:20: "[The church is] built on the foundation of the apostles and prophets, Christ Jesus himself being the cornerstone, . . ."

Wagner believes Ephesians 4:11 teaches that apostles and prophets have ongoing equipping roles in the church. And he believes Ephesians 2:20 makes it clear that these ongoing apostles and prophets hold governmental offices: "Equipping the saints is one thing, but some will say that is not necessarily governing. True, so let's go back a couple of chapters to Ephesians 2:20, where Paul describes the church as the 'household of God.' . . . According to this Scripture, after He ascended and sent the Holy Spirit, He left the nuts and bolts of building the church to the leadership of apostles and prophets."[29] Wagner believes that the apostles and prophets, then, have been tasked with building the church. He apparently believes that task requires that they hold governmental offices.

Historically, many Protestants have understood Ephesians 2:20 as referring to Old Testament prophets and New Testament apostles.[30] According to this historic position, Ephesians 2:20 teaches that the Old Testament prophets and the New Testament apostles—that is, the various human authors of the Bible, writing under the inspiration of the Holy Spirit—provided the doctrinal foundation of the church.

Today, however, nearly all Protestant interpreters believe that Ephesians 2:20 refers to first-century apostles and first-century (not Old Testament) prophets who jointly established the first churches of the Christian era.[31] Notably, their activity included the writing of New Testament Scripture, and thereby establishing foundational doctrine of the church.

According to both of these long-standing Protestant views, a major contribution of the apostles and prophets was to write Scripture or to provide

---

[28] Ibid., 256, 259.

[29] Wagner, *Church in the Workplace*, 23.

[30] Calvin, *Galatians, Ephesians, Philippians, and Colossians*, 154–55.

[31] Arnold notes that this is the predominant contemporary interpretation of Eph. 2:20 in *Ephesians*, 169.

needed revelation to the church until the New Testament Scriptures were completed. Thus, with the completion of the biblical canon, the apostolic mediation of revelation was concluded. Neither of these views understands Ephesians 2:20 as prescribing ongoing offices in church government.

1 Corinthians 12:28

In addition to Ephesians 4:11 and 2:20, a third verse is often cited by NAR leaders in support of the present-day offices of apostle and prophet, 1 Corinthians 12:28: "And God has appointed in the church first apostles, second prophets, third teachers, then miracles, then gifts of healing, helping, administrating, and various kinds of tongues."

According to Wagner, this verse teaches that apostles today occupy the first office in the "order or sequence" of church government (and, by implication, prophets are second).[32] But since present-day apostles have not, historically, been recognized in Protestant churches, teachers (pastors) have wrongly risen to the first position in church government.

> Protestant denominationalism over the past 500 years has been, for the most part, governed by teachers and administrators, rather than by apostles and prophets. . . . It is fascinating that even though we have had church government backward over the past two centuries according to 1 Corinthians 12:28,

---

[32] Wagner, *Apostles Today*, 12. Wagner allows that apostles are first "not necessarily in importance or hierarchy." Yet, this cautious nuance seems to make no real difference in NAR. Wagner's teachings do seem to establish a hierarchical church structure with apostles at the top since, as we have shown, he teaches that pastors are subject to the authority of apostles. Wagner also claims that "apostles hold one of the most exalted offices in the church"; see *Apostles Today*, 44. And he has endorsed many books teaching that apostles hold hierarchical positions in church government. For example, a book written by Héctor Torres—featuring a foreword written by Wagner—says, "The apostles of the New Testament are the judges of the Old Testament." Torres also teaches that "God has placed apostles in authority over prophets"; see Torres, *The Restoration of the Apostles and Prophets: How It Will Revolutionize Ministry in the 21st Century* (Nashville: Thomas Nelson, 2001),115, 196. And John Eckhardt—in another book with a foreword written by Wagner—states that apostles are "first in rank," and goes on to define "rank" as possessing "authority and power" in the "army of God"; see Eckhardt, *Moving in the Apostolic: God's Plan to Lead His Church to the Final Victory* (Ventura, CA: Regal Books, 1999), 45.

we have evangelized so much of the world! Think of what will happen now that church government is getting in proper order.[33]

Numerous Protestant interpreters across denominational lines believe that apostles are listed first in the above verse—and prophets second—because they are first in rank or importance.[34] Of these interpreters, some believe that the apostles and prophets identified in this passage held a temporal office—of highest authority or ranking—in the early church. They deny that this verse establishes ongoing offices in church government. Others believe that the apostles and prophets referenced in 1 Corinthians 12:28 did not hold a limited, temporal office. Rather, they see the apostles and prophets as a wider, non-temporal group of individuals. On this view, apostles and prophets are not listed as first and second because they sit at the top of a hierarchical church structure. Rather, they are first and second because of important functions they have in proclaiming the gospel and establishing churches.

SUMMARY

Apostles in NAR have a number of functions, including receiving revelation from God, casting new vision for the church based on the revelation they have received, and governing within the church. Their authority, though sweeping, does have some limits. They have limited spheres of authority, they must work together with prophets, and they cannot author Scripture. The key Scriptures used to support the existence of present-day apostles are Ephesians 4:11, Ephesians 2:20, and 1 Corinthians 12:28.

In the next chapter we review biblical teaching about the most prominent apostles: the Twelve and Paul.

---

[33] Wagner, *Apostles Today*, 12.

[34] Anthony C. Thiselton, *First Epistle to the Corinthians,* New International Greek Testament Commentary (Grand Rapids: Eerdmans, 2000), 1013–15.

6

Apostles in the Bible: The Twelve and Paul

> He appeared to Cephas, then to the twelve. Then he appeared to
> more than five hundred brothers at one time, most of whom are
> still alive, though some have fallen asleep. Then he appeared to
> James, then to all the apostles. Last of all, as to one untimely born,
> he appeared also to me.
>
> —The Apostle Paul, *1 Corinthians 15:5–8*

DEFINITION OF AN APOSTLE

An apostle—as the word is used frequently in the New Testament—is one whom Christ commissioned as his authorized representative. The Greek word *apostolos* literally means "one who is sent." The English word *apostle* is a virtual transliteration of the Greek. Jesus first used *apostolos* in reference to his original twelve disciples, those whom he commissioned to preach the "kingdom of heaven" to the Israelites (Matt. 10:1–7). Following his resurrection, Jesus recommissioned eleven of those twelve to preach the gospel to all nations (Matt. 28:16–20).[1] Jesus later commissioned Paul, who was then called Saul, to be his authorized delegate to preach the gospel to the Gentiles (Rom. 1:5, 14–15).[2] The Twelve and Paul have historically enjoyed unmatched status in the eyes of Christians, for they were commissioned personally by the Lord and given unique roles in founding the church.

---

[1]   At this point, there were only eleven apostles, not twelve. A substitute had not yet been appointed for Judas Iscariot, who betrayed Jesus and killed himself. See Matt. 26:47–50; 27:3–5.

[2]   See three accounts of Paul's commissioning in the book of Acts (9:1–19; 22:1–21; 26:12–18).

THE TWELVE

The Unique Calling of the Twelve Apostles

That the Twelve held a unique calling is shown by the fact they were designated as the Twelve in the Gospels and in the early church. This honorific set them apart as a distinct and distinguished group (see Acts 6:2; 1 Cor. 15:5). In addition, two more facts demonstrate their unique role: (1) the limitation of their number, and (2) the criterion for inclusion in their group.

The Limitation of Their Number

When their number was reduced to eleven because of Judas's demise, Peter and the others judged, on the basis of Scripture, that they should replace him with another and thus restore the number in their group to twelve (Acts 1:15–26). During a special gathering that followed the ascension of Jesus, Peter cited two Old Testament passages that he believed foretold the need to fill Judas's vacant office: Psalm 69:25 and Psalm 109:8.[3]

It is generally agreed that the number twelve is significant because it parallels the number of the ancient tribes of Israel. The twelve apostles thus serve as a symbolic bridge representing continuity between God's work in and through the nation of Israel and God's new work in and through the church. Jesus told the Twelve that, when his kingdom came, they would sit on twelve thrones and judge the twelve tribes of Israel (Matt. 19:28). The book of Revelation teaches that the New Jerusalem will have a wall with twelve gates bearing the names of the twelve tribes of Israel; the wall will also have twelve foundation stones, bearing the names of Christ's twelve apostles (Rev. 21:12, 14).

In line with this symbolism, the Twelve were sent, initially, to preach exclusively to the Israelites because they were an extension of the first part of Jesus's earthly ministry (Matt. 10:1–7), which, prior to his death and resurrection, was directed to the Israelites so as to reveal himself as their long-awaited Messiah (Matt. 15:24). Only later, following his death for the sins

---

[3] We believe that Peter was correct in his interpretation and that he may even have been instructed by Jesus, on the basis of these predictive passages, to find another to replace Judas. During his brief time on the earth following his resurrection, Jesus instructed his apostles in the significance of Judas's betrayal and in the meaning of much that is taught in the Hebrew Scriptures. See Luke 24:27 and elsewhere.

of all humanity, did Jesus broaden the commission of the Twelve and send them to preach the gospel to all nations (Matt. 28; 1 Tim. 2:4–6). Yet, due to their symbolic significance, they continued to have the leading role in presenting the gospel to the Jews as well. Peter, the most prominent member of the Twelve, was appointed by Christ as the apostle to Jews (Gal. 2:7–8). He, along with John (another influential member of the Twelve) and James (an influential leader in the Jerusalem church), resolved to preach to the Jews. The apostle Paul, on the other hand, was commissioned to minister among the Gentiles (Gal. 2:9).

The Criterion for Inclusion in Their Group

The unique role of the Twelve following Jesus's ascension is also revealed by the criterion used for determining Judas's replacement. Peter stipulated that the man they selected must come from among "the men who have accompanied us during all the time that the Lord Jesus went in and out among us, beginning from the baptism of John until the day when he was taken up from us—one of these men must become with us a witness to his resurrection" (Acts 1:21–22).

The remaining eleven apostles were able to identify two candidates who met this requirement: Barsabbas, also known as Justus, and Matthias. Before making their choice, they prayed and said, "You, Lord, who know the hearts of all, show which one of these two you have chosen to take the place in this ministry and apostleship from which Judas turned aside to go to his own place" (Acts 1:24–25). Following this prayer, they cast lots and unceremoniously selected Matthias.

While the selection process was simple, the felt need for a substitute was serious. It would fall to twelve, no more and no less, to fulfill a unique role. And they were fully convinced that it was God's will that they should make their circle complete and that God would make his own choice clear. Of course, it mattered who was selected. This is the point of Peter's stipulation about the man's qualifications. Like the eleven, Judas's replacement is to serve as a witness to Jesus's resurrection (Acts 1:22).

It's clear, then, that the Twelve functioned as official eyewitnesses of Jesus's earthly ministry—witnesses to all the things he did and taught, culminating in the resurrection. Their singular role as uniquely authoritative eyewitnesses is a recurring theme in the book of Acts. During a sermon preached to the Israelites at the temple, Peter refers to himself and John as witnesses to Jesus's resurrection (Acts 3:15). Later, when Peter and John stand trial before the Jewish leaders for preaching about Jesus, they reply to their accusers that they cannot stop speaking about what they have seen and heard as eyewitnesses (Acts 4:20). During another sermon Peter tells a group of Gentiles: "We are witnesses of all that he did both in the country of the Jews and in Jerusalem. They put him to death by hanging him on a tree, but God raised him on the third day and made him to appear, not to all the people but to us who had been chosen by God as witnesses, who ate and drank with him after he rose from the dead (Acts 10:39–41)." The apostle Paul—not one of the Twelve—also referred to the Twelve as "those who had come up with him from Galilee to Jerusalem, who are now his witnesses to the people" (Acts 13:31).[4]

The Functions of the Twelve Apostles

Proclaiming the Resurrection. As the uniquely appointed eyewitnesses of Jesus's earthly ministry, the Twelve proclaimed the resurrection (Acts 2). They also performed miraculous signs and wonders that confirmed their status as God's special messengers (Acts 2:43; 3:4–8; 5:12).

Governing Churches. As an institution, the group of twelve, who were headquartered in Jerusalem, were the earliest leaders in the church, and they saw it as their duty to oversee all missionary efforts. Thus, they had governing authority extending to churches in other regions. This authority included resolving doctrinal matters and issuing commands, as they did— in conjunction with the elders of the Jerusalem church—at the Council at Jerusalem (Acts 15:2, 6, 22–23).

Providing Eyewitness Testimony for Scripture. Because their eyewitness testimony about Christ's earthly ministry was seen as uniquely authoritative, the Twelve played a unique role in the production of the New Testament Scripture. Their teachings were continually sought by the first believers (Acts 2:42). They passed on Jesus's teachings and the events of his life and ministry, which were preserved in Scripture.

Before he was crucified, Jesus alluded to the Twelve's future role in producing Scripture. He spoke of the "Helper"—that is, the Holy Spirit—whom

---

[4]   Paul did not specifically name the Twelve. But, as official eyewitnesses, they were, no doubt, chiefly who he had in mind, even though there were others who were eyewitnesses of Jesus's entire earthly ministry (shown by the pool of candidates from which Matthias and Barsabbas were selected in Acts 1:21–23).

he would send to help them testify about Jesus and remember all the things he had taught them (John 14:26; 15:26–27). Their divinely inspired accounts of Jesus's ministry formed the biographical content of the four New Testament Gospels—Matthew, Mark, Luke, and John.

Matthew and John wrote the Gospels bearing their names. It is generally believed that John Mark received the material for his Gospel from the apostle Peter. In this way, Mark's report had the authority of an apostle. Luke, at the beginning of his Gospel, directly states that he received his material from "those who from the beginning were eyewitnesses" (Luke 1:2); those eyewitnesses would naturally include the twelve apostles, Christ's official eyewitnesses.[5] Both Mark and Luke, then, recognized that it was imperative that their accounts be properly authorized by the apostolic community. Additional books are attributed to the apostles Peter and John: the first and second letters of Peter, written to the church at large; three letters by John, also distributed to the churches; and the book of Revelation, also called the Apocalypse, written by John at the end of his life.

While Matthew, John, and Peter are the only members of the Twelve who actually penned documents of Scripture, the entire group functioned to preserve, transmit, and certify the authentic teachings of Jesus. When books were being recognized as authoritative for inclusion in the New Testament canon of Scripture, those that were written by one or another of the Twelve— or by their close associates, like Mark and Luke—were safely judged to be divinely inspired. As such, these texts bore the stamp of approval from Jesus's authorized eyewitnesses, those he specifically commissioned as apostles. And by extension, these materials had the authority of Jesus himself.

In short, the Twelve had a unique role as eyewitnesses of Jesus's earthly ministry as revealed by their special designation as "the Twelve," by their closed circle of membership, and by the criterion used for their selection. Their functions included proclaiming the resurrection, governing the church, and providing eyewitness testimony for the production of Scripture.[6]

---

[5]   Furthermore, Luke's close connection with the apostle Paul, a colleague in ministry, was seen to validate his Gospel and the book of Acts. See Bruce M. Metzger, *The Canon of the New Testament: Its Origin, Development and Significance* (Oxford: Oxford University Press, 1987; repr., 2009), 253.

[6]   Later in this chapter we note that the apostle Paul also governed in the early church, and, of course, is the author of the largest portion of what we know as the New Testament Scriptures.

THE APOSTLE PAUL

The Unique Calling of the Apostle Paul

The unique role of the Twelve was grounded in their calling as eyewitnesses of Jesus's entire earthly ministry. In contrast, Paul's unique role was defined by his calling to preach the gospel to the Gentiles. The uniqueness of Paul's role is shown by two facts. First, his commission occurred at an abnormal point in time as compared with other apostles. Second, his commission had a unique scope to spread the gospel throughout the Gentile world.

The Abnormal Timing of Paul's Commission

The Twelve received their commission when Jesus appeared to them in the forty days following his resurrection (Acts 1:3–8). This was before Jesus ascended to heaven. But Paul was not even a follower of Christ at the time and could not have been sent as an apostle until sometime later—at least one or two years after the ascension and perhaps as many as several years later.[7] In due course, Jesus Christ, the ascended Lord, confronted Paul and commissioned him to preach the gospel to the Gentiles, saying:

> *But rise and stand upon your feet, for I have appeared to you for this purpose, to appoint you as a servant and witness to the things in which you have seen me and to those in which I will appear to you, delivering you from your people and from the Gentiles—to whom I am sending you to open their eyes, so that they may turn from darkness to light and from the power of Satan to God, that they may receive forgiveness of sins and a place among those who are sanctified by faith in me.* (Acts 26:16–18)

This was a new development in two respects. First, it inaugurated God's movement among Gentiles in the formation of his church; second, it enlisted a providentially prepared ambassador to the Gentiles, one having the full authority of an apostle, to secure meaningful Gentile outreach.

The result of Paul's encounter with the risen Christ was his immediate and radical conversion. The once violent persecutor of Jesus's followers would become one of their most influential leaders. Paul came to see himself,

---

[7] P. W. Barnett, "Apostle," in *Dictionary of Paul and His Letters*, ed. Gerald F. Hawthorne and Ralph P. Martin (Downers Grove, IL: InterVarsity Press, 1993), 48. Barnett states that Paul's commissioning occurred one or two years after Christ's first post-resurrection appearances. Others place the event later than Barnett.

above all, as an "apostle to the Gentiles" (Rom. 11:13, see also Rom. 1:5; Gal. 1:16; 2:7–9). He believed that God had called him to this unique role even before he was born, just as God had called the Old Testament prophets Isaiah and Jeremiah to their own unique roles before they were born (Gal. 1:15–16).

Paul was keenly aware that his commission occurred at an abnormally late point in time as compared with other apostles. In recounting the many appearances Christ made after his resurrection, in the order of their occurrence, he wrote: "He appeared to Cephas [Peter], then to the twelve. Then he appeared to more than five hundred brothers at one time, most of whom are still alive, though some have fallen asleep. Then he appeared to James, then to all the apostles. Last of all, as to one untimely born, he appeared also to me" (1 Cor. 15:5–8). By referring to himself as "one untimely born," Paul acknowledged that the timing of Christ's appearance to him—in comparison with other apostles—was unprecedented. It didn't occur in the days immediately following Christ's resurrection at the same time he appeared to the Twelve and "all the apostles."[8] The unusually late timing indicated that Paul's commission was atypical and that he had a particular role to fulfill.

In verse 8 of the same passage, Paul also stated that Christ appeared to him "last of all." The majority of New Testament commentators understand his use of the word *last* to be chronological in sense. That is, it is intended to indicate that Paul was the last person to whom Christ made a first-time appearance.[9] Seeing the resurrected Christ was a requirement for being an

---

[8]   An alternative interpretation is presented by some interpreters, like Anthony C. Thiselton and others whose views he outlines. See Thiselton, "First Epistle to the Corinthians," 1208–10. Thiselton believes the Greek phrase, which is translated "one untimely born" in the New American Standard Bible, is better interpreted in other ways, such as a "miscarried" or "aborted" fetus or as a "stillborn child." Thiselton interprets the phrase to be a reference to God's gracious appointment of Paul as "giving life" to one who, in his pre-converted state, was "beyond all hope." Though Thiselton apparently does not see this phrase as a reference to the timing of Paul's commission, he does understand the phrase "last of all," found in the same verse 7, to state that Paul was the last and final apostle (p. 1210).

[9]   Jesus later appeared to John (Rev. 1:9–17), but, of course, John had already been with Jesus, both before and after the resurrection. This time John was revisited by Jesus. Some commentators argue that Paul was only claiming to be the last apostle to whom Christ had appeared up to that point. For a refutation of this argument,

apostle. Paul knew this (1 Cor. 9:1). This suggests that Paul saw himself as the last and final apostle—of the same sort and having the same authority as Jesus's first commissioned apostles.[10]

New Testament scholar Peter Jones[11] argues that Paul was an eschatological figure who played a major role in the unfolding of God's end-time plans. Paul's view was that before Christ's second coming, the gospel would be offered to the Israelites first and to the Gentiles last.[12] Paul saw this sequence foretold in the Old Testament prophecy of Isaiah 49:1–6. Jones believes that Paul alluded directly to this prophecy in 1 Corinthians 15:10—just two verses after verse 8, where his phrase "last of all" occurs—by using language similar to that found in Isaiah 49:4.

According to Jones, Paul recognized that the first part of Isaiah's prophecy (Isa. 49:4–6a) was fulfilled by the Twelve, who were given an apostolate to the Jews; that is, they were sent foremost to preach the gospel to the Jews.[13] And he recognized that the second part of the prophecy (Isa. 49:6) would be fulfilled by himself, the apostle to the Gentiles. Paul's eschatology, then, explains why he saw himself as the last apostle: because he was the apostle to the Gentiles, who would be *last* to be presented with the gospel.[14]

The revelation Paul received about the Gentiles' inclusion in the church, according to Jones, completed the "foundational revelation of the gospel."[15] It also set in motion the last event before the end—the proclamation of the

---

see Peter R. Jones, "1 Corinthians 15:8: Paul the Last Apostle," *Tyndale Bulletin* 36, no. 1 (1985): 19–28.

[10] We later argue that Paul's requirement was only for apostles of a certain type.

[11] Jones taught for seventeen years at the French seminary Faculté de Théologie Réformée in Aix-en-Provence. He presently teaches at Westminster Seminary California.

[12] Jones, "1 Corinthians 15:8," 22–28. According to Jones, Paul saw his mission to the Gentiles as ultimately resulting in turning the Jewish people to Christ (see p. 23).

[13] Ibid., 22–23.

[14] Jones points out that Peter was mentioned first on Paul's list of eyewitnesses to the resurrected Lord while Paul received the last resurrection appearance and was sent to the Gentiles. Jones sees this as further support of Paul's view of Jews first-Gentiles last. Ibid., 22.

[15] Ibid., 32.

gospel to Gentiles, which would be carried on after Paul's death. As a result, there is no need for more apostles after Paul.

> If Paul's gospel, as he says, is the "gospel of the uncircumcision" (τὸ εὐαγγέλιον τῆς ἀκροβυστίας Gal. 2:7), for which he was granted a special revelation of the mystery (Eph. 3:3) concerning the Gentiles (Eph. 3:8), and if according to Isaiah 49:6 (as we have seen), Matthew 24:14, Luke 21:24, and Romans 11:25 the preaching to the Gentiles is the last event before the end, it would appear that the revelation concerning the Gentiles would complete the apostolic gospel for the period preceding the end. [16]

If the conclusion can be drawn from 1 Corinthians 15:8 that Paul was the final apostle, then this shows the uniqueness of Paul's role. We believe Jones makes a compelling case, though we hold that there were later apostles of a different kind than Paul.

The Unique Scope of Paul's Commission

The uniqueness of Paul's role is also shown by the scope of the commission he received: to spread the gospel throughout the Gentile world. Just how momentous Paul's commission to the Gentiles was is often lost on contemporary readers of the New Testament. But it was shocking at the time. When Paul presented his commission to the Jewish leaders—explaining that Christ had sent him away from the Jews because they had rejected Jesus, and sent him to the Gentiles instead, they became irate and wanted to kill Paul. "They listened to him up to this statement, and then they raised their voices and said, 'Away with such a fellow from the earth! For he should not be allowed to live'" (Acts 22:22). The reason for their strong reaction was that many of them viewed Gentiles as evil pagans, even though the Old Testament foretold a time when Gentiles would be included in God's kingdom. The idea that righteous Jews would reject one of God's messengers, as Paul claimed to be, and yet evil Gentiles would receive him, was highly insulting.

The Jewish leaders were not the only ones who were scandalized by Paul's commission. Even the twelve apostles—themselves sent to preach the gospel to *all nations*—did not yet fully grasp that Christ's work on the cross had put Jews and Gentiles on equal footing. It was not until the Council at Jerusalem that they agreed with Paul that the Gentiles did not have to become circumcised or follow other requirements of the Jewish law to be saved (Acts 15).

---

[16]   Ibid., 28.

The Functions of the Apostle Paul

Announcing a New Development in Salvation History

As an apostle to the Gentiles, Paul was authorized to announce a radically new development in salvation history: the gospel was to be preached equally to the Gentiles (Rom. 1:16). His Damascus Road commission marks a turning point in the book of Acts, the focus of which shifts from this point to Paul's work among the Gentiles. Paul told the Ephesians that his commission to the Gentiles played a major role in unfolding God's eternal plan.

> When you read this, you can perceive my insight into the mystery of Christ, which was not made known to the sons of men in other generations as it has now been revealed to his holy apostles and prophets[17] by the Spirit. This mystery is that the Gentiles are fellow heirs, members of the same body, and partakers of the promise in Christ Jesus through the gospel.
>
> Of this gospel I was made a minister according to the gift of God's grace, which was given me by the working of his power. To me, though I am the very least of all the saints, this grace was given, to preach to the Gentiles the unsearchable riches of Christ, and **to bring to light for everyone what is the plan of the mystery hidden for ages** in God who created all things. (Eph. 3:4–9, our emphasis)

In addition to his authorization to announce this new work of God, Paul was to play a strategic role in the fulfillment of it. Paul led extensive missionary campaigns directed toward Gentiles. He traveled across the ancient world, preaching the gospel and planting churches in Gentile regions. His message was confirmed by God with miraculous signs and wonders (Acts 14:3; 19:11–12; Rom. 15:19), and his ministry bore much fruit.

Governing Churches

Like the Twelve, Paul exerted great authority over churches. This is seen in his freedom to issue commands and stern warnings to them, sometimes including discipline (see, for example, 1 Cor. 5:4–5 and 2 Cor. 13:2, 10). Paul even asserted apostolic authority over churches he had not founded. This is seen in his letter to the Romans. The Twelve also acknowledged Paul's

---

[17] Other apostles and prophets also received revelation about the Gentiles' inclusion in the gospel, but Paul was the chief recipient of this revelation.

authority, as demonstrated, for example, when Peter referred to Paul's letters as "Scriptures" (2 Peter 3:16).

Producing Scripture

Paul's most significant function was writing Scripture. He received a number of revelations directly from Christ, including insight into the mystery of Jews and Gentiles being united in the church (Eph. 3:3–6). This revelation—along with Paul's instructions for the early Christians and his other teachings—were contained in letters he sent to churches under his oversight. These letters were eventually included in the New Testament Scriptures. Paul, more than any other New Testament author, explicated the church's doctrinal foundation. He composed more of the New Testament than any other person—thirteen books of the twenty-seven. [18]

In short, Paul had a unique role as an apostle—most likely as the final apostle in a specific category of apostles. This uniqueness, as we have seen, is revealed by the unusual timing and the unprecedented scope of his commission to spread the gospel throughout the Gentile world. In this role, Paul announced a radically new development in salvation history, governed churches with authority, and wrote a significant portion of the New Testament.

SUMMARY

The Twelve and Paul enjoyed unmatched status and authority in the early church. The Twelve had a unique role as eyewitnesses of Jesus's earthly ministry, while Paul had a unique role as an apostle who was sent to preach the gospel to the Gentiles. Their functions included proclamation of the resurrection, government of the church, and responsibility for the writing of Scripture.

In the next chapter we review biblical teaching about the other apostles and false apostles.

---

[18]   Some believe Paul also wrote Hebrews, though the majority of scholars today doubt this.

7

Apostles in the Bible:
The Other Apostles and False Apostles

> Then he [Christ] appeared to James, then to all the apostles.
>
> —The Apostle Paul, *1 Corinthians 15:7*

> For such men are false apostles, deceitful workmen, disguising themselves as apostles of Christ.
>
> —The Apostle Paul, *2 Corinthians 11:13*

In addition to the Twelve and Paul, the New Testament also refers to others as apostles. Some of these other apostles were considered genuine and some were not. Very little information is provided about most of them.

THE OTHER APOSTLES

Paul mentions an untold number of other apostles in 1 Corinthians 15:7, where he listed Christ's resurrection appearances to various groups of people. After listing Peter and the Twelve, and the five hundred to whom Jesus appeared at one time, Paul says: "Then he appeared to James, then to all the apostles." It is clear from the context that the phrase "all the apostles" does not refer to the Twelve or to Paul himself. Who, then, were these other apostles?

Other apostles are also mentioned by name elsewhere in the New Testament. They include Barnabas (Acts 13:2–3; 14:4, 14; 1 Cor. 9:6), Andronicus, and Junia (Rom. 16:7). Still others who may have been called apostles include James the half-brother of Jesus (1 Cor. 15:7; Gal. 1:19; 2:9), other unnamed half-brothers of Christ (1 Cor. 9:5), and Silas (Acts 15:40; 1 Thess. 2:6).

At least some of these individuals had important and prominent functions in the early church. Barnabas was a recognized leader in the church at Antioch and an effective missionary and church planter. Andronicus and Junia are described by no less an authority than Paul as "outstanding among the apostles" (Rom. 16:7).[1] James—if he was an apostle[2]—was an influential leader in the Jerusalem church and the author of a book of Scripture that bears his name. The judgment he issued during the Council at Jerusalem held great sway (Acts 13:1–22).

When were these other apostles commissioned? If 1 Corinthians 15:7 were the only Scripture that referred to them, then it would appear that they were all commissioned during the period of Jesus's post-resurrection appearances. This is a reasonable assumption since both the Twelve—with the exception of Matthias—and Paul received their commissions when Christ appeared to them.[3]

Ephesians 4:11 also refers to other apostles. This verse lists apostles among other gifted leaders that Christ gave the church. Composed about AD 60—some thirty years after Jesus's post-resurrection appearances recalled in 1 Corinthians 15:7—the letter indicates that the Lord was continuing to provide apostles to the churches in Ephesus at this later date. What are we to make of this? How could there be additional apostles if Paul claimed to be the last apostle? The mystery is compounded by the fact that Paul was the author of this letter!

The answer is that there were different types of apostles during the first era of the Christian church. The word *apostle* had a somewhat flexible range of meaning at this time. It could be compared to the English word *messenger*, which is used with some flexibility today. A messenger can be sent by

---

[1]   This phrasing is used by the New International Version and the New American Standard Version. The English Standard Version, consulted elsewhere throughout this book, translates Rom. 16:7 differently, saying that Andronicus and Junia were "well known to the apostles." Some scholars who argue that is doubtful that Andronicus and Junia were apostles are Michael H. Burer and Daniel B. Wallace, "Was Junia Really an Apostle? A Re-examination of Rom 16.7," *New Testament Studies* 47 (2001): 76–91.

[2]   It seems likely, based on Gal. 1:19, that James, the half-brother of Christ, was considered an apostle. Some think he was not, but instead only an influential leader in the Jerusalem church.

[3]   Matthias was an exceptional case, since he received his appointment by Christ through the casting of lots (Acts 1:24–26).

a human individual, by an institution, or by God. In a similar way, apostles could be people sent directly by God, or they could be people who were sent by churches. The type of apostles they were—including the specifics of their roles and the levels of their authority—was determined by the identity of their senders.

Paul may be making such a distinction in the introduction to his letter to the Galatians, where he seems to be describing his own type of apostleship in contrast to other types: "Paul, an apostle—not from men nor through man, but through Jesus Christ and God the Father, who raised him from the dead . . ."(Gal. 1:1). Here Paul appears to describe a difference between an apostle sent out by men and an apostle sent out by Jesus Christ *and God the Father*. He may well be insisting on his own elevated authority above those apostles commissioned merely by churches. Sometimes it pays to examine the original biblical language for nuances that may be significant. This is one of those times.

Here is Paul's statement to the Galatians in Greek:

Παῦλος ἀπόστολος, οὐκ ἀπ' ἀνθρώπων οὐδὲ δι' ἀνθρώπου ἀλλὰ διὰ Ἰησοῦ Χριστοῦ καὶ θεοῦ πατρὸς

Transliteration: *Paulos apostolos, ouk ap anthropon oude di anthropou alla dia Iesou Christou kai theou patros*

The first thing we notice is that Paul's actual diction here is more compact than it is in some English translations. The closest word-for-word translation would be: "Paul an apostle, not from men nor through man, but through Jesus Christ and God the Father." Apart from a relatively trivial difference in punctuation, this is precisely how the passage is translated in the English Standard Version: "Paul an apostle—not from men nor through man, but through Jesus Christ and God the Father."

This is helpful because it reflects the way in which the notion of *being sent*—whether from men or from Jesus Christ and God the Father—is packed into the one word *apostolos*, or apostle. There is no verb in the Greek, no word corresponding to our English word *sent*. Some translators supply the past tense verb *sent* because it's implied in Paul's choice of the term apostle when identifying himself in his greeting. He's an apostle—that is to say, he is one who is sent. The significance of the Greek word *apostolos* is the only basis for interpolating the additional word *sent* found in some English translations, such as the New International Version and New American Standard

Bible, which renders the verse as: "Paul, an apostle (not *sent* from men nor through the agency of man, but through Jesus Christ and God the Father, who raised Him from the dead)."

Translators believe they're doing English readers a favor in making this sense of *apostle* explicit. But something is lost in translation. By calling himself an apostle, Paul has provoked the question, "But who has sent you?" In effect, "Whose apostle are you?" The nature of his apostleship will depend on the answer to this line of questioning.

And Paul answers before the question is raised (perhaps because he believes the question has been raised by some in Galatia). He answers first in the negative, then in the positive, drawing a sharp contrast: "I am not an apostle from men, but from God." He is emphatic as well. He does this through virtual repetition when he answers in the negative: "Make no mistake, I am not an apostle *from* men; I am not an apostle *through* men. Men have nothing to do with my apostleship." Paul's positive answer is equally emphatic: "I am an apostle through Jesus Christ *and* God the Father." Paul is absolutely unequivocal about that.

So, here in this passage in Galatians, if Paul is distinguishing between types of apostles, then the distinction is going to turn on what agency is doing the sending. Clearly, he claims superlative authority by virtue of being sent through powerful divine agency, rather than from or through some human agency. On this interpretation, Paul sets himself apart from other kinds of apostles. Paul doesn't denigrate the idea of being sent by or through some human entity or agency. One could be sent in such a way and thus be a kind of apostle. But this is not the kind of apostle Paul is, for he is sent through divine agency. And this difference makes all the difference in the world.

Others have given this verse careful attention and acknowledged the distinction that Paul makes between types of apostles.[4] Numerous commentators have also identified different types of apostles in the New Testament.[5]

---

[4] An example is R. C. H. Lenski in his commentary on Galatians in *The Interpretation of St. Paul's Epistles to the Galatians, to the Ephesians and to the Philippians* (Minneapolis: Augsburg Publishing House, 1961), 19–24.

[5] I. Howard Marshall, "Apostle," in *New Dictionary of Theology*, ed. Sinclair B. Ferguson and David F. Wright, Master Reference Collection (Downers Grove, IL: InterVarsity Press, 1988), 40; Craig L. Blomberg and Jennifer Foutz, *A Handbook of New Testament Exegesis* (Grand Rapids: Baker Academic, 2010), 222–23.

Kenneth Berding, for example, identifies four distinct categories of apostles.[6] Some who are designated apostles belong to more than one category:

1. The Twelve, who were "appointed by Christ himself and set apart to share in his mission" (Matt. 10:1ff.; Mark 3:13–19; Luke 8:1; 9:1; John 6:70; Acts 1:26; 6:2; 1 Cor. 15:5).

2. A larger group that included the Twelve, James the half-brother of Jesus, Paul, and all "those who were eyewitnesses of Christ's post-resurrection experiences" (1 Cor. 9:1; 15:5–9).

3. "Those who were not necessarily eyewitnesses of the resurrection (although they may have been), but were specially appointed as missionaries for a broader ministry," including Paul (Acts 13:2–3; Eph. 3:7–9), Barnabas (Acts 13:2–3; 14:4, 14), Silas (Acts 15:40; 1 Thess. 2:6), and perhaps Timothy (cf. 1 Tim. 4:14; 2 Tim. 1:6), Titus (2 Cor. 8:19), and others unknown to us today.

4. "Those who were simply messengers or representatives of particular churches sent out on short-term ministry tasks" (1 Cor. 8:16–24; Phil. 2:25; cf. Acts 15:22; 8:14; 11:22; 15:3, 33; 19:22; 1 Cor. 4:17; Eph. 6:22; Col. 4:8; 1 Thess. 3:2; 2 Tim. 4:12).

Berding describes the first two categories of apostles as "formal"[7] and "authoritative."[8] The apostles of Christ were all eyewitnesses of Christ's post-resurrection appearances. The second two categories he describes as "functional," meaning that they met "particular needs at particular times."[9] The functional apostles (in Berding's categories 3 and 4) were not necessarily eyewitnesses, but were commissioned by churches to fulfill functions similar to missionaries, church planters, and church representatives.

There can be no doubt that there were different types of apostles. This fact implies that Paul's statement in 1 Corinthians 15:7—that Christ appeared to *all* the apostles—refers not to everyone who is called an apostle in the New Testament, but rather to everyone who was an apostle in the formal sense. To keep this distinction clear, we'll follow the practice of Paul and refer to

---

6   Kenneth Berding, *What Are Spiritual Gifts? Rethinking the Conventional View* (Grand Rapids: Kregel Publications, 2006), 206–7.

7   Ibid., 207.

8   Ibid., 325 (Appendix A, note 2).

9   Ibid., 207, 325 (Appendix A, note 2).

those formal apostles as "apostles of Christ" (2 Cor. 11:13) and to those who were functional apostles as "apostles of the churches" (2 Cor. 8:23).

Notice, the apostles of Christ were not limited to the Twelve and Paul. They included the other, unidentified apostles Paul mentions in 1 Corinthians 15:7. Since they're unidentified, we can't say who the other apostles of Christ were. Berding speculates that Barnabas may have been an apostle of this type since he appears so early in the book of Acts.[10] There really is no way to know for certain. Whoever the apostles of Christ were in addition to the ones named, they were part of a limited circle of people who had seen the resurrected Christ and operated with special authority in the first Christian era. Presumably, however, there continued to be a special reason for an intimate group of disciples to be exactly twelve in number. It was judged imperative by eleven of the Twelve that they find a replacement for Judas Iscariot, and Matthias filled the bill of strict requirements.

Also notice that being an eyewitness was a necessary condition for being an apostle of Christ. In other words, apostles of Christ only received their recognition as apostles based on an appearance from the Lord. This is consistent with Paul's view. He cited having "seen Jesus our Lord" as evidence of his own apostleship (1 Cor. 9:1).

Being an eyewitness was not a sufficient condition, however. Paul states in 1 Corinthians 15:6 that Christ appeared to "more than five hundred brothers at one time." These brethren, though they were blessed with an eyewitness appearance, are not called apostles—in clear contrast to those who are called apostles in the immediately surrounding verses. Presumably, then, one could have been an eyewitness without receiving the status of an apostle of Christ.

So, what criteria, other than an eyewitness experience of Christ, qualified one as an apostle of Christ and differentiated one from those who were eyewitnesses? In addition to an eyewitness encounter, the Twelve and Paul also received a personal commission from Christ. We can infer, then, that the others referred to as apostles of Christ also received a personal commission from Christ when he appeared to them.

Apostles of Christ would thus naturally have greater stature and authority than apostles of the churches. This could explain why James—if he was indeed an apostle of Christ—had such great authority in the early church. Even though he wasn't included among the Twelve or specially called in the

---

[10]   Ibid., 325 (Appendix A, note 1).

manner that Paul was, he is singled out by name in 1 Corinthians 15:7 as having witnessed an appearance from Christ. Paul thought it significant to mention James by name, and he surely had a reason for doing so.[11]

As significant as their role surely was, none of the other apostles of Christ, including James, appears to have exercised the level of authority that the Twelve and Paul had. We have already demonstrated that the Twelve had great authority, governing the early churches and providing official eyewitness testimony to Christ's earthly ministry—testimony that was crucial to the production of Scripture. Paul shared a level of authority equal to theirs, as is shown in at least two ways: (1) he publicly rebuked Peter, the most prominent member of the Twelve, to his face for actions that Paul considered counter to the way of the gospel (Gal. 2:11–14); and (2) the Twelve acknowledged Paul's authority as equal to theirs when they acknowledged that God had sent Paul to the Gentiles in a way parallel to God's sending of Peter to the Jews. Peter also referred to Paul's letters as "Scriptures" possessing authority equal to the Scripture of the Old Testament (2 Peter 3:16).

Though some apostles of Christ—specifically, the Twelve and Paul— clearly had greater authority than others, it is not clear if all apostles of Christ performed miracles. Paul stated that the signs of a true apostle included "signs and wonders and miracles" (2 Cor. 12:12). He evidently did not mean to imply that miracles were necessary signs of those considered to be apostles of the churches. But were they a necessary sign of *all* considered to be apostles of Christ, or just of himself and the Twelve? Scripture doesn't say. We've already noted that the Twelve and Paul performed miracles. Others who performed miraculous signs and wonders in the early church included Stephen (Acts 6:8), Philip (Acts 8:6), and Barnabas (Acts 14:3; 15:12). Stephen and Philip—who are called deacons, not apostles—appeared to receive their ability to perform miraculous signs after the twelve apostles laid hands on them (Acts 6:6). Whether Barnabas could perform miracles due to possible status as an apostle of Christ or for some other reason—perhaps because Paul, his close colleague, had laid hands on him—is not known. Notice that we're not saying that apostles of Christ, or their close colleagues, were the

---

[11] James was a half-brother of Christ, which would have given him stature in the early church. But Jesus's other half-brothers did not appear to have the same stature. Something was different about James.

only Christians who performed miracles.[12] We're saying that, according to Paul, miracles were performed by all true apostles of a certain kind—by the Twelve, Paul, and possibly (though we can't know for sure) by all apostles of Christ.

In short, other apostles—in addition to the Twelve and Paul—are named in the New Testament. Some of these others were apostles of Christ, commissioned personally by Christ to preach the gospel. Because of their divine commission, they probably exercised a significant degree of authority, though not at the level of the Twelve or Paul. Others were apostles of the churches—selected by the churches to perform important services—who need not have seen the resurrected Lord and probably did not exercise great authority. They functioned during the first Christian era much as missionaries, church planters, and church representatives do today.

We pause here to emphasize how little we know of the details that naturally interest us and other readers of the New Testament. That there were different kinds of apostles, we can be sure. That these distinctions mattered also is clear. We're confident that what's needed for the church to flourish today has been revealed in the New Testament. It's presumptuous, therefore, to claim that more is needed, and it is a threat to the integrity of Scripture to force an interpretation that is not warranted by the evidence.

With this in mind, we now look at another group of apostles present in the early church.

FALSE APOSTLES

In addition to the different types of genuine apostles recorded in the New Testament, we also find another group known as "false apostles." These imposters claimed status as apostles of Christ though they had not been sent by Christ. Paul spoke of false apostles who had infiltrated the church at Corinth, where they tried to usurp his status as an apostle: "For such men are false apostles, deceitful workmen, disguising themselves as apostles of Christ. And no wonder, for even Satan disguises himself as an angel of light. So it is no surprise if his servants, also, disguise themselves as servants of righteousness. Their end will correspond to their deeds (2 Cor. 11:13–15)."

---

[12]   1 Cor. 12:29 indicates that there were other workers of miracles in the early church.

Paul's late commissioning no doubt made him vulnerable to attacks from those who were trying to discredit him as an apostle.

False apostles had also tried to infiltrate the church at Ephesus. In this they failed. We know of their attempt because Jesus spoke about it through the revelation he gave to the apostle John, recorded in the book of Revelation. In a letter Jesus dictated to the church at Ephesus, he praised the Ephesian Christians for thwarting these false apostles: "I know your works, your toil and your patient endurance, and how you cannot bear with those who are evil, but have tested those who call themselves apostles and are not, and found them to be false (Rev. 2:2)."

How did the Ephesian Christians recognize the false apostles in their midst? They must have observed some of the same characteristics as were displayed by the false apostles at the church at Corinth. These characteristics are found in Paul's second letter to the Corinthians, which was written specifically to refute these false apostles. Paul contrasts his own motivations and manner of ministry with theirs. They were motivated by a desire for money (2 Cor. 2:17) and self-promotion (2 Cor. 4:5), and were concerned with superficialities—like physical appearance and polished speaking skills—rather than true inner spirituality (2 Cor. 5:12; 10:10). They were arrogant, boasting that they were super-apostles (2 Cor. 11:5; 12:11). They twisted Scripture deceptively to serve their own purposes (2 Cor. 4:2). Most alarmingly, they did not teach the truth about Christ and his saving work, but instead preached another Jesus and a different gospel (2 Cor. 11:4).

In addition, they falsely claimed that they received visions and revelations from God. By doing so, they asserted that their ecstatic experiences were the equivalent of the requirement for all apostles of Christ of having seen the resurrected Lord. This explains why Paul feels compelled to boast, against his humble instincts, about his own visions and revelations, which, in contrast to theirs, were genuine (2 Cor. 12:1–4).

The false apostles also were apparently unable to perform miracles to authenticate their claims to apostolic status. In contrast to these powerless apostles, Paul said of his own ministry to the Corinthians, "The signs of a true apostle were performed among you with utmost patience, with signs and wonders and mighty works" (2 Cor. 12:12).

These false apostles weren't claiming merely to be apostles of the churches, but to have a status greater than that of Paul himself. Paul and Jesus's references to false apostles, made to two different churches, indicate that these pretenders were both numerous and influential in the early church.

Thus, in addition to the different types of true apostles present in the early church, there were also false apostles. These false apostles preached not from sincere hearts, but from selfish desires for personal gain and status. Theirs was a false gospel that did not convey accurately the truth about Christ and his saving work. They lacked the required credentials of all apostles of Christ—having seen the Lord and received a personal commission from him. They also, in contrast to the Twelve and Paul, couldn't perform miraculous signs.

SUMMARY

In addition to the Twelve and Paul, other apostles are named in the New Testament. Though they had important roles, they did not exercise great authority like the Twelve and Paul. Rather, they functioned during the first Christian era much as missionaries, church planters, and church representatives do today. In addition to the different types of true apostles found in the Bible, there are also false apostles, who were both numerous and influential in the early church.

In the next chapter we compare genuine apostles in the Bible to NAR apostles.

8

NAR Apostles Compared to the Bible's Apostles

> It is important to be exceedingly clear that no one today possess-
> es the same level of authority as the Twelve or Paul.
>
> —Clinton E. Arnold, *Ephesians*

Now that we've described the different apostles in the New Testament, we must ask how NAR teachings on apostles line up with Scripture. Does the Bible teach that apostles have an ongoing role in the church? If so, then what does that role look like? Is there a present-day *office* of apostle, as taught by NAR leaders, or something more like a *ministry function*, as Pentecostals believe?

OFFICE OR FUNCTION?

The answer depends on which type of apostle is being referred to. Apostles of the formal kind—including the Twelve, Paul, probably James, and all the other apostles to whom Christ appeared following his resurrection—do not continue today. The apostle Paul's statement in 1 Corinthians 15:8 suggests that he was the final apostle of this kind. With the passing of the first generation of Christians, there can be no more living eyewitnesses who could add to the Gospel records of Jesus's life and teachings. This closes the door on any apostles, since the time of the Twelve, who would claim to share in their unique contribution and office. Paul also had a unique role as the apostle to the Gentiles.

All the apostles of Christ, except Paul, received appearances from Christ in the forty days following Jesus's resurrection. This is an important point, because it shows that Jesus had a particular purpose for remaining on earth during those forty days rather than ascending immediately to heaven. He had work to do. What was he doing? He was making sure that leaders were set in place and equipped to carry on the work he had begun. He appeared to them, commissioning them as eyewitnesses to the fact of his resurrection. He explained the Scriptures to them and told them what to do after he was gone. Luke spoke of Jesus's leadership-building activities at the beginning of the book of Acts.

> *In the first book, O Theophilus, I have dealt with all that Jesus began to do and teach, until the day when he was taken up, after he had given commands through the Holy Spirit to the apostles whom he had chosen. He presented himself alive to them after his suffering by many proofs, appearing to them during forty days and speaking about the kingdom of God.* (Acts 1:1–3)

Jesus determined that he needed to be physically present to raise up the church's first leadership. Paul was an exception. That Jesus felt he needed to be present to commission the apostles of Christ suggests that he would not typically commission them after he ascended to heaven.

The apostles of Christ understood that their role in governing the church was temporary. As they aged, and in preparation for their departure, they appointed elders to govern the church (Titus 1:5; 1 Peter 5:1–3; Acts 14:23) rather than ordaining any new apostles of Christ to succeed them. So, contrary to the claims of NAR leaders, the church did not intentionally suppress, or even unintentionally neglect, the office of apostle. It followed the system of church government that had been established by the apostles of Christ themselves—that is, a government led by elders (later called bishops).

Apostles of the functional kind, however, do continue. The apostle Paul made this clear in Ephesians 4:11, where he listed the types of gifted leaders that God has given the church in its ongoing structure. Ephesians 4:11 does not list every type of gifted leader, but only those that are essential to the establishment of local churches and the proclamation of the Word of God.[1] There's no reason to believe that leaders of this type—including the untold number of functional apostles who served the early church as missionaries and church planters—would no longer be needed by the church. This fact is so obvious that the church has intuitively recognized it; missionaries and church planters have functioned throughout church history to the present day. They simply have not always been called apostles.

This avoidance of the word *apostle* when referring to present-day missionaries and church planters is appropriate. In New Testament times, people would have realized that the word carried a flexible range of meaning.

---

[1] Clinton E. Arnold, *Ephesians*, Zondervan Exegetical Commentary on the New Testament (Grand Rapids: Zondervan, 2010), 256.

But calling people apostles today, when the majority of Protestants think of apostles in the formal sense—as apostles of Christ—would no doubt cause confusion. On this point, theologian Wayne Grudem (himself a charismatic) apparently concurs when he says, "It is noteworthy that no major leader in the history of the church—not Athanasius or Augustine, not Luther or Calvin, not Wesley or Whitefield—has taken to himself the title of 'apostle' or let himself be called an apostle."[2]

But we agree with the position that people exist today who function as "apostles of the churches." And we emphasize that these people have essential roles to play. This seems clear from the way they're listed first in Ephesians 4:11 and 1 Corinthians 12:28. Reading these verses in the contexts of their surrounding passages shows that they refer to a temporally unrestricted group of individuals whom God has gifted to make ongoing contributions on behalf of the church. The importance of their contributions stems from what they do: they proclaim the gospel and establish new churches.

Yet, for several reasons, we disagree with the NAR position that an office of apostle—a formally recognized position in church government—exists today.

First, the fact that NAR churches are growing quickly is not necessarily a sign of God's approval of them. All church growth isn't necessarily healthy growth. The New Testament contains multiple warnings about false apostles, false prophets, and false teachers who will accumulate many followers (Matt. 24:4–5, 11; Acts 20:29–30; 2 Peter 2:1–2; 1 John 2:18–19; 2 John 7; Jude 3–4). Wagner's argument from church growth is glaringly insufficient.

Second, there's no indication from Scripture that today's "apostles" hold formal, governmental offices. The three key Scriptures that Wagner cites do not support present-day offices. Ephesians 4:11—the linchpin verse for NAR leaders—does not list all the various types of gifted leaders God has given the church. It certainly doesn't prescribe five governmental offices. In fact, it doesn't speak of "offices" at all.

Nor does 1 Corinthians 12:28. The other ministries included in Paul's list in 1 Corinthians 12:28–29 appear to be more functional rather than official. This would indicate that the apostles in this list are also of the functional kind. As Berding states, "A list, after all, usually includes items that fit

---

[2] Wayne Grudem, *Systematic Theology: An Introduction to Biblical Doctrine* (Grand Rapids: Zondervan, 1994), 911.

together under a single conception."[3] The functional apostles in this list are ranked as first in importance because their functions—proclaiming the gospel and establishing churches—are of fundamental importance, not because they are powerful figures in a hierarchical church government.

Finally, Ephesians 2:20 also does not prescribe ongoing offices as NAR leaders often claim. This verse says nothing about governing offices. Furthermore, it is speaking about the time period at the beginning of the church, when it was founded by first-century apostles and prophets. So it cannot properly be used to teach that there is an ongoing office of apostle.

Indeed, there is no attempt to replace the Twelve after their deaths.[4] Scripture doesn't provide any instruction for the appointment of future apostles of Christ to govern the church. If the appointment of apostles to a formal governmental office is essential to the health of the church, then surely Scripture would contain such instruction. In addition, there would need to be church officials, themselves apostles, to make such appointments. Evidence of a hiatus in the stream of apostles of Christ is evidence that there are no longer apostles of Christ.[5]

We acknowledge that Scripture is not specific about all details concerning church governance. Thus, there is room for divergent forms. But any claim that churches *must* observe a form of church governance that includes the present-day office of apostle—or otherwise be lacking in some important way—goes well beyond Scripture. Wagner emphatically states, "Churches that fail to recognize the position of apostles and prophets, not in a hierarchy but in a divine order, cannot expect to be everything that God originally designed them to be."[6] He goes even further, referring to church leaders who object to apostle-led governance as "unanointed leaders of old

---

[3]   Kenneth Berding, *What Are Spiritual Gifts? Rethinking the Conventional View* (Grand Rapids: Kregel Publications, 2006), 207. Berding allows that, in Paul's mind, there may have been some overlap in concept between the formal and functional categories.

[4]   We have already noted that Judas was replaced after his death, but once his vacant office was filled and the circle of twelve was completed, there was no attempt to replace others of the Twelve after their deaths.

[5]   This has always been part of the rationale behind the doctrine of apostolic succession for Roman Catholics, the Orthodox Church, and Anglicans.

[6]   C. Peter Wagner, *Church in the Workplace: How God's People Can Transform Society* (Ventura, CA: Regal Books, 2006), 23.

wineskins."[7] He asserts that they are under the influence a powerful demon known as the "corporate spirit of religion."[8]

Granted, Wagner claims that NAR is not establishing a hierarchy. But his claim appears to be undermined by his own teachings. It's difficult to imagine how a hierarchy is not formed when he writes about "the unusual amount of authority entrusted to apostles."[9] Indeed, Wagner seems to tacitly acknowledge a hierarchy when he speaks of one benefit of having apostolic networks as "pain-free church government."[10] By "pain-free," he seems to imply that, since pastors call all the shots in their local churches—and apostles call the shots in apostolic networks—NAR churches will not have to experience the bureaucratic hurdles that accompany more democratic systems of government. Yet, the cost of such pain-free church government is that there is little room for dissent.

Wagner also seems to tacitly acknowledge a hierarchy when he writes about the need for apostles to submit themselves voluntarily to the authority of an overseeing apostle so they can have some system for accountability. Yet he admits that he doesn't know to whom the overseeing apostle will submit. Furthermore, his suggestion that apostles submit to an overseeing apostle raises an even larger concern about accountability. Since overseeing apostles wield far-reaching authority that extends to multiple other apostles—each overseeing their own network of churches and ministries—what will prevent these overseeing apostles from joining up with other overseeing apostles, ultimately leading to the emergence of one apostle with pope-like authority? And even if such a figure should emerge, there is no guarantee that apostles would submit to his authority. Indeed, there is no guarantee that all apostles will voluntarily submit to the authority of *any* overseeing apostle. Wagner acknowledges the crucial protection afforded by checks and balances in civil government.[11] But, for some reason, he sees these as a hindrance and not a protection in church government. This seems to us to be inconsistent.

---

[7]   C. Peter Wagner, *Changing Church* (Ventura, CA: Regal Books, 2004), 21.

[8]   Ibid., 18–22.

[9]   C. Peter Wagner, *Apostles Today: Biblical Government for Biblical Power* (Ventura, CA: Regal Books, 2006), 43.

[10]   C. Peter Wagner, *Dominion! How Kingdom Action Can Change the World.* Grand Rapids: Chosen Books, 2008), 34.

[11]   Ibid., 15.

All of this unchecked power could lead to apostles exercising abusive leadership and promoting heretical teachings. So the question of account-ability for apostles is significant and remains unanswered. Even during the first generation of the Christian church, provisions were made for discern-ing whether this or that person was an apostle, and this depended on his relationship to apostles of Christ, whose authority was traceable to Christ's direct commissioning of them. Accountability for them was not the prob-lem that it is for NAR apostles.

NAR leaders might respond that accountability is not as big a problem as it might seem because NAR churches join apostolic networks voluntari-ly and, thus, can withdraw at any time if they feel that an apostle is being abusive or promoting heretical teachings. But one must understand that, ac-cording to NAR teachings, failure to submit to a NAR apostle is seen as fail-ure to submit to God. Recall Bill Hamon's words: "It is almost impossible for individuals to humble themselves under God without humbling themselves in submission and relationship to Christ's delegated representatives of Him to His Church."[12] Also recall Wagner's statement that a pastor rarely leaves an apostolic network because "apostolically oriented pastors . . . are con-vinced that they would not be able to reach their full destiny in serving God apart from the spiritual covering of the apostle."[13] In any case, how could any pastor be sure that he was discerning correctly that this or that apostle within the network had disqualified himself or really was not an apostle to begin with? Thus, there is subtle but powerful pressure for pastors to remain under an apostle's authority.

INADEQUATE SCRIPTURAL SUPPORT FOR THE NAR POSITION

Through his interpretation of Scripture, Wagner has shown that he be-lieves that apostles continue today. But he hasn't made an adequate case. He speaks of all New Testament apostles as if they were all apostles of Christ, like the Twelve and Paul. But this clearly is not so. After building his argu-ment for the continuation of apostles (without distinguishing between kinds of apostles), Wagner, whether knowingly or unknowingly, has extended that

---

[12]   Bill Hamon, *Apostles, Prophets, and the Coming Moves of God: God's End-Time Plans for His Church and Planet Earth* (Santa Rosa Beach, FL: Destiny Image Publishers, 1997), 153.

[13]   Wagner, *Changing Church*, 36.

idea to include the NAR office and associated this office with extraordinary authority to govern.

To be fully consistent, Wagner must not only show that apostles continue today. He must show also that apostles of the formal kind—"apostles of Christ," to recall New Testament language—continue today. This means that he must more adequately address Paul's statement in 1 Corinthians 15:8, where Paul regards himself as the final apostle. In his six books about apostles, Wagner nowhere addresses this verse.[14] That he would neglect a verse with such obvious bearing on his teachings is inexplicable. Many see it as a key verse marking Paul as the final apostle. Even if Wagner disagrees with our interpretation—as he certainly does—he should acknowledge it and offer a better interpretation.

But if Wagner should decide to address this statement, then he cannot simply argue, with a minority of interpreters, that Paul did not say that Christ appeared to him *last*, but rather *least*. Jones has given a number of reasons why this translation is flawed, including the fact that it is virtually impossible from a grammatical standpoint.[15] Wagner must also address Jones's argument that Paul saw himself as fulfilling an eschatological role that made any further apostles—at least those of a certain type—unnecessary.

Further, Wagner must deny that there is any significance to the fact that Jesus personally appointed all the New Testament apostles—and all of them while he was physically present on earth. Wagner has taken the apparent exceptions of Matthias and Paul and made then into a rule, throwing open the door to an unlimited number of apostles of Christ.

Even if Wagner can overcome these obstacles and show that Scripture supports the continuation of apostles of Christ, he still has not made his case for NAR apostles. The authority of such an apostle—especially one on the level of the Twelve or Paul—would be so considerable that anyone who claims it would have a significant burden of proof.

That burden is not lessened by Wagner's claims that the Twelve and Paul had limited, territorial spheres of authority. This is not supported by Scripture. Paul and Peter both wrote letters to churches they didn't found: Romans, and 1 and 2 Peter. Each opens his letter by identifying himself as an

---

14   It is conceivable that we have overlooked some obscure discussion of it in his writings.

15   Peter R. Jones, "1 Corinthians 15:8: Paul the Last Apostle," *Tyndale Bulletin* 36, no. 1 (1985): 17.

apostle (Rom. 1:1; 1 Peter 1:1), thereby asserting his authority over these churches. Their authority is so far-reaching that it extends over all churches, worldwide, to this day, through the Scriptures they wrote.

On the one hand, Wagner's teaching about "spheres of authority" appears to ease the tension caused by "apostolic overlap"—the problem that occurs when numerous apostles pop up in the same city or the same sector of society. But it also challenges the traditional view of New Testament apostles whose authority, in some sense, extended over the entire church.

Also, in apparent contradiction to his teaching about limited spheres of authority, Wagner states that some NAR apostles—called "broadband apostles"—receive new revelation for the corporate church,[16] which would seem to imply that they do assert authority over the entire church. The existence of such broadband apostles undermines Wagner's claim that apostles cannot write new Scripture—or so it seems to us. In claiming to give new revelation that is binding on all Christians, are they not claiming, in effect, that their revelation should be treated on a par with Scripture, even if their words aren't physically appended to a Bible?

SUMMARY

Scripture indicates that apostles of Christ—including the Twelve, Paul, and the other apostles to whom Christ appeared and specially commissioned following his resurrection—do not continue today. Other apostles— the apostles of the churches—have an ongoing role, but they do not govern. Their functions are similar to those of today's missionaries and church planters. Since the scriptural evidence indicates that the New Testament governmental office of apostle no longer exists, NAR leaders who claim to hold this office must first demonstrate that the office is ongoing. This they have failed to do.

In the next chapter we explain five biblical tests for determining whether an alleged apostle is a genuine apostle of Christ or not.

---

16   Wagner, *Dominion!*, 36–37.

9

Testing NAR Apostles

> I know your works, your toil and your patient endurance, and
> how you cannot bear with those who are evil, but have tested
> those who call themselves apostles . . .
>
> —Jesus, speaking to the church in Ephesus, *Revelation 2:2*

NAR apostles do not claim merely to be missionaries and church planters, groups that, as we have seen, could be considered types of present-day apostles according to the evidence of Scripture. Rather, NAR apostles claim to hold a formal office in church government similar to that of the "apostles of Christ in the New Testament." In our assessment, leaders of the NAR have failed to produce biblical support for their teaching that present-day apostles must govern the church. But even if they could provide the needed support, such apostles must still pass five biblical tests for being genuine apostles.

First, apostles must quite literally have seen the resurrected Lord. Second, they must have received a specific commission by Christ in the fashion of those first commissioned during the Apostolic Age. Third, they must perform miracles that attest to their authority as apostles of Christ. Fourth, any new teachings or practices they promote must be supported in Scripture. Fifth, they must exhibit an exemplary quality of ministry and lives of the highest level of virtue and integrity. We will now consider each of these tests briefly.

AN APPEARANCE FROM CHRIST

Peter Wagner believes that a personal appearance from Christ should not serve as a litmus test for determining whether a person is truly an apostle or not.[1] This is curious. For Paul, having "seen Jesus our Lord" was a criterion for all apostles of Christ (1 Cor. 9:1). Why, then, are NAR apostles exempt?

---

[1] C. Peter Wagner, *Apostles Today: Biblical Government for Biblical Power* (Ventura, CA: Regal Books, 2006), 30.

Wagner doesn't say. (He does maintain, however, that about 20 percent of the apostles he knows have seen Jesus personally.[2])

To satisfy this requirement, it's not even enough, really, to claim to have seen Christ. If such a claim is to be believed, one must be able to demonstrate that the appearance occurred. How would an apostle do that today? In the case of the apostle Paul, others could provide testimony to corroborate his claim. His traveling companions were on the scene when Christ appeared to him. They didn't see Christ, but they saw the bright light that appeared and heard the sound of his voice. They also saw the powerful effect Christ's appearance had on Paul—how it blinded him for three days and caused a complete reversal in his plans to persecute the church at Damascus. After he appeared to Paul, Christ also appeared to Ananias in a vision and told him of his appearance to Paul. Ananias, then, could provide further testimony to substantiate Paul's claim. Also, and this is crucial, Paul took counsel with the other apostles of Christ after a lengthy period of reflection and self-examination. Three years into his Christian life, he "went up to Jerusalem" to see Peter and "remained with him fifteen days" (Gal. 1:18). Paul recounts his meeting in the context of establishing his credentials as an apostle. Evidently his time with Peter was critical to confirmation of Paul's status as an apostle of Christ. This was evidence that he was the real deal.

Paul's instantaneous, radical conversion from a persecutor of the Christians to one of their most vocal leaders suggested that he had had a genuine encounter with Christ. Christ's appearance to Paul was not an empty claim with no independent validation. Others could attest to it and to the life-changing effects it had on him (Gal. 1:11–24).

NAR apostles cannot dismiss the requirement to have seen Christ. And if they truly have received an appearance from him, then others should be able to confirm it. These corroborating witnesses would have to be of comparable stature to those we read about in the New Testament, as was Peter in the case of Paul. The logic of this situation would require an unbroken chain of apostolic officials going back to the original apostles. Surely, God, who appointed no less than twelve official eyewitnesses to contribute to the writing of four separate Gospel accounts of Christ's life—and to vouch for Paul— would be as concerned to provide multiple voices of testimony to verify that a modern-day apostle had experienced a literal visitation from Jesus Christ.

---

[2]   Ibid., 30–31.

A Specific Commission by Christ

An appearance from Christ, however, is not enough in itself to guarantee apostleship. According to Scripture, Jesus appeared after his resurrection to more than five hundred "brothers" at one time (1 Cor. 15:6). These individuals were not recognized as apostles of Christ, presumably because Jesus had not specifically appointed them as such.

Jesus expressly commissioned the twelve apostles twice, both before and following his resurrection (Matt. 10:1–7 and Acts 1:8). When filling the apostolic office left vacant by Judas, the apostles submitted to the selection Christ made through the unusual device of casting of lots (Acts 1:24–26).

NAR leaders do teach that apostles are appointed directly by God. But they're publicly affirmed as being apostles when they're commissioned into the office by other apostles. Thus, the appointment of a NAR apostle by God is not necessarily a public event that can be confirmed with outside validation, as when Christ appointed the Twelve and Paul. These appointments by Christ were objective events allowing for public verification.

The appointment of NAR apostles by God seems very different from the appointments of the apostles of Christ. The unverifiable nature of NAR appointments may explain why they feel the need to hold public commissioning ceremonies to affirm that they are truly apostles. But there can be little doubt that a vital connection with one or more of the original apostles would need to be corroborated for such a commissioning to be valid.

In our view, and based on our understanding of Scripture, a genuine apostle who shared the status of the apostles of Christ would be appointed specifically by Christ in a manner that allowed for outside verification of the event—and there would be no need for a separate public commissioning ceremony.

The Performance of Miracles

Wagner doesn't believe that working miraculous signs and wonders is required of NAR apostles.[3] Again, this is curious. The apostle Paul distinguished himself from false apostles—who were only pretending to be apostles of Christ—in part by his ability to work *bona fide* miracles (2 Cor. 12:12). So why are NAR apostles exempt from this requirement? Wagner doesn't say.

---

[3]   Ibid., 30–31.

If Paul did not mean to say that miracles authenticated all true apostles of Christ, then at the very least he meant that they authenticated the Twelve and Paul. And since NAR leaders look to the Twelve and Paul as models for NAR apostles it would seem logical to suppose that NAR apostles must also be able to perform miracles.

Other prominent NAR leaders, such as Bill Hamon, do believe that miracles are required of all today's apostles.[4] And even though Wagner doesn't believe miracles are required, he does claim that "almost" every apostle he knows has seen physical healings in their ministries.[5] Yet he adds, "but not many have seen mass healings through the casting of their shadow as did Peter (Acts 5:15)." And, of course, it's one thing to have "seen" a miracle take place; it's quite another to perform signs and wonders oneself. (See the diagram later in this chapter, which illustrates the different ways miracles might occur. They may be direct acts of God with the involvement of no human agent at all, divine acts in response to petitionary prayer, or divine acts mediated through the signs and wonders of human agents.)

What should go without saying bears repeating: mere claims to have performed physical healings do nothing to support claims of extraordinary authority. Alleged miracles must be spectacular and they must be verifiable.

The miraculous signs that were performed by the Twelve and Paul were not easy to miss. Their awe-inspiring works included raising the dead and healing the paralyzed. Their powers were not limited to healing conditions that it would be difficult to verify, such as backaches or emotional pain. Moreover, their miraculous signs were accomplished publicly so there would be no doubt they had occurred. No one was expected to settle for merely taking the apostles of Christ at their word.

Notice that we're not arguing against gifts of healing (1 Cor. 12:9) that may be used to cure backaches or emotional pain. Healings of these types of conditions certainly would bless those who experience them, even though they may not be as dramatic as healings of paralysis or blindness. Nor are we arguing that miracles of other types do not occur. Our point is simply that a very high standard of supernatural endowment must be met if we are to be convinced that a modern-day apostle is among us.

---

[4]   Bill Hamon, *Apostles, Prophets, and the Coming Moves of God: God's End-Time Plans for His Church and Planet Earth* (Santa Rosa Beach, FL: Destiny Image Publishers, 1997), 32–34.

[5]   Wagner, *Apostles Today*, 31.

Nor are we arguing that all healings must be conducted publicly. Healings experienced in private settings may serve, mainly, for the benefit of the persons healed and not as a miraculous sign for others. We suspect, in fact, that God does, in the typical case, heal in response to petitionary prayer, and that this is as common among non-charismatic believers as it is among charismatics, Pentecostals, or members of NAR churches. Unlike these less dramatic and less verifiable types of healings, when an apostle claims to have performed a miraculous sign it should be impressive and it should be confirmed by evidence that can be publicly verified. Reliable eyewitness testimony and, if at all possible, medical documentation are reasonable requests regarding any miraculous sign that is expected to provide evidence for someone's claim to be a special representative of God.

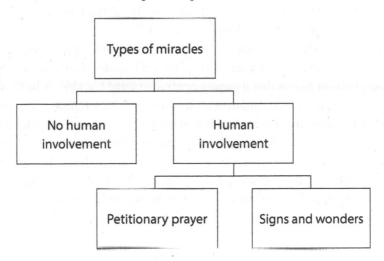

Diagram 1. Providentia Extraordinaria

When God brings about events that otherwise would not happen, i.e., miracles,[6] these are of two general types, one of which subdivides into two types:

- miracles wrought by God without human involvement of any kind and

---

[6] R. Douglas Geivett and Gary R. Habermas, eds., *In Defense of Miracles: A Comprehensive Case for God's Action in History* (Downers Grove, IL: IVP Academic, 1997), 594.

- two types of miracles wrought by God with human agency or involvement: (a) petitionary prayer, and (b) signs and wonders.

SUPPORT IN SCRIPTURE FOR ANY NEW TEACHINGS AND PRACTICES

Any new teachings and practices taught by NAR apostles must be supported in Scripture. Even the apostle Paul was not exempt from this criterion. When he brought new teachings to the Jews in Berea, they examined the Scriptures to see if his teachings found support there (Acts 17:11). The Bereans determined that they did. The fact that even Paul—the great apostle—could only give new teachings if they had the support of Scripture shows how crucial this criterion is for testing present-day apostles. It becomes even more crucial in light of Paul's warning about false apostles who disguise themselves as true apostles (2 Cor. 11:13).

Of course, Wagner says the extrabiblical revelation taught by NAR apostles doesn't *contradict* Scripture: "The one major rule governing any new revelation from God is that it cannot contradict what has already been written in the Bible. It may supplement it, however."[7] This reflects a desire to uphold the authority of Scripture. But to say that it is enough if NAR revelations *do not contradict Scripture* is setting the bar too low. First, there ought to be traces of past revelation in anything new that follows. These traces must be substantial and consistent with the results of the best standards of biblical interpretation. As we show in this book, NAR exposition of Scripture is routinely impressionistic, impatient to draw lessons and principles that aren't in the text, and casual about standard alternative interpretations of the passages they invoke. What biblical traces they see of major elements of NAR teaching are fictions. New revelation always extends the knowledge of God beyond what was known before. But it is always a recognizable extension of what has already been revealed. This was true of Jesus when he fulfilled messianic prophecy, and it was true of the New Testament apostles who were directly commissioned by Jesus to preach his message to the world, the very word that the Father had given to the Son (see John 17).

Second, what is new should to some degree be anticipated in what already has been revealed. Jesus predicted that there were prophets of God

---

7   C. Peter Wagner, "The New Apostolic Reformation Is Not a Cult," *Charisma News*, August 24, 2011; accessed June 6, 2014, http://www.charismanews.com/opinion/31851-the-new-apostolic-reformation-is-not-a-cult.

yet to come (Matt. 23:34; Luke 11:49). He thereby created the expectation of further revelation. So far, so good. But to connect this prophecy with its fulfillment—that is, with the emergence of these same prophets of God—we need additional clues. We need ways to recognize these prophets of God to be the ones Jesus predicted. And we have the clues we need. Notably, Jesus says, "I send you prophets and wise men and scribes" (Matt. 23:34).[8] These prophets of God are his disciples. We have confirmation of this when he forecasts their suffering and martyrdom. Jesus had already warned his disciples that this would happen (Matt. 10:16–23). "For so they persecuted the prophets who were before you," he had said (Matt. 5:12; see Acts 7:52). In fact, grave physical persecution and often martyrdom are the expected consummation of a prophet's ministry.[9]

We find in John 17 a striking prayer from Jesus for those who will be his apostolic witnesses—his disciples. He says, "They have believed that you sent me" (v. 8). "And I am no longer in the world, but they are in the world" (v. 11). "As you sent me into the world, so I have sent them into the world" (v. 18). *The baton is passed.* Their authority is ensured: "Sanctify them in the truth; your word is truth" (v. 17). And we, who are not apostles, are beneficiaries of their faithful execution of this high office, for Jesus prayed not for them only, "but also for those who will believe in me through their word" (v. 20)! They are the foundation of the church (Eph. 2:20).

And so it is with new revelation. We are given cause to expect it, but we are also given terms by which to test it when it comes. If we are not given cause to expect it, then we should not expect it; and if we are to expect it, we should accept it as the recognizable fulfillment of terms set forth in earlier revelation.

So any new revelation is to be anticipated in earlier revelation; and new revelation must show traces of the old. If we think of these two points together, we see a kind of reciprocity that is crucial to the confirmation of new revelation. Any genuinely new revelation is tethered to past revelation in both directions. (See diagram 2.)

---

[8]   In the Luke passage Jesus refers to himself as "the wisdom of God," a fitting metaphor for the one who prepares for the future revelation of divine wisdom.

[9]   This will be true for the two witnesses of Revelation 11 as well. "And when they have finished their testimony," they will be killed, though it is revealed that they will be raised up after three and a half days (Rev. 11:7–11).

Revelation Old & New

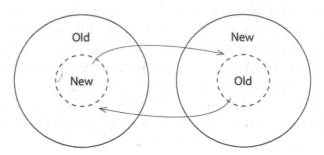

Diagram 2

Third, new revelation should amplify already existing revelation. Any new revelation should extend what is already revealed in ways that can - be identified as such extensions of earlier revelation. This is in addition to traces of the old in the new. Earlier truths that are amplified in new revelation don't appear so much as trace elements; rather, they fill out what is contained in the old. What is filled out or amplified may not itself suggest that further revelation is to be expected. But with further revelation, what is already known comes to be known better, and this relation is clearly discernible. An inspection of what is new will, for anyone already familiar with the old, call to mind the old that is present in it but will show it in more amplified form. This is a third form of continuity between earlier revelation and new revelation that we should look for when assessing new revelation claims. (See diagram 3.)

Revelation Old & New

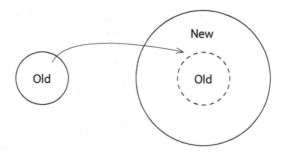

Diagram 3

Revelation claims within NAR lack these elements of continuity. NAR revelation strikes out in a radically new direction, with neck-snapping re-orientation and a jarring intensity. NAR leaders have pioneered a radically new theology. It is systematic and far-ranging, both for doctrine and for Christian practice. In some respects, it bears comparison with the creation of a distinct worldview. It is, in effect, too much all at once. If its essential tenets and practical admonitions were drawn together and packaged into a single document with alleged apostolic authority and set alongside the documents of the New Testament, it would stand out as a stunning novelty with only the most tenuous ties with the New Testament or with the biblical tradition more generally. NAR apostles and prophets expect us to acknowledge the authoritative status of their revelation claims with little or nothing to go one. They don't provide the means of seeing their deep connection with existing revelation.

We believe that the sum of revelation we have available today was completed when the apostle John wrote the book of Revelation. John's book is filled with prophetic truth. It gives us an idea of what to expect in the future. If two witnesses arrive, under the conditions described in Revelation 11, and they perform the actions predicted there, and their prophetic message has the characteristics indicated, then it will be known that they are authentic prophets of God. The anticipation of them is informed with detail we now have that will permit them to demonstrate their credentials. What they prophesy will be new; but that they will come has been revealed already. Here, past revelation begets expectation of new revelation, with clear criteria for discerning the new when it comes through future prophets of God.

The book of Revelation also offers a very telling climax. John writes, "He who testifies to these things says, 'Surely I am coming soon.' Amen. Come, Lord Jesus!" (Rev. 22:20). The one who testifies to these things is Jesus Christ himself (Rev. 1:1), and his testimony includes all that is in this book. It is Jesus, then, who says—at the end of this revelation of "things that must soon take place"—"Surely I am coming soon." This is the Second Advent. The Second Coming of Christ, which follows the composition of the chronologically last book written by a New Testament apostle, is *the next event on God's revelatory calendar.* The interval between the last book written by a New Testament apostle and the Second Coming of Christ brings forth *no new revelation.*[10] With the conclusion of John's revelation we have the anticipation of what to expect when new revelation comes.[11]

So, revelation claims of the nature and scope set forth by NAR apostles and prophets are not innocent simply by virtue of being logically compatible with whatever other revelation we already have. This condition is too weak. The Wagner test for defending the new truths of the New Apostolic Reformation is unacceptable. It is too permissive. We've examined this tactic in some detail because it is often used as a convenient device for deflecting criticism of NAR revelation claims. But if NAR claims are not linked in the right ways to biblical revelation, then it's safe to ignore them and potentially dangerous to embrace them.

QUALITY OF LIFE AND MINISTRY

A genuine apostle of Christ will have an exemplary quality of ministry and a distinctly virtuous character.[12] The fruit of an apostle of Christ's ministry, like that of the apostle Paul, will be people responding to the gospel and becoming true disciples of Jesus, reflected in lives changed by the work of the Holy Spirit (1 Cor. 9:12, 16–18; 15:1, 14; 2 Cor. 3:2–3; 1 Thess. 2:1–13).

Genuine apostles of Christ will be willing to endure great suffering in fulfillment of their commission, as did the apostle Paul (2 Cor. 1:5, 8–9; 11:23–28). They will not use methods that are deceitful or that "tamper" with Scripture (2 Cor. 4:2). They will be motivated by sincerity (2 Cor. 1:12) and marked by the character traits of self-sacrifice (1 Cor. 9:1–15, 19) and humility (2 Cor. 11:7). It is noteworthy that Wagner refers to character as

---

[10] The two witnesses of Revelation 11 are forerunners of the return of Jesus, rather like John the Baptist was at the first advent. They, too, will be clothed in sackcloth (Rev. 11:3).

[11] John recorded his vision of revelation when he was old and living alone on the island of Patmos. He had ministered to the churches of Asia Minor. His flock would have wondered about the fate of the church as the death of the last living apostle was at hand. This book is meant to strengthen God's people and prepare the church for a time of future persecution.

[12] Michael W. Austin and R. Douglas Geivett, eds., *Being Good: Christian Virtues for Everyday Life* (Grand Rapids: Eerdmans, 2012).

"the *sine qua non*" of an apostle of Christ.[13] The one character trait he speaks of at length is humility. But other tests are just as critical for evaluating alleged apostles of Christ.

In light of these several tests, how do NAR teachings about apostles of Christ fare? Screening their claims by multiple biblical criteria, such teachings fall short.

Summary

If individuals claim to be apostles of Christ, they must pass five biblical tests for genuine apostleship. As far as we can tell, many NAR leaders either disregard these tests or fail to present convincing evidence that they have passed these tests.

In the next chapter we explain NAR teachings about the nature of a prophet.

---

[13] Wagner, *Apostles Today*, 44–45.

10

NAR Prophets: The Secret Intelligence Agents

> We are the hidden prophets who have been kept for this hour.
> We are the eyes of those who have been given the divinely pow-
> erful weapons. We have been shown all that the Lord is doing,
> and all that the enemy is planning against you. We have scoured
> the earth and together we know all that needs to be known for
> the battle.
>
> —Rick Joyner, *The Final Quest*

NAR apostles are viewed as the generals in God's army. But NAR prophets
are the secret intelligence agents. They receive secret information about the
enemy's plans, the ways God is working, and strategies the church needs to
defeat Satan and advance God's kingdom.

In support of this view of prophets, NAR leaders often cite Amos 3:7.

> *For the LORD God does nothing*
> *without revealing his secret*
> *to his servants the prophets.*

They believe this verse teaches that God always reveals his plans in advance to prophets. Some major events that US prophets claim God revealed
to them before they occurred include the September 11, 2001, terrorist attacks on the United States;[1] the 2008 U. S. financial crisis;[2] Sarah Palin's po-

---

[1]   Brian Tashman, "Bakker and Jacobs Claim to Have Prophesied September
11th Attacks," *Right Wing Watch*, August 23, 2001; accessed February 21, 2014.
On *The Jim Bakker Show*, televised on August 12, 2011, NAR prophet Cindy Jacobs
claimed that God revealed these attacks to multiple NAR prophets in the Apostolic
Council of Prophetic Elders.

[2]   Sharon Stone and Cindy Jacobs, "Sharon Stone and Cindy Jacobs: 'Prophetic Words about the Current Economic System and Political Crisis," The Elijah List,
September 24, 2008; accessed January 28, 2014, https://www.elijahlist.com/words/
display_word/6884.

litical rise;[3] and the 2010 earthquake in Haiti[4].

NAR prophets regularly release their new revelations at conferences or publish them in alerts e-mailed to their followers. They also write entire books containing panoramic visions of the end time. Two examples are Wendy Alec's *Journal of the Unknown Prophet* (Warboys Media, 2002) and Rick Joyner's *The Final Quest* (MorningStar Publications, 1996).

Individual prophets have banded together to form what they call "prophetic councils," which are like central intelligence agencies. Prophetic councils analyze all the pieces of information coming in from various prophets so they can see the bigger picture of what God is supposedly revealing to the church. Some national and regional prophetic councils are the Netherlands Prophetic Council, the UK Prophetic Council, and the Canadian Prophetic Council.

The most prominent council is the Apostolic Council of Prophetic Elders (ACPE), founded in 1999, which, at any given time, consists of 20 to 25 prophets, mostly from the United States. The ACPE—convened by Cindy Jacobs—meets before the start of each year to determine, by consensus, what God has told the prophets about the upcoming year.[5] Their revelations are compiled in a single annual document called the "Word of the Lord," which is distributed through their own organizations and is published in *Charisma* magazine. The council's "Word of the Lord for 2014" revealed, among other things, that:[6]

- "God is opening a door of hope" so that many "will receive new joy and hope in this coming season";

---

[3] Ibid.

[4] Chuck Pierce, Cindy Jacobs, and Kim Clement, "Chuck Pierce, Cindy Jacobs and Kim Clement: Highways Are Buckling! His Glory and Unity Will Come!," The Elijah List, January 19, 2010; accessed February 28, 2011, http://www.elijahlist.com/words/display_word/8407.

[5] The ACPE typically attaches a disclaimer to the beginning of their "Word of the Lord" documents stating that their prophecies do not necessarily have to be fulfilled within the upcoming calendar year, but may find fulfillment over a "season"—that is, a longer, unspecified period of time.

[6] "ACPE Word of the Lord for 2014," *Generals News*, Generals International, January 29, 2014, accessed February 1, 2014, http://www.generals.org/news/single-view/article/acpe-word-of-the-lord-for-2014.

- God will give the United States a "second chance" after the nation has turned away from him and lost a measure of its greatness;
- a new party will arise in the United States having a heart for social justice and biblical values and a fiscal plan that will eliminate the national debt;
- the ending of abortion for the United States will be a spiritual factor leading to a new "move" of miracles, and a curse that was put on the United States after the nation legalized abortion in 1973 will begin lifting with the ending of 2013;
- a new Jesus People movement will result in mighty miracles, medical breakthroughs for cancer and other incurable diseases, and entire sports teams kneeling down to pray, capturing the attention of the news media;
- a Third Great Awakening will take place in such colleges as Harvard and Yale;
- young children will prophesy and receive visions and dreams that will give direction to the adults in their lives;
- Satan will try to release a new, virulent strain of flu;
- churches will begin to incorporate 24/7 [non-stop, round-the-clock] prayer;
- Iran's nuclear power will eventually topple; and
- the one-child policy in China will crumble.

One prominent prophet-guided organization is the International House of Prayer (IHOP), which was founded based on prophetic words—described as IHOP's blueprints—given by US prophet Bob Jones.[7] IHOP is advised by a prophetic network made up of about 250 people under the oversight of a Prophetic Council.[8]

Individual prophets also provide guidance for apostolic networks of hundreds, and sometimes thousands, of churches. One such US prophet is

---

[7] Mike Bickle, "Session 8: The Blueprint Prophecy and the Black Horse," *Encountering Jesus: Visions, Revelations, Angelic Visitations from IHOP-KC's Prophetic History*, transcript, September 19, 2009, MikeBickle.org, accessed August 15, 2014, http://www.mikebickle.org.edgesuite.net/MikeBickleVOD/2009/20090919C-T-The_Blueprint_Prophecy_and_the_Black_Horse_IPH08.pdf.

[8] Mike Bickle, *Growing in the Prophetic: A Practical, Biblical Guide to Dreams, Visions, and Spiritual Gifts*, rev. ed. (Lake Mary, FL: Charisma House, 2008), 65, PDF e-book, http://mikebickle.org/books.

James Goll, the official prophet for Harvest International Ministry (HIM), an apostolic network of more than 20,000 churches in 50 nations.

DEFINING PROPHETS

But are there really prophets today? And, if so, what do they do? It depends on who you ask.

At one end of the spectrum are those Protestant Christians who describe themselves as cessationist since they believe that prophets' roles ceased after Scripture was written.[9] Some of these Protestants believe that a gift of prophecy is given to certain Christians today, but it is not a gift for giving divine revelation; rather, it's a gift for expositing Scripture.

In the middle of this spectrum are those, including classical Pentecostals and charismatics, who believe that there are people today who give revelation to individuals and to local churches. But those who hold this view don't believe that present-day prophets reveal new truths for the church. And most of these people do not speak of a present-day office of prophet as NAR leaders do. Rather, they speak of a present-day ministry function or ministry gift of prophet, or, more commonly, the spiritual gift of prophecy—ways of speaking that do not entail a specially recognized official position in church government.

At the far end of the spectrum are NAR leaders who affirm the existence of prophets comparable to the great Old Testament prophets and who possess extraordinary authority extending to individuals, churches, and nations. NAR leaders hold that these prophets govern the church and reveal new truths, which are often described as strategies for advancing God's kingdom.

Before examining this audacious NAR view of prophets, we must take a closer look at the more moderate view, as expressed by the world's largest

---

[9]   The Protestant Reformers, notably Martin Luther and John Calvin, were, on the whole, cessationists, as was Jonathan Edwards. A benchmark book arguing for cessationism is B. B. Warfield's *Counterfeit Miracles* (New York: Charles Scribner's Sons, 1918; repr., Edinburgh: Banner of Truth, 1982). Contemporary cessationist scholars include John MacArthur, O. Palmer Robertson, and Richard B. Gaffin Jr. A moderate cessationism perspective is advanced in Daniel Wallace and M. James Sawyer, eds., *Who's Afraid of the Holy Spirit? An Investigation into the Ministry of the Spirit of God Today* (Dallas: Biblical Studies Press, 2005). For multiple perspectives by different authors, see Wayne A. Grudem, *Are Miraculous Gifts for Today? Four Views* (Grand Rapids: Zondervan, 1996).

Pentecostal denomination, the Assemblies of God. The contrast between these two views will highlight what makes NAR distinct.[10]

PENTECOSTAL VIEW: THE PRESENT-DAY GIFT OF PROPHECY

A white paper released by the governing body of the Assemblies of God (AG) identifies two groups of people who prophesied in the New Testament.[11] The first group consists of recognized prophets in the early churches who often worked closely with the apostles (and included the apostles themselves), traveled occasionally from church to church, included both men and women, and exercised spiritual influence with the apostles and elders, though these prophets were never appointed to ruling functions as were elders.[12]

The second—and more pervasive—group is made up of a broad distribution of laypeople who had received the spiritual gift of prophecy and prophesied to varying degrees.[13] This group is seen as a fulfillment of a prophecy made by the Old Testament prophet Joel that God would pour out his Holy Spirit on all people (Joel 2:28–29).

The denomination maintains that prophecy is a continuing gift of the Holy Spirit "that will always be broadly distributed throughout a holy and responsive church until Jesus comes."[14]

What is the purpose of the gift of prophecy, and what does it look like, according to the Assemblies of God? In the early church, the gift served "to edify and build up the body of Christ through encouragement, consolation, and correction."[15] Similarly, today the gift functions when Christians "speak under the anointing of the Spirit to strengthen, encourage, or comfort

---

[10]   We believe NAR claims have confused some Pentecostals who believe that the New Apostolic Reformation is simply a natural expression of Pentecostalism. One goal of this book is to demonstrate how far this is from the truth.

[11]   "Apostles and Prophets," General Presbytery of the Assemblies of God, August 6, 2001; accessed September 29, 2010, http://ag.org/top/Beliefs/Position_Papers/pp_downloads/pp_4195_apostles_prophets.pdf.

[12]   Ibid., 8–9.

[13]   Ibid., 9.

[14]   Ibid., 10.

[15]   "Prophets and Personal Prophecies," Assemblies of God, accessed August 9, 2014, http://ag.org/top/Beliefs/topics/sptlissues_prophets_prophecies.cfm.

(1 Cor. 14:3)."[16] The documents referenced do not specify the types of content these prophecies may include, though they apparently may sometimes include predictions of future events and even directions for an individual's personal life. Yet the Assemblies of God cautions against the abuse of attaching "final-word authority" to such directions.[17]

The AG church does not allow that those with the gift of prophecy hold a formal church office: "Prophets in the New Testament are never described as holding a recognized office or position as in the case of pastors and evangelists. . . . When they prophesied under the inspiration of the Spirit, their ministry was noted, but they were not ordained to hold a position, title, or office. They could indeed have been called prophets without designating them as filling an office."[18]

Because those with the gift of prophecy do not hold a formal office, the governing body of the Assemblies of God disapproves of using the title of prophet in churches. Since the New Testament doesn't provide for establishing the prophet in a hierarchical governing structure of the church, the Assemblies of God disapproves of formally naming or declaring individuals as prophets in the church.[19]

NAR VIEW: THE PRESENT-DAY OFFICE OF PROPHET

NAR leaders—in contrast to Assemblies of God officials—believe that today's prophets hold a formal office. In the NAR view, it's essential that prophets govern, for these prophets must direct the church to adopt their new strategies. Bill Hamon, an influential US prophet, writes: "God has ordained that the apostles and prophets will receive the revelations, creative ideas, and divine strategy for bringing transformation to this world as God has ordained from the foundation of the world."[20]

Just as Peter Wagner is widely regarded as a leading authority on present-day apostles, Bill Hamon—the founder of Christian International Ministries

---

[16] "Apostles and Prophets," Assemblies of God, 11.

[17] "Prophets and Personal Prophecies," Assemblies of God.

[18] Ibid.

[19] Ibid.

[20] Bill Hamon, *Prophetic Scriptures Yet to Be Fulfilled: During the Third and Final Church Reformation* (Shippensburg, PA: Destiny Image Publishers, 2010), 247.

Network in Santa Rosa Beach, Florida—is regarded as a leading authority on present-day prophets. Hamon is often called the father of the modern "prophetic movement" and is featured regularly as a leading prophet in *Charisma* magazine.[21] Hamon's prophetic résumé is impressive. In the sixty years he purports to have held the office of prophet, he claims he has personally prophesied to more than 50,000 individuals, including presidents of nations.[22] He's written seven major books on prophets and apostles that have influenced the views of numerous NAR leaders and have been endorsed by many of those same leaders, including Peter Wagner. Hamon also wrote a 300-page manual that, according to his figures, has been used to train more than a quarter of a million people around the world for prophetic ministry.[23] While that number may be difficult to verify, there's no doubt that his influence is far-reaching.

Though other NAR prophets are better known on a popular level—Rick Joyner and Cindy Jacobs, for example—we look closely at the teachings of Hamon because they have been formative to the new NAR theology. When explaining Hamon's views we do not mean to imply that they are shared by every leader associated with NAR. But we have observed significant overlap between many of his views and those of other NAR leaders.

THE NATURE AND SCOPE OF A PROPHET'S AUTHORITY

For Hamon, present-day prophets have the same extraordinary authority as Old Testament prophets. "So why do some teachers declare that the New Testament prophets are different from the Old Testament prophets? The prophets are the same as the one eternal God whom they represent. . . .

---

[21]   The phrase "prophetic movement" refers to the movement that began in independent charismatic churches in the 1980s to restore prophets to the church. The movement to restore apostles began in the 1990s.

[22]   "Dr. Bill Hamon's Story," Christian International Ministries Network, accessed February 27, 2014, http://christianinternational.com/dr-bill-hamon; Hamon, *Prophetic Scriptures Yet to Be Fulfilled*, 211.

[23]   Ibid., 54–55. Hamon's training manual is titled *Manual for Ministering Spiritual Gifts*. Only those certified to teach fee-based courses, offered through Hamon's ministry, can purchase the manual.

Present-day prophets have the same anointing, authority and ministry they had in the Old Testament."[24]

Hamon claims that present-day prophets also have "administrative authority" in the church.[25] In other words, through their prophetic words they govern. They give words of guidance, instruction, rebuke, judgment, and revelation—"whatever Christ chooses to speak for the purifying and perfecting of His Church."[26]

To support his teaching that NAR prophets hold governing roles in the church, Hamon appeals to what he calls a "divine principle in biblical interpretation."[27] The principle "is that whatever was established in the Old Testament remains proper as a principle or practice unless the New Testament does away with it." In defense of his method of interpreting Scripture, which is required to support this claim, he says that tithing is practiced in the church because nothing stated in the New Testament abolished it.

Hamon says the same holds true for the office of prophet. He claims that governing was a key function of several Old Testament prophets—including Abraham, Moses, Samuel, David, and Daniel—and these governing prophets serve as models to today's prophets. "These examples of just a few biblical prophets should be sufficient to show that God has invested much more ability within His prophets than just enough to make them a mouthpiece for guidance."[28]

In Hamon's view, those with a prophetic office can give specific, directive words not only to churches, but also to individuals regarding their personal lives—prefaced with the extraordinarily authoritative phrase "Thus saith the Lord."[29] In contrast, people who have only the spiritual gift of prophecy but have not been formally ordained to the office by a "prophetic presbytery" are

---

[24]   Bill Hamon, *Apostles, Prophets, and the Coming Moves of God: God's End-Time Plans for His Church and Planet Earth* (Santa Rosa Beach, FL: Destiny Image Publishers, 1997), 127–28.

[25]   Bill Hamon, *Prophets and Personal Prophecy: God's Prophetic Voice Today* (Shippensburg, PA: Destiny Image Publishers, 2001), 36.

[26]   Ibid.

[27]   Bill Hamon, *Prophets and the Prophetic Movement: God's Prophetic Move Today* (Shippensburg, PA: Destiny Image Publishers, 2001), 157.

[28]   Ibid., 159.

[29]   Hamon, *Prophets and Personal Prophecy*, 73.

discouraged from giving directive prophecies to individuals, especially ones prefaced with this authoritative phrase.[30]

But Hamon believes that the authority of the prophetic office is more far-reaching than this; it even extends to nations. "Those who are truly commissioned prophets have the right to prophesy direction, correction, guidance and new revelation to a person, church or nation."[31]

The extraordinary authority claimed for NAR prophets is difficult to overstate: "To reject God's prophets is to reject God," warns Hamon, and "to fail to recognize the prophets, or to keep them from speaking, is to refuse God permission to speak."[32] The consequences of such rejection are dire. Hamon declares: "It has always been true—and in this Prophetic Movement will be especially true—that the way we respond to God's divinely established prophets will determine our success or failure, life or death, captivity or freedom. Whole nations have arisen or fallen based on their response to God's word through His prophets."[33]

In the next chapter we take a closer look at NAR prophets.

SUMMARY

Many Protestants believe that prophets' roles ceased after Scripture was written. Others—including Pentecostal and charismatic Christians—believe prophets do continue today who minister primarily in local churches, speaking words that strengthen, encourage, or comfort. These prophets do not govern the church or reveal new truths. In contrast, NAR leaders claim that the prophets of today reveal new truths and hold a formal office in church government, with extraordinary authority that extends to individuals, churches, and nations.

---

[30]   A prophetic presbytery is a group of two or more prophets or prophetic ministers whose functions include the formal ordination of individuals to the fivefold ministry offices. See Hamon, *Prophets and Personal Prophecy*, 38–39; Hamon, *Apostles, Prophets, and the Coming Moves of God*, 283.

[31]   Hamon, *Apostles, Prophets, and the Coming Moves of God*, 123–24.

[32]   Hamon, *Prophets and Personal Prophecy*, 8.

[33]   Hamon, *Prophets and the Prophetic Movement*, 178.

11

NAR Prophets: A Closer Look

> Jesus still needs His prophetic voices to speak His specific personal messages to individuals and nations.
>
> —Bill Hamon, *Prophetic Scriptures Yet to Be Fulfilled*

Now we take a closer look at NAR prophets, explaining what exactly they do, the limits to their authority, and the Scriptures used in support of their claim for a present-day prophetic office.

THE FUNCTIONS OF NAR PROPHETS

The key functions prophets are authorized to perform for individuals, churches, and nations, include the following.

Prophesying to Individuals

Specific functions prophets perform for individuals include:

- revealing, imparting, and "activating" spiritual gifts through the laying on of hands and prophecy;[1]
- revealing and confirming those with a call to one of the fivefold ministry offices;[2]
- revealing God's personal will to individuals on major life decisions that are not addressed directly in Scripture, including whom to marry, which business decisions to make, and where to live;[3]
- confirming what God has already told an individual;[4]

---

[1]   Bill Hamon, *Prophets and Personal Prophecy: God's Prophetic Voice Today* (Shippensburg, PA: Destiny Image Publishers, 2001), 14–15.

[2]   Ibid.

[3]   Ibid., 53, 81, 131–32.

[4]   Ibid., 3.

- giving prophecies that result in physical healing, including creative miracles;[5] and
- identifying the root cause of psychiatric and psychological problems, resulting in the immediate inner healing of individuals.[6]

Prophesying to Churches

Specific functions prophets perform for local churches include:

- revealing a change of direction or personnel changes in church leadership;[7]
- clarifying a church's vision, giving prophetic direction to that church, and revealing whether it is fulfilling God's purpose for that specific church;[8]
- revealing when demons have been sent to thwart the work of a church;[9]
- revealing whether a church was truly founded by God, what God's original purpose for that church was, and whether it should develop a new purpose;[10] and
- preventing church splits by revealing what is going on in the spirit realm and confirming that a pastor is God's choice for a church.[11]

Prophesying to Nations

Specific functions prophets perform for nations include:

---

[5] Ibid., 23. "Creative miracles" refers to miracles that actually create something out of nothing; for example, a new limb where there was none before.

[6] Ibid., 24.

[7] Bill Hamon, *Apostles, Prophets, and the Coming Moves of God: God's End-Time Plans for His Church and Planet Earth* (Santa Rosa Beach, FL: Destiny Image Publishers, 1997), 142.

[8] Ibid., 143.

[9] Ibid.

[10] Ibid., 143–44.

[11] Ibid., 144.

- identifying the high-ranking demons that rule over nations, then leading strategic "prophetic intercessory warfare prayer" to destroy those demons;[12]
- giving national leaders prophecies for their nations;[13]
- accurately predicting earthquakes, tidal wives, and other catastrophes of nature, instilling the fear of God in people and turning entire nations to God;[14]
- executing God's judgments on nations;[15]
- speaking into existence the plagues of the book of Revelation that will torment God's enemies in the last days;[16] and
- confronting all false religious groups that practice supernatural spirit communication, including witches, occultists, spiritualists, New Agers, and Satan worshipers.[17]
- How the nations respond to the messages of the prophets will determine whether they are declared "sheep nations" or "goat nations" on judgment day.[18]
- Prophets to nations will have an increasingly critical role, according to Hamon. He believes they will increase in miraculous power to such a degree that heads of other nations, including the president of the United States, will begin to seek out these prophets for their guidance.[19] Hamon himself claims to have given prophetic words to heads of nations, including the former president of Columbia,

---

[12] Ibid., 9–10.

[13] Ibid., 183.

[14] Ibid., 232

[15] Hamon, *Prophets and Personal Prophecy*, 8.

[16] Hamon, *Apostles, Prophets, and the Coming Moves of God*, 139.

[17] Bill Hamon, *Prophets and the Prophetic Movement: God's Prophetic Move Today* (Shippensburg, PA: Destiny Image Publishers, 2001), 85.

[18] Hamon, *Apostles, Prophets, and the Coming Moves of God*, 117. "Sheep nations," according to Hamon, are the nations referenced in Matt. 25:31–46, in which the majority of people will have become "born-again Christians." See Hamon, *Prophetic Scriptures Yet to Be Fulfilled: During the Third and Final Church Reformation* (Shippensburg, PA: Destiny Image Publishers, 2010), 257–58.

[19] Hamon, *Prophets and the Prophetic Movement*, 131.

Álvaro Uribe, whom he advised to support a particular political candidate.[20] Cindy Jacobs has met with national leaders, including then Mexican President Felipe Calderón.[21]

Revealing New Truths

In addition to these functions with regard to individuals, local churches, and nations, NAR prophets also claim to perform a critical function for the broader church: the revelation of new truths for doctrine and practice, which are often described as "strategies" the church needs in order to advance God's kingdom on earth.

Ephesians 3:4–5 is important to Hamon's argument for the provision of new revelation: "When you read this, you can perceive my insight into the mystery of Christ, which was not made known to the sons of men in other generations as it has now been revealed to his holy apostles and prophets by the Spirit." Hamon says of verse 5 that the apostle Paul teaches that both apostles and prophets are given the revelation ministry for the church. Just as Paul received divine revelation about the inclusion of Gentiles in the church—a major topic for Paul in the Ephesians 3 passage—present-day apostles and prophets continue to receive new truths from God for the church. Hamon says: "He [Paul] also reveals that this anointing for divine revelation was not just given to the prophets of old but has now been equally given to Christ's holy apostles and prophets in His Church."[22]

Hamon claims that God gave him just such revelation for the church in a prophetic vision:

> He showed me a great Book. Its title was *The Book of the Mortal Church on Earth*. He flipped through the Book until He came to a page entitled "The Last Chapter of the Mortal Church." . . .
>
> He said some of His ministers would only be shown one page or paragraph, which would become their major message and ministry . . .

---

[20]   Rachel Tabachnick, "NAR Apostles' Brand of 'Transformation' to be Promoted at Conference at Harvard," *Talk to Action*, March 24, 2011; accessed January 28, 2014, http://www.talk2action.org/story/2011/3/24/142629/678.

[21]   Cindy Jacobs, "Cindy's Mexico Report," *Generals News*, Generals International, May 2011; accessed January 28, 2014, http://www.generals.org/news/single-view/article/cindys-mexico-report.

[22]   Hamon, *Apostles, Prophets, and the Coming Moves of God*, 140.

He said He was showing me an overview and highlights of the whole chapter because He was giving me the responsibility of keeping an overall perspective and making the progressive purpose of God known to His corporate Church.[23]

Some things God permitted Hamon to see include:[24]

- "God is activating the second phase of apostles and prophets and is fully restoring them to their rightful place of power and function";
- that "it is now time to activate the Joseph and Daniel Company of apostles (Joseph) and prophets (Daniel) within the business field and political arena"; and
- prophets and apostles to the nations "will be some of the main instruments God uses to reap the great end-time harvest."

Hamon also claims that God has called him to raise up a great company of end-time prophets.[25] These prophets will corporately prepare the way for Christ's second coming, just as an individual prophet, John the Baptist, prepared the way for his first coming. God showed Hamon that there are 10,000 prophets in North America alone.[26]

Prophets prepare the way for Christ's return by giving more and more vital truths to the church. But Hamon claims that these new truths don't add to Scripture. "Instead, the prophet brings illumination and further specifics about that which has already been written."[27]

Furthermore, their revelation is not actually new, according to Hamon—this despite the fact that he routinely uses the phrase "new truths."[28] Instead, this revelation is made up of what he calls "restored truths." These are teachings and practices that were known and understood by early Christians but were lost during the so-called Dark Ages of the church.[29] Now, they're being progressively restored, and this will continue until the church finally employs

---

[23] Ibid., 17–18.

[24] Ibid., 18–21.

[25] Hamon, *Prophetic Scriptures Yet to Be Fulfilled*, 210.

[26] Hamon, *Prophets and Personal Prophecy*, 9.

[27] Ibid., 3.

[28] See an example of his use of this phrase in *Prophets and the Prophetic Movement*, 160.

[29] Hamon, *Prophets and the Prophetic Movement*, 60.

all the strategies God has given for advancing his kingdom. Hamon states: "The Scriptures definitely teach there will be 'line upon line, precept upon precept,' restoration of truth upon restoration of truth until the Church comes to its divinely predestined purpose."[30]

The restoration of the church is a key NAR teaching. NAR leaders are continually talking about all they are "restoring"—teachings and practices, the fivefold ministry offices, and supernatural power. How are these critical truths restored? Through "prophetic illumination" of the Scripture, according to Hamon. Prophetic illumination is when God gives a prophet supernatural insight into the correct interpretation and application of a specific passage of Scripture. It's like a light going on—suddenly the church, through a prophet, develops an understanding of a specific verse that it did not have prior to that time. Hamon writes: "They [the proper understanding and application of specific Scriptures] are hidden from the eyes of men until God's time for that truth to be restored and established."[31]

For example, Hamon claims that it was through prophetic illumination of Malachi 4:5—"Behold, I will send you Elijah the prophet before the great and awesome day of the LORD comes"—that God revealed to him that a great company of end-time prophets—who have the "anointing of Prophet Elijah"[32]—will prepare the way for Christ's second coming. Hamon believes God showed him that this verse has two fulfillments: one that was recognized by all Christians in John the Baptist, and a second in NAR prophets.

Hamon believes the first truth to be restored by prophetic illumination was the Protestant understanding of salvation by grace through faith. Martin Luther's recovery of this teaching around 1517 occurred after he received prophetic illumination of Ephesians 2:8–9. Hamon teaches that the Protestant Reformation that resulted from Luther's revelation launched a five hundred-year restoration period during which teachings and practices have been restored to the church, gradually, progressively, and in piecemeal fashion, but with escalating speed. He calls this the "snowball" principle of restoration.[33] By Hamon's calculations, it's possible that all truths will be restored

---

30   Bill Hamon, *Day of the Saints: Equipping Believers for Their Revolutionary Role in Ministry* (Shippensburg, PA: Destiny Image Publishers, 2002), 66.

31   Hamon, *Prophets and Personal Prophecy*, 10.

32   Hamon, *Apostles, Prophets, and the Coming Moves of God*, 111.

33   Hamon, *Prophets and the Prophetic Movement*, 29.

by the year 2030. He bases this calculation on the fact that the church was up and running by about AD 30, and his belief that God has ordained a period of 2,000 years for the "Mortal Church" to endure until Christians receive their "immortal" bodies.[34]

The following list shows the truths that have been restored to date, according to Hamon, along with the major movements that restored them:[35]

1500—Salvation by grace through faith (Protestant movement)

1600—Water baptism, separation of church and state (Evangelical movement)

1700—Sanctification, the church set apart from the world (Holiness movement)

1800—Divine physical healing in the atonement (Faith Healing movement)

1900—Holy Spirit baptism with unknown tongues (Pentecostal movement)

1950—Prophetic presbytery, singing praises, and Body of Christ membership ministries[36] (Latter Rain movement)

1950—Evangelist ministry and mass evangelism reactivated with miraculous healings (Deliverance Evangelism movement)

1960—Renewal of all restored truth to all past movement churches.[37] "Pastors were restored to being sovereign head of their local churches." (Charismatic movement)

1970—Faith confessions, prosperity, and victorious attitude and life. "Teacher ministry reestablished as a major fivefold ministry." (Faith movement)

1980—Prophetic, activating gifts, warfare praise, prophets to nations. "Prophet ministry was restored, and a company of prophets brought forth." (Prophetic movement)

---

[34]   Ibid., 82.

[35]   This list has been adapted from a list featured in Hamon, *Prophetic Scriptures Yet to Be Fulfilled*, 127–28.

[36]   "Body of Christ membership ministries" is a reference to the teaching that each member of the body of Christ has a spiritual gift or fivefold ministry office; that is to say, each member has a ministry to fulfill in the church.

[37]   This means that Charismatic groups began to develop within most traditional denominations that had previously rejected charismatic practices, such as speaking in tongues and prophesying.

1990—Apostolic, miraculous, networking, great harvest. "Apostle ministry restored to bring divine order, finalize restoration of fivefold ministers for full equipping of the saints." (Apostolic movement)

2007—"Saints manifesting mightily, and harvest reaped!" (Saints movement)

Notice that, during the last five decades of the twentieth century, God began restoring teachings about the place of the fivefold ministry offices in the church—starting in the 1950s with evangelists, in the 1960s with pastors, in the 1970s with teachers, in the 1980s with prophets, and in the 1990s with apostles. With all of the fivefold ministry officers now governing and equipping lay-Christians for their roles in ministry, the church has entered its present stage of restoration, which Hamon calls the "Saints movement."

A major truth being restored during the Saints movement is that all Christians —and not paid clergy only—are ministers of the Lord. This means that, very soon, those everyday Christians who have been trained by the fivefold ministry officers will begin to perform miracles and produce other supernatural manifestations as part of their normal lives. This will lead to a great end-time harvest of souls, as they demonstrate Jesus's miraculous power as witnesses of the kingdom of God. Hamon says, "We are going to see a mighty spiritual army of professionals, laborers, students, homemakers, and retirees demonstrating Christ Jesus' ministry and overcoming power over all the forces of darkness."[38]

Following the Saints movement—which will likely last for several years[39]—two more restorational movements will precede Christ's return: the "Army of the Lord Movement"—when the church will execute God's written judgments until all Christ's enemies are subdued under his feet— and the "Kingdom Establishing Movement"—when the church will demonstrate God's miraculous power until every person will have to acknowledge Jesus Christ as the true Lord God over all the earth.[40]

All the truths that have been restored by prophets to date—from the Protestant Reformation to the Saints movement—are what Hamon refers to as "present truth." He urges Christians to attend churches where the entirety of present truth is embraced so that they do not miss out on what God wants to do through them and the church.

---

[38] Hamon, *Day of the Saints*, 31.

[39] Ibid., 42.

[40] Hamon, *Apostles, Prophets, and the Coming Moves of God*, 251–78.

Some families have been camped in the Catholic church for numerous generations and have never, to this day, advanced on to the first restoration truth that was established some 500 years ago. Likewise, some have been historic Protestants for years and have never experienced Evangelical-Holiness Movement truths. In like manner, some Pentecostals have not advanced beyond what was restored in the Pentecostal Movement a hundred years ago. Even many Charismatics have not advanced into the Prophetic/Apostolic Movement truths and spiritual experiences. No doubt many who are now involved in the Prophetic and Apostolic will not move on to be leaders and participants in the Saints Movement.

As for me and my house, I do not want to stop anywhere short of the fullness of restored truth. [41]

Those who do not advance in present truth will miss out on leading and participating in the next great movements of God on earth.

LIMITS OF A PROPHET'S AUTHORITY

Despite the tremendous authority of prophets, even Hamon allows that they have some limitations.

Prophets Must Be Invited into a Church

Prophets or apostles can't barge into a church and call the shots, says Hamon. They must be invited in by the pastor. Furthermore, if a prophet receives revelation that suggests a change in direction for a church or a change in its leadership, then the prophet should share that information with the pastor privately and not with the entire congregation. A prophet must allow the pastor to decide whether to share it with the church. The exception would be if gross sin is occurring in a church that has submitted itself to the authority of a prophetic or apostolic overseer.

But Hamon warns pastors against acting the part of lone rangers who submit to no one. If they don't submit to the overseeing authority of prophets and apostles, they will not have anyone "to turn to in their hour of need."[42]

---

[41] Hamon, *Day of the Saints*, 49.

[42] Hamon, *Apostles, Prophets, and the Coming Moves of God*, 142–43.

Prophets are Fallible

Genuine prophets can make mistakes when they prophesy.

> We must not be quick to call someone a false prophet simply because some-
> thing he said was inaccurate or did not seem to apply to us. The man may
> be honest, righteous, and upright, yet immature in his prophesying. He may
> have misinterpreted what the Lord was saying.
>
> In this case we should say that he gave an inaccurate word or a false
> prophecy, but we cannot properly call him a false prophet unless we can
> prove that *the man himself* is false [Hamon's emphasis]. Missing it a few
> times in prophecy does not make a false prophet. No mortal prophet is infal-
> lible; all are liable to make mistakes.[43]

This teaching—that genuine prophets can err—is promoted by many
NAR leaders, including Mike Bickle. In his popular book *Growing in the
Prophetic*, Bickle teaches that four levels of prophecy are being progressively
restored to the church. These include the highest "Level IV prophets" who
have a "prophetic office" comparable to the great Old Testament prophets.
Bickle writes, "What I have called 'the Level IV prophetic office' represents
a maturity and power in prophetic ministry that parallel the Old Testament
ministries of men like Samuel and Elijah."[44]

Despite their high office, prophets may still make mistakes. "This [their
high degree of accuracy] doesn't mean that prophets are 100 percent infal-
lible," Bickle explains, "but their words are to be taken seriously. Unlike the
Old Testament ground rules for prophets, where 100 percent accuracy was
required upon the penalty of death, the New Testament doesn't require the
same standard of its prophets."[45]

Though NAR prophets can err, NAR leaders teach that they will do so
less and less as the days go by. A common NAR teaching is that the accuracy
of prophets will increase. This teaching is reflected in an advertisement for a
prophetic conference sponsored by the Elijah List.

---

[43]   Hamon, *Prophets and Personal Prophecy*, 125–26.

[44]   Mike Bickle. *Growing in the Prophetic: A Practical, Biblical Guide to Dreams,
Visions, and Spiritual Gifts*, rev. ed. (Lake Mary, FL: Charisma House, 2008), 42, PDF
e-book, http://mikebickle.org/books.

[45]   Ibid., 41.

This year's guest speakers are Dutch Sheets, James Goll, Jane Hamon, Denny Cline, and myself, Steve Shultz. . . .

The accuracy level by these prophetic voices has always been very high on what God is about to do, and it gets more accurate each year as the "prophetic ear" of the Church grows in accuracy.[46]

Prophets' Revelation Does Not Have the Authority of Scripture

NAR prophets cannot place their revelation on par with Scripture. Only a false prophet would claim that his or her words "would ever be equivalent to Scripture in inspiration or authority."[47]

In addition, Hamon says that no individual prophet can establish a new doctrine that is binding on all Christians. Such universal revelation must be submitted to other apostles, prophets, and fivefold-ministry officers, and church councils should be convened to evaluate the new doctrine. [48]

Despite these cautious statements, Hamon's teachings about "new truths" or "restored truths" do, in our view, elevate the authority of NAR revelation to that of Scripture. Disclaimers to the contrary give us little confidence that there is a real difference on this point.

In contrast to the allowance made by Hamon for new doctrine to be established by church councils, other prominent prophets, such as Rick Joyner, state emphatically that contemporary prophetic revelation never establishes doctrine.[49] Joyner teaches that revelation today serves two purposes: (1) "revealing the present or future strategic will of the Lord in certain matters" (as in the apostle Paul's vision in Acts 16:9 guiding him to go to Macedonia); and (2) "illuminating doctrine that is taught in the Scripture, but is not clearly seen" (as in the apostle Peter's trance in Acts 10, which illuminated biblical teaching about the Gentiles' inclusion in the gospel).

Despite Joyner's teaching, the revelations of many NAR prophets—including his own—do seem to establish doctrine. Indeed, it is difficult to

---

[46] "Final Day to Register for Our 'What Is God Saying for 2014?' Conference," The Elijah List, January 8, 2014; accessed January 28, 2014, http://www.elijahlist.com/words/display_word.html?ID=12976.

[47] Hamon, *Prophets and the Prophetic Movement*, xxiii.

[48] Ibid., 144.

[49] Rick Joyner, *The Final Quest* (Charlotte, NC: MorningStar Publications, 1996), 12.

imagine how one could write entire books containing panoramic visions about the end time and the nature of God's kingdom, such as we find in Joyner's works, without introducing new doctrine. In *The Final Quest*—the same book in which Joyner teaches that contemporary prophetic revelation never establishes doctrine—Joyner presents a number of them, including the doctrine of a coming "great spiritual civil war" in the church; the doctrine that the church must receive prophets to have victory in the end-time battle; and the doctrine that the Gospels should be used as the lens for interpreting the apostle Paul's New Testament writings, not the other way around.[50] If these do not qualify as doctrines in Joyner's mind, then one must wonder what does. And Bill Hamon claims that God showed him the last chapter of *The Book of the Mortal Church on Earth* so that Hamon could make "the progressive purpose of God known to His corporate Church."[51] Making God's "progressive purpose" known—including the next major movements of God on earth—is, we argue, nothing short of providing new doctrines.

It's also difficult to reconcile NAR claims that a prophet's words do not have the authority of Scripture with other statements made by NAR prophets. For example, in his introduction to *The Final Quest*, Joyner claims that the majority of the revelation he received for his book was through a higher and more accurate "level of revelation," which he describes as a trance-like state, than that which was probably experienced by the apostles of Christ when they wrote New Testament Scripture.[52]

Prophets' Revelation Is Often Conditional

Many NAR prophecies are conditional because their fulfillment is often dependent on human behavior. Conditional prophecies, according to Hamon, "are those prophetic promises and declarations made by God to individuals that *can* be cancelled, altered, reversed, or diminished [Hamon's emphasis]." These prophecies "may fail and never be fulfilled," he said. The reason they can fail is because "for prophecy of this kind to come to pass requires the proper participation and cooperation of the one who receives the prophetic word."[53]

---

50 Ibid., 37, 58–59, 134.

51 Hamon, *Apostles, Prophets, and the Coming Moves of God*, 18.

52 Joyner, *The Final Quest*, 10–11.

53 Hamon, *Prophets and Personal Prophecy*, 120.

This does nothing to distinguish NAR prophets from Old Testament prophets, who often prophesied future divine blessing or judgment that would or would not come to pass depending on the conduct of recipients of that revelation. These were conditional prophecies that depended on the obedience of God's people. The NAR proviso is no help in qualifying the sense of authority they attribute to prophets today.

Prophets Must Work Together With Apostles

Prophets and apostles are "co-laboring ministries" and should maintain a "close working relationship."[54] As complementary foundational ministries upon which the church is built, they are the two—out of the five ministry offices—"that are paired together in ministry and that have similar anointed abilities," especially the anointing to receive revelation of new truths.[55] Prophets and apostles should not view each other as competition, but should see themselves as equally needed.[56]

Prophets Have Varying Levels of Authority

Prophets with long-lasting, proven ministries and greater maturity speak with more authority than new prophets.[57] Elijah is an example of an Old Testament prophet who had greater authority than other prophets, according to Hamon. Elijah stopped the rain and called down fire from heaven. Meanwhile, one hundred other prophets were forced to hide from Jezebel in caves (1 Kings 18:4). Hamon also cited Samuel as a prophet whose words never failed and who oversaw an entire company of less authoritative prophets (1 Sam. 19:20).

The varying levels of authority found among NAR prophets result in differing functions. Thus, Hamon identifies different types of prophets,

---

[54] Hamon, *Prophets and the Prophetic Movement*, 160.

[55] Ibid.

[56] Ibid., 159. Hamon stresses that prophets share authority equal to the apostles, but he also teaches that every prophet "needs to submit to someone" who can provide him or her with instruction and correction. See Bill Hamon, *Prophets, Pitfalls and Principles: God's Prophetic People Today* (Shippensburg, PA: Destiny Image Publishers, 2001), 45.

[57] Hamon, *Prophets, Pitfalls and Principles*, 142.

including prophets to the nations, prophets to the entire church, and prophets to local churches only.

Scriptures Used to Support the NAR Office of Prophet

Peter Wagner emphasizes three key Scriptures in support of the present-day office of *apostle*—Ephesians 4:11, Ephesians 2:20, and 1 Corinthians 12:28. Hamon cites these same three verses to support the present-day office of *prophet*. Like Wagner, Hamon believes that these verses teach that the office of prophet, along with the office of apostle, is a perpetual office appointed by Christ to govern the church. Since we've already explained NAR interpretations of these passages we need not review them again here.[58]

Summary

NAR prophets are authorized to perform a number of functions for individuals, churches, and nations. A critical function is the revelation of "new truths" to the church, which are often described as "strategies" the church needs for it to bring transformation to the nations. Yet the extraordinary authority of a present-day prophet is limited in several ways, including the stricture that NAR revelation does not have the authority of Scripture (though we argue that their revelation *is* treated as having the authority of Scripture). The three main Scriptures used to support a present-day office of prophet are the same Scriptures used to support the present-day office of apostle: Ephesians 4:11, Ephesians 2:20, and 1 Corinthians 12:28.

In the next chapter we examine the biblical teaching about prophets.

---

[58] For an explanation of how NAR leaders understand these verses, see chapter 5.

12

Prophets in the Bible

> The testimony of Jesus is the spirit of prophecy.
>
> —The Apostle John, *Revelation 19:10*

Now that we've described the NAR view of prophets, we review biblical teaching about prophets.

DEFINITION OF A PROPHET

In the Bible a prophet was a person who spoke for God. In the Old Testament, the most common term for prophet, *nābî*, referred to "a person called and designated by God to be his spokesperson."[1] The New Testament uses *prophētēs*, which, in the Greek, meant "a proclaimer or expounder of divine matters or concerns that could not ordinarily be known except by special revelation."[2] *Prophētēs* was also the term chosen by the Jewish translators of the Septuagint—the Greek translation of the Old Testament—to translate the Hebrew term *nābî*.

OLD TESTAMENT PROPHETS

Prophets' Messages

Throughout Israel's history, God commissioned prophets to guide his chosen nation and give instruction, correction, warnings of judgment, and consolation. These prophets received their messages from God in diverse

---

[1]   Bruce K. Waltke and Charles Yu. *An Old Testament Theology: An Exegetical, Canonical, and Thematic Approach* (Grand Rapids: Zondervan, 2007), 805.

[2]   Walter Bauer, *A Greek-English Lexicon of the New Testament and other Early Christian Literature* (BDAG), 3rd ed., rev. and ed. Frederick William Danker (Chicago: University of Chicago Press, 2000), 890.

ways—through visions and dreams, from angelic messengers, and by hearing his audible voice.

The prophets shared common messages. Their major message was a call for the Israelites to keep the Mosaic covenant. For this reason, they've often been referred to as "covenant enforcers."[3]

The Mosaic covenant was a special relationship that God arranged with Israel. God promised to make Israel into a "kingdom of priests" that would serve as a light to the rest of the nations (Exod. 19:5–6). If the Israelites obeyed the laws God revealed to them through the prophet Moses, they would reflect God's righteousness and justice, and they would channel God's presence and blessings throughout the world.

To help the Israelites remain faithful to the covenant, God promised to raise up a series of prophets, culminating in a specific great prophet like Moses (Deut. 18:15).[4] The message of these prophets—a call to covenant faithfulness—is summarized by the unknown author of 1 and 2 Kings:

> Yet the LORD warned Israel and Judah by every prophet and every seer, saying, "Turn from your evil ways and keep my commandments and my statutes, in accordance with all the Law that I commanded your fathers, and that I sent to you by my servants the prophets." (2 Kings 17:13)

The Israelites, however, did not heed this message. So the prophets foretold the coming of a new covenant (Jer. 31:31–34) and a Messiah who would initiate that covenant (Heb. 12:24). The coming of the Messiah was the ultimate message of the Old Testament prophets. Jesus said as much when he told his disciples:

> O foolish ones, and slow of heart to believe all that the prophets have spoken! Was it not necessary that the Christ should suffer these things and enter into his glory?" And beginning with Moses and all the Prophets, he interpreted to them in all the Scriptures the things concerning himself. (Luke 24:25–27)

---

[3] Philip S. Johnston, ed., *The IVP Introduction to the Bible* (Downers Grove, IL: InterVarsity Press, 2006), 38, 118.

[4] Many Old Testament interpreters see in this verse a promise that after Moses died God would raise up a series of prophets in succession. At the same time, they also see it—in light of the larger passage of Deut. 18:15–19—as a prediction of the coming of a specific great prophet like Moses. Thus, many Israelites through the centuries were awaiting the arrival of this great prophet.

Prophets' Backgrounds

Certain Old Testament prophets stand out, like miracle-working Moses, fiery Elijah, and weeping Jeremiah. But there also were many more lesser-known prophets, some of them unnamed (Judg. 6:7–10; 1 Sam. 2:27–36; 1 Kings 13:1–3). Some prophets' words were not even recorded in Scripture and their books have been lost, like those of Iddo and Ahijah the Shilonite (2 Chron. 9:29). And others prophesied only once, like the seventy elders appointed to assist Moses (Num. 11:24–25).

Prophets came from varied backgrounds. Amos was a shepherd,[5] Jeremiah a priest, and Isaiah a royal court official. Women, as well as men, were prophets, including Miriam, Deborah, and Huldah.

Prophets' Functions

Guiding

Prophets were often consulted by Israel's leaders, who were seeking divine guidance on national matters, including war plans (1 Kings 22:5). King David consulted Nathan about his plans to build the temple (2 Sam. 7:1–7). King Jehoram asked Elisha if he should kill an army of captured Aramean soldiers (2 Kings 6:21–22).

Kings were the primary recipients of most prophetic guidance in the Old Testament. This may be due to the focus of the Old Testament—on national Israel—and not because of any "absence of this ministry in the life of common folk."[6] It seems that prophets also guided private citizens about personal matters. Before Saul was king he sought out a prophet to help him locate his lost donkeys (1 Sam. 9:6–10). His servant's suggestion to seek out a prophet indicates that this was not unusual.

Prophesying to Other Nations

A prophet's ministry didn't always stop at the borders of Israel. Prophets often pronounced judgments on other nations (Isa. 13–23). Some were actually sent by God to other nations, like Jonah, who was sent to the Assyrian

---

[5] Some translators maintain that Amos was not a shepherd, but a sheep breeder.

[6] John W. Hilber, "Diversity of OT Prophetic Phenomena and NT Prophecy," *Westminster Theological Journal* 56, no. 2 (1994): 245.

city of Nineveh to warn its people of looming judgment. And Jeremiah was appointed to be a prophet to the nations (Jer. 1:5).

Receiving Revelation

Old Testament prophets were given revelation, which was preserved in Scripture. The Writing Prophets—all of what we call the Major and Minor Prophets—spoke oracles that were written down in books bearing their names. And Moses is traditionally regarded as the author of the Pentateuch, the first five books of the Old Testament.

Even those books that haven't been tied to a specific prophet still show prophetic influence, according to Bruce Waltke, coauthor of *An Old Testament Theology* and a leading Old Testament scholar. Waltke notes, for example, that scholars often neglect the prophetic status of writers of the historical books of the Old Testament. Though these historians drew their material from various sources, and though they never claimed to have experienced divine revelation like the Writing Prophets, they were prophets nonetheless.

> The prophetic status of these writers is clear from the nature of their work. From Genesis through Kings, these anonymous[7] writers communicate their thoughts from the perspective of the omniscient narrator. They know what God in heaven is thinking and what a couple says in the privacy of their bedroom; they know the thoughts, intentions, and feelings of their characters, including God; and they evaluate events from God's perspective. In essence, they are as omniscient as God; they speak for God, the classic definition of a prophet. If we deny their prophetic status, then we have to conclude that their work is fiction; there is no middle ground. These authors could not have written trustworthy historical annals about events beyond human epistemology without divine inspiration.[8]

This expresses well the outlook of the Old Testament itself regarding the diverse responsibilities of God's prophets.

---

[7] In a footnote, Waltke notes that Moses, although the author of much of an earlier form of the Pentateuch, was not the final author, i.e., the one who wrote Moses' obituary in Deuteronomy 34. None of these historical books name their first author or their inspired editors. Waltke, *An Old Testament Theology*, 60.

[8] Ibid., 60.

Interceding before God

Prophets made intercession to God on behalf of individuals and the nation of Israel. For example, when the Israelites sinned by demanding a king, they asked Samuel to pray for their forgiveness so that God would not smite them (1 Sam. 12:19). And Moses' prayers influenced God to relent from destroying the Israelites in the desert (Exod. 32:10–33:17).

Worshipping

Prophets also contributed to Israel's worship. Some Levites, while serving at the temple, delivered spontaneous prophetic oracles that caused the Israelites to worship God (2 Chron. 20:14–17).[9] Some prophesied in the form of song (1 Chron. 25:1–6), including the prophetess Miriam (Num. 15:20–21). A group of prophets prophesied to the accompaniment of musical instruments (1 Sam. 10:5).

Prophetic Companies

The Old Testament mentions prophetic companies, called "sons of the prophets," whose functions aren't fully known.[10] These companies were sometimes very large, with more than one hundred members (1 Kings 18:4). They were based at specific locations, including Bethel, Jericho, and Gilgal. They often served under a master prophet, like Elisha (2 Kings 4:1, 38; 6:1; 9:1), yet their own words were also authoritative. They're shown pronouncing judgment on Israel's kings (1 Kings 20:35–42), anointing kings (2 Kings 9:1–13), and predicting future events (2 Kings 2:3, 5).

In summary, Old Testament prophets called the Israelites to covenant faithfulness and proclaimed a new covenant. Their functions included the provision of divine guidance for kings and private individuals, prophesying to other nations, and receiving revelation. They also interceded with God on behalf of the Israelites, contributed to Israel's worship, and performed unknown functions as part of prophetic companies.

---

[9] A number of the Levites' oracles came to be included in the book of Psalms (Pss. 39, 50, 62, 73–83, and possibly 88). See Hilber's discussion of prophets' contribution to worship in "Diversity of OT Prophetic Phenomena and NT Prophecy," 246–47.

[10] Hilber, "Diversity of OT Prophetic Phenomena and NT Prophecy," 247–48.

New Testament Prophets

When people think of prophets, they often think of the great Old Testament prophets, like Moses and Elijah. Yet figures are also identified as prophets in the New Testament (some are not expressly called prophets, but are only described as prophesying). These personages include John the Baptist, Simeon, Anna, Jesus of Nazareth, those present at Pentecost, prophets at the church in Antioch, Judas and Silas, Agabus, the four daughters of Philip, prophets at the church in Corinth, and the "two witnesses" in the book of Revelation.[11]

In addition, Paul, Peter, and John received special revelation from God. John received an entire book of prophecy, the book of Revelation. For this reason, some scholars conclude that these three apostles of Christ[12] were both apostles and prophets.

Prophets' Message

Prophets in the New Testament—ministering under the New Covenant—didn't call people to obey the Mosaic covenant. They did, however, concur with the Old Testament prophets about the same ultimate message—the message of the Messiah. Jesus Christ was proclaimed by the first prophet of New Testament history, John the Baptist, and the last living apostle, John. The apostle John confirmed that Jesus was the ultimate message of all the Bible's prophets, from both the Old Testament and the New, when he said that all prophecy points to Jesus: "For the testimony of Jesus is the spirit of prophecy" (Rev. 19:10).

Prophets' Purpose and Functions

The primary purpose of New Testament prophets was to edify (that is, to build up) the church. According to Paul, edification of the church was the purpose of all spiritual gifts, including the gift of prophecy (1 Cor. 12:7;

---

[11] Others are also described as prophesying, such as Zacharias and Elizabeth. We do not list every person who prophesied, but only several especially noteworthy people.

[12] Recall our definition of "apostles of Christ"—that is, those apostles mentioned in 1 Cor. 15:1–7 who had seen the resurrected Christ and operated with special authority in the first Christian era.

14:3–5, 12, 26). In Ephesians, prophets are listed among the types of gifted leaders whom God has provided for "building up the body of Christ" (Eph. 4:11–12). To edify the church, New Testament prophets performed various functions.

Receiving Revelation

We already noted that Paul, Peter, and John received special revelation from God, which was preserved in Scripture.

Guiding the Early Church

Prophets' revelation guided the growth of the early church. This is reflected in the activity of prophets at critical junctures in the book of Acts. Prophets at the church in Antioch revealed that God had chosen Barnabas and Paul for a special mission to the Gentiles (Acts 13:1–3). Two other prophets, Judas and Silas, traveled with Paul and Barnabas to Antioch, where they delivered the letter containing the decision made by the Council at Jerusalem (Acts 15:22, 32). While there, these two prophets spoke words that "encouraged and strengthened the brothers" in that particular church. Agabus predicted a famine that took place during the reign of the Roman emperor Claudius. His prophecy prompted the Christians at Antioch to send relief to the church at Jerusalem so the church could survive (Acts 11:28–30).

Prophets were active at the church in Corinth, where they contributed prophecies during worship meetings. Paul advised the church to allow two or three prophets to give revelations "so that all may learn and all be encouraged" (1 Cor. 14:31). Though the exact content of their prophecies isn't stated, we know from this last verse that it included words of teaching and exhortation. And from 1 Corinthians 14:3, we know that "one who prophesies speaks to people for their upbuilding and encouragement and consolation."

Worshipping

Worship was a function of New Testament prophets, just as it was for prophets in the Old Testament. At Pentecost, those who prophesied spoke of "the mighty works of God" (Acts 2:11). Others in the New Testament delivered prophetically inspired oracles of praise, similar to the oracles of the Levites in the Old Testament—including Elizabeth (Luke 1:41–45), Mary (Luke 1:46–55), Zacharias (Luke 1:67–79), and Simeon (Luke 2:28–32).

Evangelism

Prophets also had an indirect function related to evangelism. Generally, their prophecies were for believers (1 Cor. 14:22). Yet prophecies could occasionally speak to unbelievers who came into their church meetings, thereby exposing the secrets of the visitors' hearts and, thus, causing them to worship God (1 Cor. 14:24–25).

Revealing Ministry Callings or Spiritual Gifting

In Paul's letters to Timothy, we learn that prophecies were given to Timothy at the time Paul and the elders at the church in Ephesus laid hands on him (1 Tim. 1:18; 4:14; 2 Tim. 1:6). Many interpreters believe the event in view is Timothy's ordination to ministry and that the prophecies about him pertained to his specific calling or spiritual gifting.

A Function Not Performed by New Testament Prophets

New Testament prophets apparently did not share a function that was typical of some Old Testament prophets—prophesying to nations.

With two notable exceptions, New Testament prophets were not sent to prophesy to nations. The exceptions are John the Baptist and Jesus. Both were sent to the people of Israel, which, within their social context and despite Roman rule, maintained a national identity. But, after Pentecost, prophets functioned mostly within local churches, traveling occasionally to deliver prophecies to other Christians, as did Agabus with Paul. These prophets didn't pronounce judgments on nations.

After John and Jesus, the next time we see prophets declaring judgments on nations is in the book of Revelation, with the two witnesses who strike the earth with plagues (Rev. 11:6).[13] According to a futurist interpretation of this book, these two witnesses won't appear until just before Christ's return.

The reason post-Pentecost prophets were not sent to proclaim judgment on the nations is likely because they were busy fulfilling the Great Commission to "make disciples of all nations" (Matt. 28:19). That is, they were preaching the gospel to the nations, not pronouncing judgments on them. Judgment is postponed until "the day of God's wrath." Meanwhile, God

---

[13]   Bob DeWaay, "John the Baptist and Prophets to Nations," *Critical Issues Commentary*, Issue 67 (November/December 2001); accessed September 2, 2014, http://www.cicministry.org/commentary/issue67.htm.

waits patiently for the repentance of all men and women who will hear and believe the gospel (see 2 Peter 3:1–10).

FALSE PROPHETS

Genuine prophets are not the only prophets found in the pages of the Bible. There are also many false prophets.

In the Old Testament, false prophets included pagan prophets claiming to speak on behalf of pagan gods, such as the 450 prophets of Baal and the 400 prophets of Asherah who served King Ahab and Queen Jezebel of Israel (1 Kings 18:19–20). In addition there were false prophets from Israel who claimed to speak on behalf of the true God. These included Zedekiah and the 400 prophets with him (1 Kings 22:5–12). Other unnamed false prophets of Israel were condemned by Isaiah (Isa. 28:7–13), Jeremiah (Jer. 23:9–40), Ezekiel (Ezek. 13), and Micah (Mic. 3:5–12).

False prophets are also found in the New Testament. Jesus specifically warned about false prophets when he said: "Beware of the false prophets, who come to you in sheep's clothing, but inwardly are ravenous wolves" (Matt. 7:15). He also said that false prophets would be numerous: "Many false prophets will arise and will mislead many" (Matt. 24:11). He explained that these false prophets would perform deceptive miracles to make it seem like they were actually true prophets. "For false Christs and false prophets will arise and will show great signs and wonders, so as to mislead, if possible, even the elect" (Matt. 24:24).

False prophets specifically identified in the New Testament are Elymas the magician (Acts 13:6–8), a woman called Jezebel (Rev. 2:20), and a miracle-working false prophet (Rev. 13:11–18; 16:13–14). Though only a few false prophets are identified by name, many were operating in the early church. Near the end of his life, the apostle John warned Christians that "many false prophets have gone out into the world" (1 John 4:1).

SUMMARY

Numerous prophets are found in the Bible, in both the Old and New Testaments. They had a variety of functions, though prophets in the New Testament typically did not prophesy to nations as did some Old Testament prophets. Many false prophets are also noted in the Bible; we find multiple warnings to be alert to their presence.

In the next chapter we compare prophets in the Bible to NAR prophets.

13

NAR Prophets Compared to the Bible's Prophets

> It would go beyond the limits of exegesis to assume that the gift of prophecy belongs any more *permanently* to some specific individual as an "office" than the gifts of faith or kinds of healings. The epistle remains silent on this matter.
>
> —Anthony C. Thiselton, *The First Epistle to the Corinthians*

In light of what the Bible teaches about prophets, how do NAR teachings compare? First, we'll make some brief comments about a more moderate view of contemporary prophets as those having only the gift of prophecy. We'll refer to these people as "prophetically gifted individuals." Then we'll turn to the more radical NAR view of prophets as those who hold a formal office in church government with authority extending to nations—and who reveal new truths. We'll refer to these individuals as "prophets of God."

THE PRESENT-DAY GIFT OF PROPHECY

Can people today have the gift of prophecy? Cessationists say no, if the gift includes continued provision of revelation, either for the church or for individuals. Cessationists don't allow for new revelation because they believe that, if revelation continues and God still speaks to people directly, the new revelation would share the authority of Scripture and thus would threaten its unique status. But continuationists say yes, that people today can be prophetically gifted in the sense of receiving new revelation from God. And they don't believe that the exercise of their gift threatens the authority of Scripture.

Who's right?

As fascinating as this question is, we will not attempt to answer it in this book because it is beyond the immediate scope of our topic—NAR teachings about the contemporary office of prophet. We don't think that continuationists are subject to the same error as those who promote a governing office.

In making an allowance for teachings about new revelation, we want to be clear. We believe such teaching should stress that any new revelation received by individuals today would be primarily for other individuals and local churches, not the universal church. Thus, it could not claim authority over all Christians, as Scripture does.

We also caution against use of the title prophet by continuationists, even though New Testament churches used the word to describe those with a spiritual gift of prophecy. The title presently carries many different connotations. It may lead to the wrong belief that prophetically gifted individuals govern the church or speak words that, like Scripture, are binding on all Christians.

We focus the remainder of our critique on NAR teachings about prophets who hold a present-day office.

THE PRESENT-DAY OFFICE OF PROPHET

One distinct emphasis of the NAR view is its promotion of a present-day office of prophet. By office, we refer to a specially recognized official position in church government.

Even those Protestants who have recognized a present-day gift of prophecy have not, by and large, recognized a present-day office of prophet. The main reason is that there is no biblical precedent for it. There's no evidence that New Testament prophets held governing offices in the early churches. If they did, both the Bible and history are completely silent about it and we have no reason to believe it.

But, says Bill Hamon, since some Old Testament prophets had governing offices in Israel—such as Samuel, a judge, and David, a king—then some prophets must have had governing offices in the New Testament church.

We take issue with Hamon's claim that Old Testament prophets governed. While it's true that some prophets in the Old Testament also had leadership roles, it's going too far to claim that these prophets held formal governing offices simply by virtue of their being prophets. Once the nation of Israel was established, it was not led by prophets, but rather by judges and kings. While some of those judges and kings may also have been prophets of God or may have, at times, spoken prophetically—like Samuel and David—their authority to govern stemmed from their offices as judges and kings, not from their role as prophets. Rather than governing, Old Testament prophets gave guidance to those who did govern, such as the prophet Nathan who served as an adviser to King David.

But even if we grant, for the sake of argument, that some Old Testament prophets governed, Hamon still has not made his case. The fact is that, even if some did govern, it's clear that not all of them did. Governing, then, is not an indispensable function of an Old Testament prophet. This means that it should not automatically be supposed that New Testament prophets held governing offices in the church.

Given the Bible's silence on the topic, it's likely that prophets spoken of in the New Testament did not govern. There seems to be no sense in which those who prophesied then also functioned as governors within the churches. In fact, there's no good evidence that the governing role attributed to prophets by NAR leaders was practiced by any leaders in the early church. If God thought it important for prophets, or anyone else for that matter, to rule churches after the fashion asserted by NAR leaders, why is this not clearly taught in Scripture? Why must NAR leaders rely on specious inferences from poorly assimilated evidence regarding the role of a prophet in the Old Testament?

It's true that Scripture teaches that God reveals "his secret to his servants the prophets" (Amos 3:7). But merely citing this verse does not substantiate NAR teachings that there is a present-day office of prophet in church government. NAR leaders claim that Scripture does teach that prophets held offices in church government. But the three main passages they cite—Ephesians 2:20, Ephesians 4:11, and 1 Corinthians 12:28—fail to support their claim.

Ephesians 2:20 notes that prophets alongside apostles had a foundational role in the church. But a foundational role is not necessarily equivalent to an office. A foundational role is inherently temporary; an office need not be. A prophet's foundational role very likely included affirmation of Gentile inclusion in the church (Eph. 3:5–6). But that does not depend on an official capacity to govern the church. NAR leaders simply cannot identify among New Testament prophets practices, activities, or roles ascribed to today's prophets by NAR leaders.

Ephesians 4:11 does not prescribe offices either, but rather lists five types of gifted leaders God has given the church. It's reading too much into this verse to claim that it prescribes formal offices rather than ministry functions.

Finally, NAR leaders hold that prophets are set apart as a distinct office—along with apostles and teachers—in 1 Corinthians 12:28. They point to a change of wording that occurs in this verse, which they claim shows that the first three items listed are offices and the remainder are spiritual gifts: "And God has appointed in the church first apostles, second prophets, third teachers, then miracles, then gifts of healing, helping, administrating, and various kinds of tongues." In our discussion of this verse in chapter 8, we noted that lists generally include items of a similar kind. The apostle Paul isn't suddenly switching gears mid-thought from a listing of offices to an inventory of spiritual gifts. While Paul does rank the contributions of apostles, prophets, and teachers as in some sense more important than the contributions of others, it's reading too much into this passage to claim that offices are being prescribed here. Commentator Anthony Thiselton agrees: "It would go beyond the limits of exegesis to assume that the gift of prophecy belongs any more *permanently* to some specific individual as an 'office' than the gifts of faith or kinds of healings. The epistle [1 Corinthians] remains silent on this matter."[1]

Other than the apostles of Christ, who held an exclusive office, the only two church offices clearly identifiable in the New Testament are elders and deacons. These are treated most expressly as offices. The apostle Paul appointed elders in every church (Acts 14:23), and he told Timothy to do the same (Titus 1:5). Paul also provided lists of qualifications for elders and deacons (1 Tim. 3:1–13; Titus 1:5–9). But there are no examples of the *appointment* of prophets, nor are instructions given appointing prophets to an office. Furthermore, neither the elders nor the deacons exercised the kind and scope of authority attributed by NAR leaders to present-day prophets.

NAR leaders may be tempted to explain this silence about the appointment of prophets as governing officials by suggesting that prophets were to be appointed directly by God. In response, we need only recall NAR teachings that those who hold an office must be commissioned to that office by a prophetic presbytery, that is, by people.[2]

In short, there are no New Testament passages that prescribe an office of prophet in church government. Nor are there any passages that so much as describe prophets as holding an office. There is, then, no biblical basis

---

[1]   Anthony C. Thiselton, *The First Epistle to the Corinthians*, The New International Greek Testament Commentary (Grand Rapids: Eerdmans, 2000), 965; emphasis original.

[2]   Bill Hamon, *Prophets and Personal Prophecy: God's Prophetic Voice Today* (Shippensburg, PA: Destiny Image Publishers, 2001), 39.

for affirming the present-day office of prophet. NAR leaders have erected a huge doctrine over a gaping hole.

OTHER FUNCTIONS OF NAR PROPHETS

Prophesying to Nations

Hamon claims that NAR prophets have authority to prophesy to nations. We've already noted, however, that prophets in the New Testament were not sent to nations, but functioned mostly in local churches. Except for John the Baptist and Jesus and the two witnesses in the book of Revelation, there's not a single example of a New Testament prophet pronouncing judgments on a nation. Their purpose was edification of the church, not the spiritual strong-arming of nations. The notion of present-day prophets to nations has no biblical support.

Revealing New Truths

NAR prophets reveal "new truths," according to Hamon. These new truths include "illumination and further specifics about that which has already been written [in Scripture.]"[3] Oddly, Hamon insists that these new truths are not equal to Scripture. He says, "Only a false prophet would ever believe or proclaim that what he speaks or writes is or would ever be equivalent to Scripture in inspiration or authority."[4]

This strong pronouncement is curious, for Hamon seems to teach that present-day prophets have the same functions as the Old Testament prophets. Why, then, can they not write new Scripture? Hamon never explains why; he simply says they can't. We can imagine some contemporary prophet coming along purporting to add to the extant Scriptures of the Christian church. What could Hamon say to counter such a claim? And with what authority? Not the authority of Scripture since, as we have seen, Scripture does not authorize the office of a prophet as envisioned by Hamon. And if on Hamon's own authority, because he considers himself to be a prophet, then new problems arise. First, members of the church would have to adjudicate between the conflicting claims of competing prophets, with no recourse to a higher authority. Second, Hamon's judgment would have a universally

---

[3] Hamon, *Prophets and Personal Prophecy*, 3.

[4] Bill Hamon, *Prophets and the Prophetic Movement: God's Prophetic Move Today* (Shippensburg, PA: Destiny Image Publishers, 2001), xxiii.

binding quality that could not be grounded in Scripture and so would itself be tantamount to scriptural authority, thus violating his own claim that no contemporary prophet speaks with an authority equal to that of Scripture.

This, however, is hypothetical. It's easy to see that Hamon's doctrine concerning modern-day prophets is confused, even contradictory. First, Hamon teaches that the new truths given by NAR prophets make up a body of teachings known as "present truth." Present-truth teachings must be embraced by every Christian who wants to take part in the Saints Movement[5] and other coming movements of God prophesied by Hamon. Indeed, Hamon teaches that present revelation is "absolutely essential for the Church to continue progressively fulfilling the will of God on earth."[6]

By claiming that present truth teachings must be embraced by all Christians, Hamon seems to be claiming that all Christians are bound by those teachings; that is, that the teachings are universally authoritative. But this claim can only be made for the teachings of Scripture. Hamon might respond by pointing to his teaching that *one* prophet can't give universally authoritative revelation. He says, "No one man or ministry should establish a doctrine as essential belief and practice for all Christians."[7] Does this resolve the problem? It does not. Hamon goes on to state that *councils* of NAR prophets and apostles can establish new doctrine as essential for all Christians. Here are his words: "But doctrines that claim to be binding on all Christians must not be established by any one apostle, prophet, or camp. There must be meetings of a Church council with other leaders of past and present restorational streams of truth."[8] So Hamon does allow for prophets and apostles to give new teachings that are binding on all Christians, provided that councils—not just one person—endorse those teachings. This plainly contradicts his claim that new truths are not equal to Scripture.

Second, Hamon claims that prophets receive "prophetic illumination" into Scripture that allows them to give new interpretations no one has seen before, like his interpretation of Malachi 4:5.[9] By insisting that all Christians

---

[5]   See our discussion of this movement and Hamon's teachings on church restoration in chapter 11.

[6]   Hamon, *Prophetic Scriptures Yet to Be Fulfilled During the Third and Final Church Reformation* (Shippensburg, PA: Destiny Image Publishers, 2010), 169.

[7]   Hamon, *Prophets and the Prophetic Movement*, 144.

[8]   Ibid.

[9]   See chapter 11 for his interpretation.

must accept prophets' new interpretations, he confers on those interpreta-tions the same authority enjoyed by Scripture.

Hamon might object to our understanding of his second example. He does claim that other Christians have received "prophetic illumination" into Scripture, such as Martin Luther with Ephesians 2:8–9. This is a false comparison. Martin Luther didn't claim to discover a new, hitherto dis-guised sense of Ephesians 2:8–9. Nor have Protestants ever suggested that discovery of the doctrine of justification by faith alone happened as a result of "prophetic illumination." On the contrary, Protestants have emphasized the perspicuity of Scripture, the doctrine that, in matters concerning salva-tion, the teaching of Scripture is clear, plain for all to see, if they can but read the Bible for themselves. And how could it be otherwise? Was the gospel so little understood that for centuries, until the arrival of Martin Luther, no one knew that salvation is by faith?

If illumination is at all needed in the effort to understand the Scriptures, it's not the illumination uniquely available to a prophet with the special of-fice of interpreting the dark sayings of Scripture. Spiritual discernment may well be needed for the full understanding of divine truth revealed in the Bible, but this discernment depends on "the obedience of faith" spoken of by the apostle Paul, and alluded to by Jesus in John 7:17.[10] Hamon cannot treat the example of Luther as evidence that present-day prophets reveal new, previously hidden interpretations of Scripture. Who can doubt that this leader of the Protestant Reformation—a movement based on the doc-trine of *sola scriptura*—would recoil from the notion that he was a prophet revealing "new truths"?

Third, Hamon cites Ephesians 3:4–5 in support of his teaching that present-day prophets continue to reveal new truths. But this passage doesn't teach that prophets in each generation would reveal new truths. It simply speaks of a specific new truth—the truth that Gentiles would be included in the church—which was revealed to prophets in the first century.

In addition to these inconsistencies and confusions, we must point out that the kinds of claims we are to expect from Hamon's present-day proph-ets are not trivial. They concern the proper ordering of lives, the effective engagement of believers with the surrounding culture, and the destinies of

---

10   For a multidimensional treatment of the doctrine of illumination, see R. Douglas Geivett and Paul K. Moser, eds., *The Testimony of the Spirit: New Essays* (forthcoming, Oxford University Press).

nations. For such exigencies, Christians accustomed to relying on the stable authority of Scripture will naturally require an equally strong basis for believing what an alleged prophet might say. If that prophet's authority is at all inferior to the unqualified authority vested in the prophets of old by God, then why should any modern-day believer believe his dictates or follow her commands?

In short, it doesn't matter how strongly Hamon denies that NAR prophets' revelation is equal to Scripture. When he demands that all Christians must accept such prophets' new truths, is he not claiming, in effect, that their words are equal to Scripture? But recall Hamon's own words, "Only a false prophet would ever believe or proclaim that what he speaks or writes is or would ever be equivalent to Scripture in inspiration or authority."[11] It is also inconsistent—as well being an irony and a delusion—to hold that, in order to be regarded as a true prophet, you must allow that your prophecies may not always be true.

We want to address a final point related to NAR teachings about new truths. Hamon claims that the truths given by NAR prophets are not actually new, but are old truths that were lost by the church and are now being restored. If this is truly the case, then NAR prophets would not be guilty of introducing new doctrines that challenge the unique authority of Scripture.

But, despite Hamon's claims that prophets are restoring the church's original belief system, he hasn't offered any evidence—at least none that we have seen—that the first Christians actually held beliefs similar to those of NAR. Hamon can't just *claim* that the first Christians held NAR beliefs. He must *show* they held those beliefs. But he has not done this. For example, Hamon claims God showed him that Malachi 4:5 has two fulfillments: one in John the Baptist and one in an end-time company of prophets. But where is the evidence that the early church had this understanding of Malachi 4:5? To our knowledge, this teaching is foreign to the apostolic and postapostolic fathers of the church. And it certainly hasn't been an emphasis in the main stream of historic Christian thought.

Hamon's claim to be restoring the church's original beliefs is similar to claims made by the Church of Jesus Christ of Latter Day Saints, Jehovah's Witnesses, and Christian Science, groups that Hamon himself would probably consider to be cults or dangerous aberrations of orthodox Christianity.

---

[11] Hamon, *Prophets and the Prophetic Movement*, xxiii.

Prophesying to Individuals

In addition to NAR prophets' roles discussed above, Hamon also teaches that they perform unique functions for individual Christians, including revealing people's spiritual gifts and ministries, guiding them on major life decisions, and giving prophecies that result in physical and emotional healing. We cannot devote much space to addressing these particular functions because they go beyond the immediate scope of our book. We simply note that even classical Pentecostal denominations, such as the Assemblies of God, express concern about prophetic words that purport to reveal spiritual gifts or provide personal life direction.[12]

Such practices are especially concerning in the New Apostolic Reformation because NAR prophets claim to hold a formal church office and therefore to possess extraordinary authority. So, when a NAR prophet prophesies to an individual, that prophet's words will be seen as carrying greater authority than the words of a person who has only the spiritual gift of prophecy without holding a formal office.

Because of the extraordinary authority attached to the words of a NAR prophet, a great danger is that people in NAR will become overly dependent on seeking personal direction from such prophets. Another danger is that they will obey the words of a NAR prophet much as they would the words of God. Recall Hamon's teaching that prophets in the office are authorized to give specific, directive words to individuals regarding their personal lives, prefaced with the extraordinarily authoritative phrase "Thus saith the Lord."[13] This teaching is particularly irresponsible given the consensus among NAR leaders that NAR prophets can err.

If a prophet qualifies his claim and says he may be mistaken in his guidance of others, problems multiply. This diminishes the authority, and with it the value, of a prophetic word of counsel. It thereby compromises one's claim to be a prophet. And it leaves believers who are counseled with provisos of this sort bewildered about what they should believe and how they should act in the face of a decision.

---

[12] "End-Time Revival—Spirit-Led and Spirit-Controlled: A Response Paper to Resolution 16," General Presbytery of the Assemblies of God, August 11, 2000, 2; accessed September 30, 2010, http://ag.org/top/Beliefs/Position_Papers/pp_downloads/pp_endtime_revival.pdf.

[13] Hamon, *Prophets and Personal Prophecy*, 73.

The irresponsibility may be lessened slightly by Hamon's caution that "We should always consider carefully any prophetic word given to us, whatever its source."[14] Nevertheless, this teaching is still irresponsible since Hamon says the authoritative words from a prophet in the office "can be taken seriously, evaluated, and acted upon immediately."[15]

GUARDING AGAINST FALSE PROPHETS

Hamon assures his followers that they need not worry too much about false prophets because there are not that many of them. He says that in the six hundred pages of prophecies that have been made about him over the years, only two—a fraction of a percent—have been "absolutely false."[16] He also says, "The percentage of false prophets is certainly much lower than the devil would have us believe."[17] That is, at least, what Hamon would have us believe.

Hamon's teaching ignores the fact that numerous false prophets were present in Israel and the early church (1 Kings 18:19–20; 22:5–12; Isa. 28:7–13; Jer. 23:9–40; Ezek. 13; Mic. 3:5–12; Acts 13:6–8; Rev. 2:20). It also contradicts the teachings of Jesus and the apostle John, who warned that "many false prophets will arise and lead many astray" (Matt. 24:11) and "many false prophets have gone out into the world" (1 John 4:1). In light of their warnings, why would a prophet encourage his followers to let down their guard?

SUMMARY

While there is a scriptural basis for an ongoing gift of prophecy, there is no basis for a present-day office of prophet that governs the church or prophets who prophesy to nations or give new truths.

In the next chapter we explain three key biblical tests for determining whether a prophet is genuine or not.

---

14   Ibid.

15   Ibid.

16   Hamon, *Prophets and Personal Prophecy*, 128.

17   Ibid.

14

Testing NAR Prophets

> Many false prophets will arise and lead many astray.
>
> —Jesus, *Matthew 24:11*

As the last chapter has shown, there is a biblical basis for an ongoing gift of prophecy, but no such basis for a present-day office of prophet that governs the church or prophets today who reveal new truths. If NAR prophets insist that they perform these functions, then they must pass the three key biblical tests for prophets.

THE FULFILLMENT TEST

One test set forth in Scripture is the fulfillment test. We will focus most of our comments on this test since many NAR leaders flatly reject it.

The fulfillment test requires that prophets' predictions must come true. The test is given in Deuteronomy 18:21–22, right after Moses predicts the rise of a series of prophets following his death. In other words, as soon as the Israelites learned that God would send them a series of prophets, God provided a clear test for distinguishing the true prophets from the imposters: "And if you say in your heart, 'How may we know the word that the LORD has not spoken?'—when a prophet speaks in the name of the LORD, if the word does not come to pass or come true, that is a word that the LORD has not spoken; the prophet has spoken it presumptuously. You need not be afraid of him" (Deut. 18:21–22).

Though Hamon acknowledges that Old Testament prophets had to be one hundred percent accurate in what they predicted, he claims that the same fulfillment test doesn't apply to NAR prophets. This is because "prophets ministering in the dispensation of the Church are extended more grace than were the prophets of the Old Testament."[1]

---

[1]   Bill Hamon, *Prophets, Pitfalls and Principles: God's Prophetic People Today* (Shippensburg, PA: Destiny Image Publishers, 2001), 101.

This teaching that genuine prophets can err is common in NAR. In support of this teaching, NAR leaders sometimes point to respected theologian Wayne Grudem, who agrees that New Testament prophets are not expected to be one hundred percent accurate in their prophecies.[2] But this is an egregious misunderstanding of Grudem. Grudem maintains that New Testament prophets need not be one hundred percent accurate since they do not have the same level of authority as the Old Testament prophets and do not hold a formal governing office in the church.[3] As shown in chapter 10, NAR leaders teach that New Testament prophets have the same level of authority as Old Testament prophets and that they hold a formal governing office. Thus, they make illicit use of Grudem's teaching to support their view that NAR prophets can err.

At points in his writings, it would seem that Hamon agrees with Grudem's view that New Testament prophets don't have the same level of authority as Old Testament prophets. For example, when explaining the reasons why today's NAR prophets are extended more grace than were the Old Testament prophets, Hamon suggests that the reason is because Old Testament prophets claimed to speak for God directly and thus ran the risk of leading entire nations astray. Hamon says, "The [Old Testament] prophets represented God to humankind with their divine judgments and decrees, prefaced with "Thus saith the Lord.". . . For that reason, the Old Testament prophets were required to speak the very word of the Lord each time they opened their mouths. They could not afford to speak falsely or presumptuously without the risk of leading the entire nation into error."[4]

Hamon here implies that NAR prophets don't claim to speak for God directly or to lead entire nations. Yet this statement appears to contradict his other teachings. Throughout his books, Hamon claims that NAR prophets do speak for God directly. They also announce divine judgments and decrees, prefaced with the phrase "Thus saith the Lord." And they act as prophets to the nations, commanding the obedience of entire nations. How, then, can Hamon seriously claim that NAR prophets are not at risk of leading the nations into error? It seems that in suggesting this Hamon is himself leading others into error.

---

[2] Wayne A. Grudem, *The Gift of Prophecy in the New Testament and Today*, rev. ed. (Wheaton, IL: Crossway, 2000, c1988), 51–94.

[3] Ibid., 27.

[4] Hamon, *Prophets, Pitfalls and Principles*, 101.

A second reason NAR prophets are extended more grace than Old Testament prophets, according to Hamon, is that today Jesus Christ—not prophets—serves as the mediator between God and his people, and we also have the completed canon of Scripture. This puts today's prophets "in a less responsible position than their Old Testament counterparts."[5]

In response, we note that Hamon's teachings about prophets undermine this statement that the canon of Scripture is complete. He teaches that NAR prophets reveal new truths that are universally authoritative, which is tantamount to claiming that the canon remains open.

Hamon also teaches that today's prophets have all the same authority and functions as the Old Testament prophets. So how can he claim that they don't share the same level of responsibility? He seems to be making a special plea to excuse present-day prophets from the fulfillment test.

A third reason NAR prophets are extended more grace and don't have to be one hundred percent accurate in their predictions is that they are mortal. "We must remember, after all" says Hamon, "that *all* mortals and their ministries are fallible."[6] To this, we simply point out that Old Testament prophets were mortals also, yet they weren't permitted to make mistakes in their prophecies. God enabled them to deliver his word without error. So if Hamon wishes to claim that today's prophets are like Old Testament prophets in every other respect, then he cannot exempt them from the fulfillment test.

This test applies to both Old Testament and New Testament prophets since there is no indication that it was ever annulled—and, by Hamon's own teaching, "whatever was established in the Old Testament remains proper as a principle or practice unless the New Testament does away with it."[7] Christians today, of course, don't customarily stone false prophets, as was lawful in the Old Testament (Deut. 13:5, 6–10; 18:20). This is partly because the church is not a theocratic nation and is not under the Mosaic law. Nevertheless, the fulfillment test remains valid.

The offense of giving false prophecies is serious. When you falsely claim to speak for God, you're guilty of breaking God's third commandment, "You shall not take the name of the LORD your God in vain, for the LORD will not

---

[5]   Ibid.

[6]   Bill Hamon, *Prophets and Personal Prophecy: God's Prophetic Voice Today* (Shippensburg, PA: Destiny Image Publishers, 2001), 126.

[7]   Bill Hamon, *Prophets and the Prophetic Movement: God's Prophetic Move Today* (Shippensburg, PA: Destiny Image Publishers, 2001), 157.

hold him guiltless who takes his name in vain" (Exod. 20:7). God, speaking through the prophet Jeremiah, condemned prophets who falsely claimed to speak for Him.

> *I did not send the prophets,*
> > *yet they ran;*
> *I did not speak to them,*
> > *yet they prophesied. . . .*

> *Behold, I am against the prophets, declares the LORD, who use their tongues and declare, 'declares the LORD.' Behold, I am against those who prophesy lying dreams, declares the LORD, and who tell them and lead my people astray by their lies and their recklessness, when I did not send them or charge them. So they do not profit this people at all, declares the LORD.* (Jer. 23:21, 31–32).

In our view, it is an injustice that NAR prophets can give mistaken prophecies without suffering great harm to their reputations or incurring personal loss. But, unlike them, their followers aren't always left unscathed.

Of course, some mistaken predictions—such as those indicating that Mitt Romney would win the 2012 US presidential election—may not have devastating consequences.[8] But that is not always the case. When predictions were made about the destruction of Southern California by the prophet Rick Joyner and a colleague, fear swept through charismatic churches of the region. Joyner's followers reportedly urged people to leave the state.[9] These are some of the consequences that can occur when someone claims to speak with the authority of an Old Testament prophet, but is not held to the same level of responsibility.[10]

---

[8] Jones, "Hold On to Your Dreams," The Prophetic Ministry of Bob and Bonnie Jones, September 7, 2012; accessed February 22, 2014, http://www.bobjones.org/Docs/Words%20of%202012/2012_HoldOnToYourDreams.htm; Rick Joyner, "Lessons Learned from the Recent Elections—The Path of Life, Part 44," MorningStar Ministries, Week 51, 2012; accessed February 4, 2014, http://www.morningstarministries.org/resources/word-week/2012/lessons-learned-recent-elections-path-life-part-44#.UvGRFbSmR8o.

[9] Cedric Harmon, "God's Lightning Rod," *Charisma*, March 31, 2001; accessed March 1, 2014, http://www.charismamag.com/life/156-j15/features/issues-in-the-church/303-gods-lightning-rod.

[10] We note that Rick Joyner continues to stand behind his prophecy about the destruction of California, claiming that it was misunderstood and that its fulfillment

The NAR notion that prophets will continue to increase in their accuracy as days go by is intended, no doubt, to make their followers feel better about the predictions that have failed. But it simply cannot be supported by Scripture.

THE ORTHODOXY TEST

Another test Scripture gives for prophets is the orthodoxy test, which requires that prophets' words must line up with the revelation already given. This test is spelled out in Deuteronomy 13:1–5:

> *If a prophet or a dreamer of dreams arises among you and gives you a sign or a wonder, and the sign or wonder that he tells you comes to pass, and if he says, "Let us go after other gods," which you have not known, "and let us serve them," you shall not listen to the words of that prophet or that dreamer of dreams. For the LORD your God is testing you, to know whether you love the LORD your God with all your heart and with all your soul. You shall walk after the LORD your God and fear him and keep his commandments and obey his voice, and you shall serve him and hold fast to him. But that prophet or that dreamer of dreams shall be put to death, because he has taught rebellion against the LORD your God, who brought you out of the land of Egypt and redeemed you out of the house of slavery, to make you leave the way in which the LORD your God commanded you to walk. So you shall purge the evil from your midst.*

The orthodoxy test shows up again in the New Testament, where we see that all teachings in the churches—including teachings given by prophets—were held to the standard of teaching that had been handed down by the apostles of Christ. Consider, for example, the teaching that circulated in the church at Thessalonica that the day of the Lord had already arrived. This teaching had come, possibly, through the revelation of a false prophet ("by a spirit," 2 Thess. 2:2). The apostle Paul countered it by reminding the Thessalonians what he had already taught them—that the day of the Lord wouldn't occur until other events took place first (2 Thess. 2:3–5).

---

is still future. Rick Joyner, "Response to *Charisma's* Article," MorningStar Ministries, May 8, 2007; accessed February 4, 2014, http://www.morningstarministries. org/about/questions-and-answers/response-charismas-article-rick-joyner#.UvG-MJbSmR8o.

Elsewhere, Paul urged his protégé Timothy to take the teachings he had learned from Paul—the apostolic teachings—and "entrust [them] to faithful men who will be able to teach others also" (2 Tim. 2:2). Note that Paul didn't tell Timothy to expect and rely on new truths from prophets. He instructed Timothy to recall truths already revealed through the apostles of Christ.

NAR leaders profess agreement with the orthodoxy test. They claim prophets' teachings must line up with Scripture. But our assessment has shown that many of their teachings do not line up.

Furthermore, many NAR leaders continue to esteem Latter Rain prophets who have promoted aberrant and even heretical teachings, including William Branham (1905–1965). The prophet Branham taught that Eve had sexual relations with the serpent (the so-called serpent seed doctrine) and that those who are descended from the serpent seed are destined for a non-eternal hell, while those who receive Branham's teachings are predestined to become the "bride of Christ." He also denied the doctrine of the Trinity.[11] These particular teachings of Branham are overlooked since he was known to have an unparalleled ministry of miracles. It's unwise to discount Branham's teachings while extolling his amazing miracles. Jesus warned about false prophets who will arise and perform miraculous signs and wonders (Matt. 24:24). If an individual can promote such strange and even heretical teachings and still be considered a true prophet within NAR, it seems that the orthodoxy test is not being applied consistently.

THE LIFESTYLE TEST

A third test Scripture gives for prophets is the lifestyle test. Jesus said that false prophets could be known by their bad fruit—that is, by their lawless conduct:

You will recognize them by their fruits. Are grapes gathered from thornbushes, or figs from thistles? So, every healthy tree bears good fruit, but the diseased tree bears bad fruit. A healthy tree cannot bear bad fruit, nor can a diseased tree bear good fruit. Every tree that does not bear good fruit is cut down and thrown into the fire. Thus you will recognize them by their fruits.

---

[11] D. J. Wilson, "William Marrion Branham," in *The New International Dictionary of Pentecostal and Charismatic Movements*, ed. Stanley M. Burgess (Grand Rapids: Zondervan, 2002), 440–41.

> *Not everyone who says to me, "Lord, Lord," will enter the kingdom of heaven, but the one who does the will of my Father who is in heave. On that day many will say to me, "Lord, Lord, did we not prophesy in your name, and cast out demons in your name, and do many mighty works in your name?" And then will I declare to them, "I never knew you; depart from me, you workers of lawlessness." (Matt 7:16–23)*

What would their lawless conduct include? Sexual immorality and idolatry are specifically associated with the false prophetess Jezebel at the church in Thyatira. Paul describes the false prophet Bar-Jesus as being a "son of the devil," an "enemy of all righteousness," and "full of all deceit and villainy" (Acts 13:10). Old Testament false prophets were characterized by greed (Mic. 3:5, 11; 2 Peter 2:15) and drunkenness (Isa. 28:7–8).

The lifestyle test is the most reliable test for prophets, according to Hamon.[12] He believes that, when evaluating a prophet, it's more important to look to the "quality of his life"—including his marriage, manners, and morality—than to the accuracy of his prophecies. Hamon acknowledges that no prophet's life is perfect, but Christians should take note when any major area of a prophet's life is "seriously out of order."[13]

Hamon is right that lifestyle is a test for prophets. But this test alone is not enough. Outwardly, false prophets can sometimes look very good, disguising themselves, as Jesus said, "in sheep's clothing, but inwardly [they] are ravenous wolves" (Matt 7:15).

Several NAR prophets whose significant moral failures have been publicly documented continue to be viewed as genuine prophets by many of their peers. In 1991, Bob Jones confessed to sexual misconduct and the abuse of his prophetic office. This misconduct reportedly "consisted of encouraging women to undress in his office so they could stand 'naked before the Lord' in order to receive a [prophetic] 'word.'"[14] Despite such a gross abuse of his

---

12   Hamon, *Prophets, Pitfalls and Principles*, 101.

13   Hamon, *Prophets and Personal Prophecy*, 125.

14   See "Jones, Bob," Apologetics Index, accessed February 22, 2014, http://www.apologeticsindex.org/j00.html#jones. A letter written by Vineyard founder John Wimber and sent to Vineyard pastors, dated November 7, 1991, states that Jones confessed to committing "serious sin," including "using his [prophetic] gifts to manipulate people for his personal desires" and "sexual misconduct." John Wimber, Letter to Vineyard Pastors, in the authors' possession. And a transcript of a taped

office, he remained influential as a prophet in NAR until his death in 2014. In a popular IHOP teaching series, Mike Bickle referred to him as one of his "two spiritual fathers through all these years."[15] Jones was so revered in NAR that his memorial service was attended by prominent NAR leaders and broadcast live, worldwide, by GOD TV.[16]

Paul Cain, Bickle's other "spiritual father," confessed in 2005 to being an alcoholic and a long-term practicing homosexual. Cain resumed public ministry in 2007.[17] To the credit of some prominent NAR leaders—Bickle, Jack Deere, and Rick Joyner—the validity of the restoration process was questioned.[18] Cain has since gone on to share a speaking platform with oth-

---

message given by Mike Bickle following Jones's confession states that Jones "used his ministry gift and position to win the confidence of two women and then he did things to them," which included "disrobing" and "fondling." Mike Bickle, "Bob Jones' Discipline," undated transcript of a recording on audiocassette, November 1991(?), in the authors' possession. Jones was removed from ministry in Vineyard churches after his confession of misconduct. Pam Sollner, "Minister Removed After Confession of Sexual Misconduct," *The Olathe Daily News*, November 13, 1991; posted on *Religion News Blog*, accessed February 4, 2014, http://www.religionnews-blog.com/16929/minister-removed-after-confession-of-sexual-misconduct.

[15]   Mike Bickle, "Encountering Jesus Disc 1," audio recording, 57:32, The Internet Archive, n.d., accessed September 2, 2014, https://archive.org/details/EncounteringJesus.

[16]   "Bob Jones Memorial Service," GOD TV, video, 88:07, February 21, 2014; accessed June 13, 2014, http://www.god.tv/bob-jones-ministries/video/bob-jones-memorial-service/bob-jones-memorial-service.

[17]   In October 2004, Paul Cain was publicly accused by his colleagues Rick Joyner, Jack Deere, and Mike Bickle of practicing homosexuality and being an alcoholic—allegations he first denied, but later confessed. See J. Lee Grady, "Prophetic Minister Paul Cain Issues Public Apology for Immoral Lifestyle," *Charisma*, February 28, 2005; accessed February 4, 2014, http://www.charismamag.com/site-archives/154-peopleevents/people-and-events/1514-prophetic-minister-paul-cain-issues-public-apology-for-immoral-lifestyle-.

[18]   Mike Bickle, Jack Deere, and Rick Joyner, "Update on Paul Cain, Part 5," MorningStar Ministries, 2007; accessed February 19, 2014, http://www.morningstarministries.org/resources/special-bulletins/2007/update-paul-cain-part-5#.UwRurYV6V8o.

er NAR leaders, including Bill Hamon.[19] This raises a couple of important questions: What type of behavior, in Hamon's mind, actually characterizes a life that is "seriously out of order"? And what are the consequences when an alleged prophet fails this test?

The lifestyle standard can be highly subjective. Hamon seems to have set aside the more objective fulfillment test. Scripture places an emphasis on the combination of these tests. If NAR leaders are going to claim that NAR prophets are genuine, they cannot simply ignore these biblical tests. The tests must be applied consistently and with due diligence since Scripture clearly teaches that false prophets pose a serious threat to the church.

Two Other Proposed Tests

The Miraculous Signs Test

Many people think that another test for prophets is the "miraculous signs test." On a popular level, many believe that if someone performs a miraculous sign, then he or she is a prophet. This is not necessarily the case.

It's true that biblical prophets sometimes performed miraculous signs to authenticate their messages (1 Kings 17:24; Isa. 38:7–8). But, unlike apostles on a par with the apostle Paul, who apparently were expected to perform miraculous signs (2 Cor. 12:12), Scripture nowhere states that all prophets had to do so. In fact, it specifically records that John the Baptist performed no miraculous signs (John 10:41). Meanwhile, some false prophets did perform apparently miraculous signs, such as Pharaoh's magicians (Exod. 7:8–8:7). So, the ability to perform such signs is neither a necessary nor a sufficient test for a prophet.

On the other hand, when a so-called prophet claims to perform a miraculous sign, the sign should be awe-inspiring. Pharaoh's magicians could replicate some of Moses' signs, but not the most impressive ones (Exod. 8:8–12:32). In light of this, one may observe that many of the so-called signs and wonders that are reported by NAR prophets and apostles are less than impressive, and often involve unverifiable claims to have witnessed the materialization of substances such as fragrant anointing oil, gold

---

[19]   Hamon and Cain were featured speakers at a conference called "Global Call School of the Prophets," held April 13–16, 2011, in Corona, California.

dust, and gemstones.[20] The bar seems pretty low for what is viewed as a miraculous sign by some leaders in NAR.

The Ancestry Test

Some people have proposed the ancestry test for prophets. We believe this test deserves careful consideration.

To date, all universally authoritative prophets—each link in the great chain of prophets—have been from Israel. Is that merely coincidental? This seems unlikely, especially considering Moses' prophecy that God would raise up a series of prophets from among their "countrymen."

The biblical prophecies concern the House of Israel, the remnant of the righteous, who are, in one way or another, to be instruments used by God to bring salvation to the nations. The apostle Paul referred to the ways God has worked through this specific line of people. "They are Israelites, and to them belong the adoption, the glory, the covenants, the giving of the law, the worship, *and the promises.* To them belong the patriarchs, and from their race, according to the flesh, is the Christ, who is God over all, blessed forever. Amen" (Rom. 9:4–5, our emphasis)." God's saving acts in history came through the Israelites. Paul specifically mentioned the promises they had received from God—promises that were revealed by the prophets. In other words, it was through Israel's prophets that canonical revelation had come to the world.[21]

We don't claim that the ancestry test is definitive. But it may at least encourage caution when someone today, who is not of Jewish ancestry, claims to give universally authoritative revelation.

---

[20]   Patricia King, "Heavenly Oil and Gemstones in Puerto Rico!," YouTube video, 10:19, posted by "Ftureman," January 11, 2012; accessed February 6, 2014, http://www.youtube.com/watch?v=tpqBYpo9WkA. In this video, Patricia King, a well-known NAR prophet, reports on signs and wonders that she believes confirm a prophetic vision God gave to Dennis Rojas, the pastor of a church in Puerto Rico.

[21]   We note that the apostles of Christ—those responsible for the New Testament canon—were also all Israelites. We believe this strengthens the case for the ancestry test since we would include them in the "great chain of prophets" (See Appendix A).

NAR LEADERS' UNBIBLICAL TESTS FOR PROPHETS

NAR leaders propose tests of their own that are not taught in Scripture. Here are two.

The Inner Witness Test

Hamon proposes what we call the inner witness test: "The inner witness of the Spirit with our spirit is one way of determining that a prophetic utterance is of the Lord."[22] Hamon says an inner witness may include physical sensations that occur in the "upper stomach or lower chest area" and let us know that a prophecy is true or false.[23] Here is his description of the sensations that indicate that a prophecy is false: "A negative spirit-witness, with a message of either 'No,' 'Be careful,' or 'Something's not right,' usually manifests itself with a nervous, jumpy, or uneasy feeling, a deep, almost unintelligible sensation that something is not right."[24] And here is his description of sensations that indicate that a prophecy is true: "There is a deep, unexplainable peace and joy, a warm, loving feeling, or even a sense of our spirit jumping up and down with excitement."[25]

In response, we point out that Scripture never says to test prophecies by an inner witness. The claim that prophecies can be tested by physical sensations that occur in the lower chest area is remarkably similar to the Mormon claim that God confirms the truth of the Mormon faith by giving people a burning sensation in their bosoms. In both examples, revelation is confirmed apart from any rational thought processes.

In fact, rational thought can interfere with the inner witness test, according to Hamon: "This sensation [the negative sensation that identifies false prophecies] can only be trusted when we are more in tune with our spirit than with our thoughts. If our thinking is causing these sensations, then it could be a soulish reaction rather than the spirit bearing a negative witness."[26] He also says: "Our reasoning is in the mind, not the spirit. So our traditions, beliefs, and strong opinions are not true witnesses to prophetic truth. In fact, these parts of us often bring doubt, confusion, resentment, rejection, and

---

22   Hamon, *Prophets, Pitfalls and Principles*, 119.

23   Hamon, *Prophets and Personal Prophecy*, 137–38.

24   Ibid., 138.

25   Ibid.

26   Ibid.

rebellion against true personal prophecy. Our head may say, 'No' while our heart says, 'Go.' Our soul may say, 'I don't understand,' while our spirit says, 'It's fine; don't lean to your own understanding.'"[27] By encouraging people to turn off their thoughts and to ignore their opinions, Hamon is repudiating their God-given ability to evaluate prophecies critically.

Hamon acknowledges that the inner witness test is subjective. "For that reason," he says, "we should not discard a word as inaccurate or incorrect simply because we do not 'witness' to it."[28] Of course, following the logic of Hamon's position, the inner witness test works only for true prophecies. Thus, it is useless for identifying false prophecies. It's troubling that Hamon would even suggest such a frankly subjective and oddly spiritualistic test. Why should anyone ever trust a "yes" answer?

The Spiritual Overseers Test

Hamon also proposes the spiritual overseers test. According to Hamon, prophecies should be submitted to spiritual overseers to determine whether the prophecies are true. He says, "We must be under the covering authority of spiritual eldership that can speak into our lives with authority and offer wise counsel about the prophecies we receive. Our pastor and other leaders can help us determine whether a prophecy is scriptural, accurate, and timely."[29]

But all this so-called test does is move back a step the process of testing prophecies. Spiritual leaders still have to apply the same tests we noted above. Plus, this test promotes irresponsibility. It encourages people to put blind faith in their leaders rather than learn to test prophecies for themselves.

Summary

The Bible identifies three key tests for determining whether a prophet is genuine or not. But the consistent application of these tests by many NAR leaders is sketchy at best, and the tests they themselves propose are subjective and irresponsible.

In the next chapter we explain new spiritual warfare strategies that are taught by NAR apostles and prophets.

---

27   Ibid., 137.

28   Hamon, *Prophets, Pitfalls and Principles*, 120.

29   Ibid., 119.

15

Strategic-Level Spiritual Warfare

> New recruits are now being drafted and trained and older sol-
> diers and generals are being updated on God's new revelations of
> our warfare weapons and prophetic-apostolic strategies.
>
> —Bill Hamon, *Apostles, Prophets, and the Coming Moves of
> God: God's End-Time Plans for His Church and Planet Earth*

A major difference between NAR leaders and other Christians is their view
on how to advance God's kingdom. According to NAR leaders, the way to
do this is not just through the historical means of evangelism and world
missions. Rather it's through the implementation of divine strategies that
have been revealed by NAR apostles and prophets for this purpose, and to
the authority of which the church is required to yield. This view is known as
dominionism or the Kingdom Now view.

NAR leaders are not the only ones who seek to advance God's kingdom,
of course. So do most other Christians, even though these other Christians
often differ from one other in how they understand the kingdom of God,
including its nature and the timing of its arrival. For example, many evangelical Christians living in the United States hold to a view known as premillennialism,[1] which understands God's kingdom to be a literal, physical
kingdom on earth ruled by Christ, but which will not be established until
after Christ's Second Coming.[2]

---

[1] "Premillennialism Reigns in Evangelical Theology: Evangelical Leaders
Survey," National Association of Evangelicals, March 7, 2011; accessed November
29, 2013, http://www.nae.net/resources/news/539-premillennialism-reigns-in-
evangelical-theology.

[2] Many premillennialists understand Christ to have inaugurated (especially
spiritual) elements of his reign at his ascension, but that his reign won't be fully and
physically present on earth until his return.

Many Protestant denominations—such as Lutherans, Anglicans, Presbyterians, and Methodists—as well as Roman Catholic and Greek Orthodox Christians generally hold to a view known as amillennialism. This view believes that Christ has been reigning in heaven spiritually through the entire church age. Unlike premillennialists, amillennialists do not look for the establishment of a literal, physical kingdom on the present earth. They look instead to the creation of a new heaven and a new earth.

Still other Christians—including Christian Reconstructionists and many American Protestants in the nineteenth century—hold to postmillennialism and believe that God's kingdom is a literal, physical kingdom and that the church will succeed in establishing this kingdom on earth prior to Christ's return. Postmillennialists believe this feat will be accomplished by Christianizing the nations of the world and converting the majority of people to belief in Christ.

Of these various views, NAR leaders—who believe in a literal, physical kingdom of God on the present earth—fall into either the premillennial or postmillennial camp. But whether NAR leaders identify as premillennial (such as Harold Eberle) or as postmillennial (such as Eberle's colleague and co-author Martin Trench)[3] many share a key NAR belief—that the way to advance God's earthly kingdom, to whatever extent that is possible prior to Christ's return, is through the employment of strategies revealed by NAR apostles and prophets.

This chapter explains some of the key strategies NAR apostles and prophets have revealed to advance God's physical kingdom, many of which are related to an overarching strategy they call "strategic-level spiritual warfare." We will also detail a few aspects of this movement's conception of the kingdom of God.

AN OVERVIEW OF STRATEGIC-LEVEL SPIRITUAL WARFARE

Strategic-level spiritual warfare is the act of confronting powerful evil spirits that are believed to rule specific geographical regions, cultural groups, and societal institutions. These spirits are called "territorial spirits" because they control different territories or cultural spheres.

---

[3]   Harold Eberle and Martin Trench, *Victorious Eschatology: A Partial Preterist View* (Yakima, WA: Worldcast Publishing, 2006), 221, 224.

This strategy is based on the belief that the people living in these regions or coming under the influence of these societal institutions are kept in bondage by these territorial spirits. NAR leaders find support for this belief in the book of Daniel, which reveals that a specific evil spirit, called the prince of Persia, exercised rule over the kingdom of Persia and that another evil spirit, the prince of Greece, exercised rule over the kingdom of Greece (Dan. 10:13, 20).

As long as the territorial spirits are in control, no major advances can be made in sharing the gospel or transforming society, according to NAR leaders. So the spirits must be neutralized or cast out. Then, entire nations of people will respond *en masse* to the gospel, and the church will reap the greatest harvest of souls in history. A common metaphor used by NAR leaders to describe this strategic-level warfare is that of an air war on high-ranking demons that must pave the way for the ground troops of evangelists and missionaries.

Teachings about strategic-level spiritual warfare began to emerge in the late 1980s.[4] They differ from more typical teachings about spiritual warfare. Traditionally, Christians have focused on resisting temptation, obeying the commands of Scripture, and, occasionally, casting out demons from individuals or relieving Christians of demonic oppression. But Peter Wagner, who has developed much of the teachings about strategic-level spiritual warfare, finds support for the direct confrontation of high-ranking demons in Ephesians 3:10: "so that through the church the manifold wisdom of God might now be made known to the rulers and authorities in the heavenly places." Of this verse Wagner writes: "Certain antiwar advocates would have us believe that, while we may command demons to leave individuals, we must not address higher-ranking spiritual beings. However, this Scripture specifically tells us that the Church—those of us who are believers—is expected to declare God's wisdom to principalities and powers."[5]

---

[4] For more about the history of strategic-level spiritual warfare from a pro-NAR perspective, see C. Peter Wagner, *Wrestling with Alligators, Prophets, and Theologians: Lessons from a Lifetime in the Church—A Memoir* (Ventura, CA: Regal Books, 2010), 158–99. A summary of the history can also be found in Wagner, *Dominion! How Kingdom Action Can Change the World* (Grand Rapids: Chosen Books, 2008), 120–122.

[5] C. Peter Wagner, *Changing Church* (Ventura, CA: Regal Books, 2004), 117.

NAR leaders say that territorial spirits cannot be ignored. And because they are so powerful, they can't be cast out by ordinary Christians. This is where apostles come in. NAR leaders teach that the apostle alone has the authority to cast out territorial spirits.[6] Apostle Héctor Torres calls the apostle "an arch rival to the forces in the heavenlies."[7] Torres writes: "Although every believer has rank to cast out devils [from individuals], apostles walk and minister in the highest rank. Evil spirits and angels recognize this rank."[8]

How do apostles cast out territorial spirits? Together with prophets, they have received from God a number of strategies for doing so. We will examine some of these strategies now.

SPIRITUAL MAPPING

Spiritual mapping is the practice of researching a specific city or nation to discover the ways territorial spirits hinder the spread of the gospel in that particular geographical region.[9] For example, John Dawson of Youth With a Mission (YWAM) believes that a "spirit of greed" was "let loose during the California Gold Rush and still dominates the culture of Los Angeles and San Francisco to this day."[10] In many cases, spiritual mapping projects seek to determine not only the nature of a territorial spirit's activity—such as the promotion of greed—but also the exact name of the territorial spirit. This is because many NAR leaders, like Wagner, believe that knowing the proper name, or functional name, of a demon gives Christians more power over that demon.[11] To help learn more about the territorial spirits ruling over

---

[6] David Cannistraci, *Apostles and the Emerging Apostolic Movement: A Biblical Look at Apostleship and How God is Using it to Bless His Church Today* (Ventura, CA: Renew Books, 1996), 169.

[7] Héctor Torres, *Restoration of the Apostles and Prophets: How It Will Revolutionize Ministry in the 21st Century* (Nashville: Thomas Nelson, 2001), 143.

[8] Ibid.

[9] The term *spiritual mapping* was coined by George Otis Jr.

[10] John Dawson, *Taking Our Cities for God* (Lake Mary, FL: Charisma House, 1989), 53–54.

[11] C. Peter Wagner, *What the Bible Says about Spiritual Warfare* (Ventura, CA: Regal Books, 2001), 63–64. Dawson, unlike Wagner, does not believe it is necessary to know the exact name of a demon. He is more concerned to know a demon's

a specific city, spiritual mapping projects seek answers to questions about the city's history: Why was the city originally settled? What were the religious practices of the early inhabitants? What religious institutions have dominated in the city?[12]

Spiritual mapping also involves surveying the present city. This includes identifying sites of occult activity (such as New Age bookstores), idolatry (such as buildings used for worship by non-Christian religions), or immorality (such as strip clubs). If many sites of a particular kind are discovered—for example, sites associated with witchcraft—then it might be decided that a territorial spirit associated with witchcraft controls a city. Oftentimes this is the site of some non-Christian place of worship, such as a pagan temple, Masonic Lodge, or an Islamic mosque. Or it may be the highest mountain in the region.

When a territorial spirit is identified by name, it's often confronted. The confrontation may take place at a site believed to be the physical seat of the spirit's rule. For example, Wagner's Spiritual Warfare Network determined that the entire 10/40 Window—the region of the world situated between the latitudes of 10 degrees and 40 degrees north, encompassing North Africa, the Middle East, and sections of Asia to Japan—was under the control of a demon named the Queen of Heaven. They also determined that this demon exerted its rule from the top of Mount Everest in the Himalayas. So, in September 1997, the network dispatched a team of people who had taken special training in Alpine climbing to scale the 29,000-foot mountain. They called the expedition "Operation Ice Castle." At 20,000 feet, the team directly assaulted the evil spirit, according to Wagner.[13]

Wagner doesn't provide details of the confrontation in his memoir, but he says it included a series of "prophetic acts"[14]—symbolic actions performed at the direction of God that are intended to release God's power. More details, however, are provided by two chroniclers of Himalayan expedition climbing, Richard Salisbury and Elizabeth Hawley. These two researchers have no known connection with NAR, but they've compiled a record of all

---

nature or type of activity. See Clinton E. Arnold, *3 Crucial Questions about Spiritual Warfare*, 3 Crucial Questions series (Grand Rapids: Baker, 1997), 147.

[12] These are some of the questions listed by John Dawson in *Taking Our Cities for God*, 58–59.

[13] Wagner, *Wrestling with Alligators, Prophets, and Theologians*, 238–39.

[14] Ibid., 238.

expeditions that have climbed the Nepalese Himalaya. They were amused by the antics of Wagner's team so they included an account of this particular expedition in their book. They reveal that the "prophetic acts" conducted by Wagner's team included using an ice ax to write the words "Jesus lives" on the mountain and making an ice altar, where they prayed. The team also reportedly found a large hole in the ice, which they declared to be the gateway to hell, and prayed that God would close it.[15]

Spiritual mapping was introduced to many Christians on a popular level in 1989 by John Dawson of YWAM through his bestselling book *Taking Our Cities for God*. It's no surprise that spiritual mapping has been practiced by the organization's missionary teams.[16] Spiritual mapping, at least in its earlier years, was a major activity of the World Prayer Center in Colorado Springs, Colorado. The center was co-founded by Peter Wagner and Ted Haggard in 1998 on the campus of New Life Church. A unit of the center, called the Observatory, was specially devoted to the practice of spiritual mapping.[17]

One of the most extensive spiritual mapping efforts was undertaken by the United States Reformation Prayer Network, led by Cindy Jacobs. The network appointed coordinators to oversee spiritual mapping projects in each of the fifty US states. The information gleaned from the projects was compiled into prayer guides to be used by people taking part in a national prayer strategy called Root 52.

For the entire year of 2010, participants used the guides to confront territorial spirits ruling in each state and issue "prayer proclamations," which, according to Jacobs, is "a form of intercession where God's will is decreed over a given situation and anything contrary is brought into alignment."[18]

---

[15]   Richard Salisbury, and Elizabeth Hawley, *The Himalaya by the Numbers: A Statistical Analysis of Mountaineering in the Nepal Himalaya* (Seattle, WA: Mountaineers Books, 2012).

[16]   In his dissertation, René Holvast describes the major role played by Youth With a Mission in the birth and dissemination of spiritual mapping practices. See Holvast, "Spiritual Mapping: The Turbulent Career of a Contested American Missionary Paradigm, 1989–2005," PhD Dissertation, Utrecht University, 2008, PDF e-book, http://dspace.library.uu.nl/handle/1874/29340, 27–28.

[17]   Wagner, *Wrestling With Alligators, Prophets, and Theologians*, 241.

[18]   Cindy Jacobs, *The Power of Persistent Prayer: Praying with Greater Purpose and Passion* (Minneapolis: Bethany House, 2010), 143.

For example, teams in California visited a number of high-profile locations throughout the state. On August 6, a team climbed to the top of the Hollywood Hills, overlooking the famous Hollywood sign. Led by apostle John Benefiel, they recited the words of a "divorce decree" between the region and a territorial spirit known as "Baal." They also prayed to "uproot the perversion associated with the symbol of Hollywood." Team members reported that, following their prayer, they "felt a swift breeze" in their midst, signaling that "God's spirit was cleansing away the perversion."[19]

The territorial spirit that was determined to rule over the entire United States was the pagan goddess Columbia. Clues that helped reveal her identity are the name of the US capitol—District of Columbia—and the statue of Columbia atop the Capitol building. In the fall of 2011, Jacobs' Reformation Prayer Network teamed with the Heartland Apostolic Prayer Network, led by Benefiel, for a forty-day NAR campaign called DC40 to wage strategic-level spiritual warfare against the spirit Columbia.[20] Prophetic acts included Benefiel's renaming the District of Columbia the District of Christ.

PRAYERWALKING

Prayerwalking is the practice of sending teams to pray at the physical locations of regions where they desire to see spiritual and social transformation. These teams walk the neighborhoods, cities, or university campuses and engage in what they call warfare prayer, commanding territorial spirits to leave.[21] NAR leaders claim they have biblical precedent for prayerwalking in the Israelites' march around the walls of Jericho (Josh. 6).

A popular definition of prayerwalking is "praying on site with insight." The first part of the definition—praying on site—often refers to the teaching

---

[19] "California Root 52 Report," Generals International, August 13–20, 2010; accessed May 6, 2014, http://www.generals.org/prayer/root-52/prayer-reports/california-report/.

[20] Cara Shulz, "Christian Group Directs 'Spiritual Warfare' Against Pagan Goddess," Pagan Newswire Collective-Minnesota Bureau, July 25, 2011; accessed December 27, 2012, http://pncminnesota.com/2011/07/25/christian-group-directs-spiritual-warfare-against-pagan-goddess.

[21] Wagner has written an entire book on this practice titled *Warfare Prayer: What the Bible Says about Spiritual Warfare* (Shippensburg, PA: Destiny Image Publishers, 2009).

that prayers delivered at the physical location of a territorial spirit's rule are more effective than prayers said from another location. Wagner says, "It is true that prayer knows no boundaries, but it is also true that on-site prayer has proven more effective in dislodging principalities and powers of darkness than distance prayers."[22] The second part of this definition—praying with insight—refers to the fact that prayerwalking often uses knowledge about the identity of territorial spirits gained through spiritual mapping or revealed directly by God to prophets.

A prayerwalk may not be limited to one's local community. Long-distance prayerwalks, requiring travel to distant places, are often called prayer journeys and prayer expeditions. Examples of prayer journeys are the 250 prayer teams sent out by Peter Wagner during AD2000 and Beyond—a massive, international missionary movement directed by Luis Bush that sought to reach the entire world with the gospel of Christ by the year 2000.[23] These prayer teams traveled to the countries of the 10/40 Window.[24]

On June 2, 2014, the United States Reformation Prayer Network announced plans to coordinate a continent-wide prayerwalk.[25] Called the USA Prayer Walking Initiative, it would span the Americas "from the tundra of Canada and Alaska to the tip of Argentina and Chile." The organization called for small teams of three to six Christian volunteers to undertake portions of the prayerwalk between the dates of June 15 and July 31, 2014, going to designated locations, including city hall buildings, college campuses, and "sites of false worship."

Prayerwalking has also become a popular practice among evangelical churches that aren't aware of the NAR teachings that often lie behind the practice.

---

[22] C. Peter Wagner, *Dominion! How Kingdom Action Can Change the World* (Grand Rapids: Chosen Books, 2008), 132.

[23] Wagner led the United Prayer Track of the AD 2000 Movement.

[24] "AD2000 United Prayer Track Launches Praying Through the Window II: 'The 100 Gateway Cities,'" *Mission Frontiers*, March 1, 1995; accessed August 11, 2011, http://www.missionfrontiers.org/issue/article/ad2000-united-prayer-track-launches-praying-through-the-window-ii-the-100-g.

[25] "Stand for Right: An RPN Update," e-mail from United States Reformation Prayer Network to USRPN mailing list, June 2, 2014. http://us2.campaign-archive1.com/?u=2c8533b164a12dac690d3544f&id=0bb9d077bf&e=02548e3d54.

IDENTIFICATIONAL REPENTANCE

Identificational repentance is the practice of demonstrating corporate repentance for corporate sins. The purpose of this practice is to close the "entry points" territorial spirits have used to gain control of geographical areas.[26]

NAR leaders believe that land can become polluted by sins committed on its soil, such as the atrocities committed by Americans of European descent against Native Americans. The polluted land gives demons access to that land, so it must be cleansed before territorial spirits can be cast out.

One way to "heal the land" is to repent of sins committed by one's ancestors—sins often uncovered through the process of spiritual mapping. For example, US citizens should identify with and take responsibility for the injustices committed by their forebears against Native Americans. In support of this practice, NAR leaders often point to Nehemiah and Daniel, two biblical leaders who repented on behalf of their national people, the Israelites (Neh. 1:4–11; Dan. 9:1–19). A key Scripture verse used to support the practice of identificational repentance is 2 Chronicles 7:14: "If my people who are called by my name humble themselves, and pray and seek my face and turn from their wicked ways, then I will hear from heaven and will forgive their sin and heal their land."

This NAR practice involves solemn assemblies of repentance and reconciliation, where Christian representatives of both the offending and offended parties are present. It is important that the representatives be Christians "because only they have the spiritual authority to apply the blood of Jesus" to national sins, says Wagner.[27] It's also important that the repentance be followed up with acts of restitution for the wrongs done, restitution usually accomplished through judicial decisions and legislative acts.[28] For example, during The Call Nashville in 2007—a NAR event reportedly attended by more than 70,000 people—then-Senator Sam Brownback of Kansas apologized to Native Americans on behalf of the people of the United States. Receiving the apology on behalf of Native Americans was ICAL apostle Jay Swallow, a Cheyenne Indian and co-founder of the Two Rivers Native

---

[26] Wagner, *Dominion!*, 130.

[27] C. Peter Wagner, "The Power to Heal the Past," *Renewal Journal*, July 28, 2011; accessed February 24, 2014, http://renewaljournal.wordpress.com/2011/07/18/the-power-to-heal-the-past-by-c-peter-wagner.

[28] Ibid.

American Training Center in Bixby, Oklahoma.[29] Brownback went further, following up the ceremony with a legislative act. He worked with the prophet Lou Engle to craft a resolution in the US Congress apologizing to Native Americans. The Native American Apology Resolution was signed on December 19, 2009, by President Barack Obama. NAR leaders saw the resolution—a formal apology on behalf of the United States government—as a big step toward healing America's land and the transformation of the nation.

WORKPLACE APOSTLES

Workplace apostles are apostles God has given specifically to govern the "church in the workplace," according to Wagner.[30] They govern Christians working in the various sectors of society, such as business, media, and government. They differ from other apostles who govern local churches and parachurch organizations.[31]

Despite all the strategic-level spiritual warfare conducted in the past couple of decades—including spiritual mapping projects, prayerwalks, and identificational repentance ceremonies—the church has not seen social transformation in most cities and nations. Something has been missing, according to NAR leaders. They've determined that the missing piece is workplace apostles, also called marketplace apostles. One of the newest strategies for advancing God's kingdom is that of "activating" workplace apostles.

What are these apostles like? In Scripture, two supposed workplace apostles were Luke, a physician, and Lydia, a "seller of purple" (an "international

---

[29]   See the ceremony on a YouTube video titled, "The Call Nashville Senator Brownback," 7:58, posted July 18, 2007 by XSTATICMOM; accessed February 24, 2014, http://www.youtube.com/watch?v=isOKfyriSfA.

[30]   C. Peter Wagner, *Church in the Workplace: How God's People Can Transform Society* (Ventura, CA: Regal Books, 2006), 16–17.

[31]   Wagner teaches that the church can be found in two major forms: the traditional "nuclear church" that typically meets in church buildings or in homes on Sundays and the "extended church" in the workplace—that is, the body of Christians who work in the various sectors of society throughout the rest of the week. See, Wagner, *Dominion!*, 141. He believes that the church in the workplace—just like the nuclear church—must be governed by apostles and prophets.

businesswoman").[32] Today's workplace apostles are Christian mayors, CEOs, filmmakers, journalists, lawmakers, and politicians—movers and shakers in society who are using their influence to transform their cities and nations. An apostle-filmmaker could make movies that promote God's kingdom values rather than movies that promote depravity. Or an apostle-Supreme Court justice could reverse *Roe v. Wade*.

When it comes to transforming society, workplace apostles will play a greater role than local church apostles. They "have considerably more influence among the movers and shakers of the city" than do local church pastors, and they have "insider access to the principal molders of culture, such as government, business, education, media and arts."[33] Also, "they control significant wealth." Wagner said, "I am convinced that without access to wealth, we will see very little social transformation over the years."[34]

Workplace apostles' access to wealth will lead to the fulfillment of a popular NAR prophecy known as the Great End-Time Transfer of Wealth. Since at least the early 1990s, NAR prophets have predicted that God will soon transfer control of the world's wealth from the wicked people of the world to the righteous. The purpose of the wealth transfer is to provide the church with the financial resources it will need to advance God's kingdom. Preparing workplace apostles for their role in the transfer of wealth and creating "kingdom financial models and infrastructure" to undergird the transfer are purposes of an annual conference called the Kingdom Economic Yearly Summit (KEYS).[35] The conference is billed as the church's counterpart to the World Economic Forum.[36]

While a growing number of Christians recognize the authority of apostles over local churches and parachurch organizations, most have yet to recognize the authority of apostles in the workplace. In fact, until recent years, workplace apostles have been overlooked even by NAR leaders, according to Wagner. That's because their focus had been on apostles who govern local

---

[32]   Wagner, *Church in the Workplace*, 26–27.

[33]   C. Peter Wagner, *Apostles Today: Biblical Government for Biblical Power* (Ventura, CA: Regal Books, 2006), 135.

[34]   Ibid.

[35]   "Purpose/Vision Statement for the Summit," Kingdom Economic Summit, accessed February 24, 2014, http://www.kingdomeconomicsummit.com.

[36]   Ibid.

churches. It never crossed their minds that apostles could also be found in secular arenas such as board rooms, film studios, and congressional offices.

Today, however, NAR leaders are seeking to "activate" workplace apostles by recognizing them, encouraging them, and even commissioning them as they have commissioned apostles in local churches.[37] Only when workplace apostles are in place can the church fulfill its mandate of advancing God's kingdom, NAR leaders say. Recognition of workplace apostles is crucial because they have the authority to cast out the territorial spirits that rule over societal institutions through the implementation of another strategy known as the Seven Mountain Mandate.

THE SEVEN MOUNTAIN MANDATE

Many NAR apostles and prophets claim that God has revealed a new strategy for advancing God's kingdom—a strategy they call the Seven Mountain Mandate.[38] According to this revelation, the way to take dominion is by taking control of the seven most influential societal institutions—called "mountains"—which are identified as government, media, family, business, education, church, and the arts. These institutions are presently dominated by secular humanists and other opinion leaders who do not share God's values. The church must take control of them if it's to fulfill its mandate to advance God's kingdom. The church's mandate to conquer these seven mountains is often compared to Israel's mandate to conquer seven nations before it could enter the Promised Land (Deut. 7:1).

In a book titled *The Seven Mountain Prophecy*, US prophet Johnny Enlow writes: "I've shared that the mountains were the infrastructural columns of our societies—that it's the Lord's plan to raise His people up to take every social, economic, and political structure of our nations."[39] Enlow identifies government as an important institution "because it can establish laws and

---

[37]   Wagner, *Dominion!*, 150. In 2006 The International Coalition of Apostolic Leaders was developing a process to recognize and commission workplace apostles. See Wagner, *Apostles Today*, 149.

[38]   This strategy is also sometimes referred to as the Seven Mountain Prophecy.

[39]   Johnny Enlow, *The Seven Mountain Prophecy: Unveiling the Coming Elijah Revolution* (Lake Mary, FL: Creation House, 2008), 43–44.

decrees that affect and control every other mountain."[40] He believes God is raising up apostles to "possess" this critical mountain.[41]

Though all NAR followers are taught to use their influence in their various places of work to transform society, workplace apostles must rise to the tops of societal institutions—to the highest positions. Only apostles have the God-given authority to cast out the territorial spirits that control those institutions. Enlow writes: "Before we can fully displace powers and principalities, apostles will have to be properly positioned on the tops of the mountains. Again, an apostle is someone who has been given authority to displace top-of-the-mountain demons and bring the reign of heaven in their place."[42]

Enlow has identified the names of territorial spirits that presently control the institutions. Apollyon, for example, controls the media. Jezebel controls the arts.[43] And because government is such a critical institution, it's controlled by none less than Lucifer.[44]

The Seven Mountain Mandate ties a number of NAR spiritual warfare strategies together. For example, to cast out the territorial spirits that rule over societal institutions, teams of individuals might conduct prayerwalks at locations associated with those institutions. To cast out the territorial spirit ruling over the media, Apollyon, Enlow suggests: "Substantial power could be released by going to the geographical stronghold of a spirit in media to pray or do prophetic acts. New York City is presently the stronghold site of Apollyon's influence. Atlanta is also important."[45]

Besides Enlow, the most visible proponents of the Seven Mountain Mandate include Peter Wagner, Lance Wallnau, and Os Hillman.

NAR leaders claim that the Seven Mountain Mandate didn't start with them. They say God has given the same revelation to other Christian leaders, starting with the founders of two well-known ministries: Loren Cunningham of YWAM and the late Bill Bright of Campus Crusade for Christ (now known as Cru). By connecting the Seven Mountain Mandate to these two

---

[40] Ibid., 62.

[41] Ibid., 67.

[42] Ibid., 66.

[43] Ibid., 52, 145.

[44] Ibid., 62.

[45] Ibid., 58.

well-known Christian leaders, they may be seeking to reinforce the credibility of their agenda.

How do NAR leaders attempt to connect Cunningham and Bright to the Seven Mountain Mandate? With Cunningham's own words. He recounts the story of how one day in August 1975 God gave him a list of seven categories of society and told him, "This is the way to reach America and nations for God."[46] The next day, Cunningham was scheduled to meet with Bill Bright. But before he could show Bright this divinely revealed list, Bright told Cunningham, "Loren, I want to show you what God has shown me!" He pulled out his own virtually identical list. In other words, according to Cunningham, God had given these two leaders the same list of societal institutions, at the same time and for the same purpose.

Since that day in 1975, YWAM has adopted Cunningham and Bright's seven-mountain revelation. According to Cunningham, it became the blueprint for YWAM's University of the Nations, a missionary training school that now has campuses in 101 nations. This university has seven colleges for each of the seven societal institutions.[47]

It may come as a surprise to many traditional evangelicals that YWAM—which has drawn thousands of Christian college-aged students to study at its university and to take part in its missionary campaigns—has adopted the Seven Mountain Mandate. But YWAM isn't the only well-known organization to do so. It also has partnered with more than two hundred organizations—including Campus Crusade for Christ, Wycliffe, and Evangelism Explosion— in a massive initiative named Call2All.

The 200 partnering organizations have pooled their resources to pursue what the Call2All website refers to as the "seven spheres of influence" as "a strategic framework for seeing nations discipled."[48] This means that in addition to traditional missionary efforts, such as evangelism and planting

---

[46]   Kelle Ortiz and Os Hillman, "Transcript of Interview of Loren Cunningham on Original 7 Mountains Vision," 7 Cultural Mountains, November 19, 2007; accessed August 11, 2011, http://www.reclaim7mountains.com/apps/articles/default. asp?articleid=40087&columnid=4347.

[47]   Ibid.

[48]   "Spheres," Call2All, accessed February 24, 2014, http://www.call2all.org/ Groups/1000090335/call2all/About/Spheres/Spheres.aspx#.UwvdoIV6V8o.

churches, Call2All is mobilizing the church to send missionaries into each of the seven institutions of unreached nations.

We must stress that many of these organizations have adopted what appears to be a much toned-down version of the Seven Mountain Mandate. The toned-down version teaches that Christians must exert influence in seven societal institutions if they are to complete the Great Commission. It does not teach, however, that workplace apostles must cast out territorial spirits that control these institutions.

Yet there is a real blurring of the lines when it comes to organizations that have embraced the Seven Mountain Mandate. That is to say, it is not always entirely clear which organizations embrace the toned-down version of the mandate and which have embraced the amped-up, NAR version. Nor is it entirely clear how fully this distinction is understood by moderate exponents and co-laborers. At one extreme end of the spectrum are NAR organizations, such as Generals International, led by Cindy Jacobs, which clearly embrace the muscular version. At the other end of the spectrum are those, like Campus Crusade for Christ, which appear to embrace a trimmed-down version. The exact stances of other organizations, like YWAM, are more muddled and can't always be clearly discerned.

Though not all the organizations participating in Call2All promote the radical NAR version of the mandate, the Call2All initiative has provided prominent platforms for those who do. For example, Call2All hosted an LA Global Congress, from November 29 to December 3, 2011, featuring Christian leaders in the seven institutions of society. Scheduled presenters included NAR prophets Cindy Jacobs, Lou Engle, and Mike Bickle, alongside more mainstream evangelicals, like Campus Crusade for Christ president Steve Douglass.[49]

---

[49]   Scott Tompkins, "California Event Mobilizes New Missions Partners," *Resonate News*, November 12, 2011; accessed June 6, 2014, http://www.resonate-news.com/home/newsheadlines/331; "Video: Steve Douglas [*sic*], Join the Movement," Call2All, May 1, 2011; accessed June 6, 2014 http://www.call2all.org/Articles/1000103667/call2all/About/E_zine_Archive/2011_Archive/0501_Video_Steve.aspx#.U5IpHSghXNt.

SUMMARY

NAR apostles and prophets claim to have revealed divine strategies for advancing God's kingdom. Many are related to an overarching strategy known as strategic-level spiritual warfare—the attempt to cast out high-ranking demonic spirits that are believed to rule over cities and nations. Less extreme forms of some of these strategies have even been adopted to some degree by various Evangelical organizations and ministries. We urge great caution and the use of biblical discernment for those involved with any of these strategies.

In the next chapter we examine, in light of Scripture, the various NAR strategies for advancing God's kingdom.

16

A Biblical Analysis of Strategic-Level Spiritual Warfare

> It appears, then, that we bear no responsibility for discerning, naming, or tearing down territorial strongholds.
>
> —Clinton E. Arnold, *3 Crucial Questions about Spiritual Warfare*

We now examine, in light of Scripture, some of the spiritual warfare strategies advocated by NAR leaders, which are related to an overarching strategy known as strategic-level spiritual warfare, which claims that powerful ruling demons, called territorial spirits, must be neutralized before a city, cultural group, or societal institution can be reached with the gospel. Scripture, however, provides no basis for such a claim.

Notice that we are not denying the existence of territorial spirits. In Daniel 10, we do see evidence that territorial spirits exist, both fallen angels and good angels who have been assigned to rule over specific nations. The "prince of Persia" and the "prince of Greece" mentioned in Daniel 10 are evil spirits shown exerting control over the kingdoms of Persia and Greece. And the archangel Michael is shown ruling over Israel (Dan. 10:13; see also 12:1). But these and like passages offer no evidence that Daniel engaged in strategic-level spiritual warfare against the evil territorial spirits or was even aware of the battle waging between them and Michael until an angel revealed it to him (Dan. 10:1–20). He was merely engaged in fasting to show his identification with the suffering Jewish exiles.

As for the New Testament, Ephesians 3:10, which Peter Wagner asserts calls Christians to address territorial spirits, in fact does no such thing. Rather, it states that God's wisdom is made known to angelic beings as they observe what God is doing through the church.

We see no indication that Christians have been given the authority or responsibility to engage territorial spirits directly.[1] Clinton Arnold points out, "We can have confidence that God will deal with these high-ranking spirits as He sees fit, just as He did for Daniel."[2]

In contrast to Wagner's teaching, Scripture indicates that rebuking such high-ranking spirits may actually be dangerous (Jude 8; 2 Peter 2:10–11). Even Wagner acknowledges that taking on territorial spirits involves risk and "can result in casualties if not done wisely, according to spiritual protocol and under the specific direction and assignment of the Holy Spirit."[3]

So, at a minimum, attempts to cast out territorial spirits are futile. At worst, those who confront territorial spirits directly may be opening themselves up foolishly to powerful demonic attack.

SPIRITUAL MAPPING

Since there is no biblical basis for confronting territorial spirits directly, there also is no basis for spiritual mapping projects that seek to aid such confrontations through the identification of territorial spirits.

One popular belief behind the practice of spiritual mapping is that knowing the name of a demon—either the proper name or a functional name—gives Christians more control over that demon. But Arnold points out that this belief, held by ancient occult practitioners, contradicts the teaching of Scripture. He writes:

> It seems to me that Paul wrote precisely against this kind of mind-set when he reaffirmed to the Ephesians that Christ had been raised "far above all rule and authority and power and dominion, *and every name that is named*" (Eph. 1:21 NASB). Why do we need to find the name of a territorial ruler if we are in union with a Lord who has been exalted high above every conceivable power, regardless of its name or title? (emphasis Arnold's)[4]

---

[1]   There has long been a part of the Christian church that believes that Christians have been authorized to cast out demons from individuals (Luke 10:17–19).

[2]   Clinton E. Arnold, *3 Crucial Questions about Spiritual Warfare*, 3 Crucial Questions series (Grand Rapids: Baker, 1997), 185.

[3]   C. Peter Wagner, *Dominion! How Kingdom Action Can Change the World* (Grand Rapids: Chosen Books, 2008), 127.

[4]   Arnold, *3 Crucial Questions about Spiritual Warfare*, 163.

Not all spiritual mapping projects include efforts to learn the names and jurisdictions of territorial spirits. Some simply create spiritual profiles of cities or nations to guide Christians to pray intelligently. These profiles may contain statistical information about people living in a region, including information about their religious beliefs. The popular prayer guide *Operation World* is such a profile. We affirm its value when used as intended.

We don't object to these types of profiles, if they're used as evangelistic aids rather than as tools of strategic-level spiritual warfare. Arnold believes this type of research—which provides knowledge for people to pray and minister with greater specificity—is helpful for the spread of the gospel.[5] We agree.

PRAYERWALKING

Prayerwalks, prayer journeys, and prayer expeditions are without scriptural warrant if they are attempts to confront territorial spirits. Also, the related practice of warfare prayer—commanding territorial spirits to leave—cannot be supported by Scripture. Prayer in the Bible is always directed to God; it never involves addressing evil spirits.

It's uncertain whether prayers said on site are more effective than prayers said from a remote location.[6] Our prayers should be directed toward God, and he is not bound to a physical location. We do, however, affirm that prayer is a weapon of spiritual warfare (Eph. 5:18-19). Arnold calls prayer "the heart and essence of spiritual warfare at any level."[7] It reflects our dependence on God to fight our battles for us. Thus, even though it is inappropriate for believers to confront territorial spirits themselves, as advocated by Wagner, it *is* appropriate to pray that God will hinder any demonic spirits that oppose the spread of the gospel in a region.[8]

The Israelites' march around Jericho cannot properly be used as an example of a NAR-type prayerwalk. The Israelites were not attempting to cast out a territorial spirit. They were demonstrating their faith in God to win a

---

5   Ibid., 176–77.

6   Some Christians believe exorcisms and prayers for healing seem to be more effective when said on site.

7   Arnold, *3 Crucial Questions about Spiritual Warfare*, 187.

8   Ibid., 188.

military victory for them. This was a one-time action, never again recounted in Scripture. It wasn't even the pattern for Israel's conquest of other cities in the land of Canaan at the time. Thus, it shouldn't be used to make prayer-walking into a normative and vital practice.

This is not to say that all prayerwalks are unbiblical. They may be biblical if they're viewed simply as opportunities to pray in a more focused, fervent manner for the needs of a community. These fervent prayers, to the degree that they reflect dependence on God, surely are more effective than half-hearted prayers said from a remote location. Perhaps it's better not to think of such practices as prayerwalks at all, because of the association with NAR doctrine, but rather as petitionary prayer for our nations and cities.

IDENTIFICATIONAL REPENTANCE

The NAR interpretation of a key Scripture verse used to support the NAR practice of identificational repentance—2 Chronicles 7:14—does not survive scrutiny. This verse cannot properly be used as a promise that if Christians confess their nation's sins, then God will heal that nation. Why not? Clinton Arnold gives two reasons.

First, this promise is addressed to the nation of Israel, with whom God has formed a special covenant relationship. Covenant promises given to Israel cannot be directly applied to America or to any other contemporary nation because God has only established a covenant relationship with one nation. [9]

Second, believers can't remove the penalty on corporate sin committed by unbelievers. Daniel and Nehemiah were able to confess the sins of their people because they were fellow members of God's covenant community. But Scripture offers no examples of believers confessing the sins of pagan nations. [10] Arnold asks:

> How can anyone confess the sins of other people and expect to accomplish anything in the spiritual realm? If a Christian leader today publicly confesses his or her city's sins of drug use and prostitution, what good does this do if those involved with these evils have not made a confession of faith in Christ—who alone can change their hearts and behavior? If the same

---

[9]   Ibid., 181–182.

[10]   Ibid., 180–81.

number of pimps and drug dealers are still walking the streets, no amount of vicarious confession will change anything. The demonic spirits will continue their insidious work in the lives of the people of the city because the welcome mat is still out on the porch, the light is on, and the door is wide open for them.[11]

At the same time, we affirm with Arnold the practice of corporate confession within the church, which represents the covenant people of God today.[12] For example, white Christian leaders may confess sins of racism that other white Christians have committed against black Christians. Daniel and Nehemiah provide biblical examples of this type of corporate confession. These godly leaders, acting as representatives for God's entire people, confessed the corporate sin of God's people. This biblical type of corporate confession may help remove feelings of bitterness and anger in the church and foster racial unity. But there's no reason to believe it results in the expulsion of territorial spirits.[13]

WORKPLACE APOSTLES

We've already shown that Scripture does not support NAR teachings about present-day apostles—including workplace apostles—who govern the church. We've also shown that Scripture doesn't support NAR teachings about casting out territorial spirits. Thus, there is no biblical support for NAR teachings that workplace apostles must govern the so-called church in the workplace and cast out territorial spirits that rule over societal institutions.

Furthermore, the idea that workplace apostles have God-given authority to govern the church in the workplace cannot be found in Scripture. The apostles of Christ had a church office with authority to govern *within* the church. Their office—and authority—did not extend beyond the church into the sphere of the state or society.

We applaud Christians who become experts in their fields and, with their influence, strive to influence society for the good. But Scripture does not support the notion of workplace apostles who claim an authority they don't have and promote spiritual warfare tactics that are not supported in

---

[11] Ibid.

[12] Ibid., 182–85.

[13] Ibid., 185.

Scripture. Some Christian leaders, who do not overtly identify with the New Apostolic Reformation, come perilously close to spreading this idea with their talk of "reclaiming the culture for Christ," "advancing the kingdom," or "fighting the culture war." We urge Christian leaders to offer a carefully crafted theology of culture, grounded in rigorous biblical exegesis. The lures of triumphalism and sensationalism are seductive, but they are unbecoming of the bride of Christ.

The Seven Mountain Mandate

We have already argued that there is no biblical support for the teaching that territorial spirits must be cast out of societal institutions before the gospel can go forth and produce fruit in a nation. Thus, there is no biblical basis for the NAR version of the Seven Mountain Mandate.

In their presentations of this mandate, NAR leaders often suggest that this strategy empowers all Christians, in whatever jobs or career fields they find themselves, to play significant roles in the transformation of society and the advancement of God's kingdom. This idea—that all Christians can impact the world for God, not just those in professional ministry—inspires many NAR followers. In truth, the Seven Mountain Mandate strategy is mostly empowering for NAR apostles, not for the average Christian. NAR leaders teach that only apostles can cast out the demons ruling over the major sectors of society, such as media and government.

The Seven Mountain Mandate strategy creates an elite class of workplace apostles. And it limits the most impactful ministry to those workplace apostles. If more NAR followers understood this, they might not embrace this NAR teaching with such enthusiasm.

Finally, we commend the methodology of sending out missionaries into the influential sectors of society, a strategy employed by organizations participating in the Call2All initiative. However, we urge these organizations to reconsider any alignment with NAR leaders and organizations whose understanding of the Seven Mountain Mandate might differ vastly from their own. And we urge those who support these ministries to hold them accountable.

In conclusion, we note that the NAR strategies of spiritual warfare we've discussed are without biblical precedent and, quite frankly, ineffective, if not also spiritually risky. They're also distracting Christians from the pursuit of biblical strategies that are effective.

SUMMARY

As we have noted, NAR apostles and prophets claim to reveal divine strategies the church needs for it to advance God's kingdom, many of which are part of an overarching strategy of strategic-level spiritual warfare. Contrary to NAR teachings on this subject, Scripture does not teach that high-ranking evil spirits must be neutralized before the gospel can go forth and God's kingdom can be advanced.

In the next chapter we explain NAR teachings on apostolic unity.

17

Unifying the Forces through Apostolic Unity

> The apostle is the one who will unify the Church into a fighting force.
>
> —John Kelly and Paul Costa, *End-Time Warriors*

In NAR, the church is an army that God is raising up to advance his kingdom. The army's strength comes, in large part, from its unity, a unity that is achieved through Christians' submission to apostles. This type of unity is referred to as apostolic unity.

In this chapter we look at NAR teachings about the ways that the church-army, under the leadership of apostles, seeks to attain unprecedented unity and transform society. We then examine these teachings about apostolic unity in light of the Bible's teachings about Christian unity.

THE NAR VIEW OF APOSTOLIC UNITY

The church is presently fractured by the bickering of denominations, and thus is practically impotent, say NAR leaders. They teach that the unity of Christians is essential for the church to transform society and advance God's kingdom. Bringing the church to unity is a major goal of the fivefold ministers, the five church leaders named in Ephesians 4:11–13: apostles, prophets, evangelists, pastors, and teachers: "And he gave the apostles, the prophets, the evangelists, the shepherds [pastors] and teachers, to equip the saints for the work of ministry, for building up the body of Christ, *until we all attain to the unity of the faith* and of the knowledge of the Son of God, to mature manhood, to the measure of the stature of the fullness of Christ" (our emphasis).

Yet NAR leaders do not seek just any kind of unity. They seek a specific type of unity under the leadership of present-day apostles. Peter Wagner calls it "apostolic unity."[1]

---

[1] C. Peter Wagner, *Apostles Today: Biblical Government for Biblical Power* (Ventura, CA: Regal Books, 2006), 127–29.

Apostolic unity occurs when the Christians in a given city unite under the leadership of apostles to transform their city. An example can be seen in The Call assemblies held in large stadiums throughout the United States. Co-founded by the apostle Ché Ahn and the prophet Lou Engle, these assemblies bring together Christians from across denominations to fast and pray for the end of societal evils like abortion and homosexuality, and for the restoration of the nation to its Christian roots.

Apostolic unity is based on the premise that apostles—not pastors—are the true "spiritual gatekeepers" in a city.[2] For cities to see transformation, Christians living in those cities must submit to the leadership of the local territorial apostles. Wagner says that failure to let apostles lead is the reason that not a single community in the United States has seen significant social transformation.

Some cities outside the United States, where apostolic unity has been achieved, have seen social transformation, according to Wagner. One such city is Almolonga, Guatemala, which has become a popular NAR tourist attraction.[3] Almolonga is among four communities profiled in a documentary video produced by George Otis Jr., called *Transformations*.[4] According to the video, Almolonga, home to about 20,000 indigenous people, was once characterized by poverty, alcohol addiction, violence, ignorance and witchcraft, occult activity, and idol worship.[5] Eventually, more than 90 percent of the population became born-again Christians. Jails were being closed because crime was down, and the city began to grow some of the finest produce in the Western Hemisphere.[6]

---

[2] Wagner, *Apostles Today*, 125. Wagner cites 1 Cor. 12:28 as support for the teaching that apostles are the spiritual gatekeepers of the city. In response, we point out that this verse says nothing about "spiritual gatekeepers of the city."

[3] Wagner, *Dominion!*, 56.

[4] Otis Jr., George, Lisa Knorr, and Michael Lienau. *Transformations: A Documentary*. Transformations Media, 1999. DVD.

[5] "Transformations: When God Comes to Town," YouTube video, 8:26, posted by "Yustos Anthony," May 21, 2011, accessed September 1, 2014, https://www.youtube.com/watch?v=nDqY29Fbu8M.

[6] Wagner, *Dominion!*, 56. Wagner cites as his source an excerpt from a news release written by Sarah Pollak, "Guatemala: The Miracle of Almolonga," *Christian*

A key to the transformation of Almolonga, according to Wagner, was the leadership of "territorial apostles" whom God had assigned to govern in that specific city.[7] One such apostle was Mariano Riscajche. Riscajche cast out from the city "numerous demons of alcoholism," planted a megachurch on the city's central plaza, and worked to help "establish a government of righteousness that succeeded in pushing Satan's government out of the territory."[8]

Prophet Chuck Pierce also teaches that apostolic leadership is the key to transforming cities: "If you want to see your city transformed, the Church in your region must understand God's use of apostles for this purpose. . . . We must recognize the divine government of the city that God is setting in place."[9]

NAR leaders attribute apostolic effectiveness to their vast resources. These resources come from the apostolic networks of churches and ministries the apostles oversee. Such a network, united in common cause under a common apostolic leader, is a powerful entity. Apostle David Cannistraci believes that Jesus spoke of the power of apostolic networking when he likened the kingdom of heaven to a net (Matt. 13:47). Cannistraci explains: "How is the Kingdom of heaven like a net? The net illustrates how increase becomes possible when God's people are joined together like the interconnecting cords of a net. As the Body of Christ links in interconnecting relationships and shares resources, we become powerful tools for catching lost souls."[10]

For all the power of individual apostolic networks, Cannistraci believes there's a more powerful force on the horizon. When apostolic networks

---

World News, June 10, 2005, https://www.cbn.com/cbnnews/CWN/061005Guatemala. aspx. This article is no longer accessible.

[7]   Wagner claims that "territorial apostles are essential for successful, proactive social transformation"; see *Apostles Today*, 124.

[8]   Wagner, *Dominion!*, 152.

[9]   Chuck D. Pierce and Rebecca Wagner Systema, *The Future War of the Church: How We Can Defeat Lawlessness and Bring God's Order to the Earth* (Ventura, CA: Regal Books, 2001), 99–100.

[10]   David Cannistraci, *Apostles and the Emerging Apostolic Movement: A Biblical Look at Apostleship and How God is Using it to Bless His Church Today* (Ventura, CA: Renew Books, 1996), 188.

work with other apostolic networks, the global church will finally achieve the unity needed to complete the Great Commission.

> Once Kingdom-networks begin to network, the possible advantages for the Church become enormous. I believe when the Body of Christ reaches this level, *entire nations can be taken*, as they were in the early decades of the Church [Cannistraci's emphasis]. This is apostolic ministry at its zenith. . . . The power of multiple networks voluntarily moving in the same direction paves the way for efforts in famine relief, ministry mobilization and sharing resources in greater dimensions than ever before.
>
> Imagine what would happen if the leading apostles came together, heard from God and committed the resources of their networks to reach a partic- ular nation or people group! This kind of power could sweep the planet and reap the worldwide harvest almost overnight. [11]

Thus, Cannistraci says, "apostolic networking is an indispensable part of God's end-time purpose in the Church."[12]

But the church has not yet achieved unity because apostles have only just begun to be re-accepted. Speaking of apostles' role in fostering church unity, Cannistraci states: "Apostles, along with the other [fivefold] ministry gifts, were given by Christ to edify the church and bring it to the *unity of the faith* (see Eph. 4:11–13) [Cannistraci's emphasis]. If the office of apostle is not restored, how can we hope for unity? The apostle is part of the fivefold cord God has created to tie the Body of Christ together in unity."[13] Cannistraci goes on to cite Latter Rain teacher George R. Hawtin, who wrote, "There shall never be any unity of faith until the ministry of the true apostle is rec- ognized and obeyed as strictly in the last days as it was obeyed in the days of the apostle Paul."[14]

So, the NAR thinking goes, now that apostles are re-emerging, they can unify the church.

Paradoxically, though, apostolic leadership, which will ultimately unite Christians, will initially divide them, according to Wagner. This initial dis- unity should not surprise. Many of the major movements in church his- tory initially caused division, including the Protestant Reformation, the

---

[11]   Ibid., 196.

[12]   Ibid.

[13]   Ibid.

[14]   Ibid.

Methodist movement under John Wesley, and the Azusa Street Revival. "All of these movements were powerful, apostolic-type movements, with each precipitating substantial disunity in the Church as a whole," said Wagner.[15]

The end result of these movements, however was unity; that is, unity within a new church structure or "new wineskin," to use NAR terminology. "The resulting unity," Wagner says, "was usually shaped into a new wineskin, much to the consternation of some of those who insisted on remaining in the old wineskins."[16] In the same way, the initial disunity caused by apostolic leadership in a city will result in unity among those Christians who embrace NAR—or so Wagner implies.

Apostolic unity, however, doesn't necessarily require unified doctrine. Many NAR leaders will work with others who may clash with their views on Calvinism versus Arminianism or the timing of the rapture. Oddly, many NAR apostles will also partner with others who deny classically orthodox Christian doctrines. Wagner notes that some NAR leaders are Oneness Pentecostals who deny the doctrine of the Trinity.[17]

In short, Wagner says NAR leaders have a "lighter view of doctrine"[18] than has been held by more traditional evangelicals. This lighter view is held despite the fact that they maintain strong personal convictions on biblical and theological issues. Wagner says, "There just don't seem to be as many doctrinal nuances as there used to be for which these leaders would choose to lay down their lives or, for that matter, for which they would refuse relationships with other brothers and sisters in Christ who may disagree."[19]

NAR leader Bill Johnson, senior pastor of Bethel Church in Redding, California, sums up well the teaching that apostolic leadership, rather than doctrine, is the foundation of true unity.

> For centuries the people of God have gathered together around specific truths. Denominations and organizations have been formed to unite these groups of Believers. Having common belief systems has helped to build unity within particular groups and define their purpose. . . . But there is an inherent problem with this approach—unity of this nature is based upon

---

[15] Wagner, *Apostles Today*, 128.

[16] Ibid., 129.

[17] C. Peter Wagner, *Changing Church* (Ventura, CA: Regal Books, 2004), 157.

[18] Ibid., 144.

[19] Ibid., 144–45.

uniformity. . . . When agreement in nonessential beliefs are considered nec-essary for fellowship, then division is natural and to be expected. While doc-trine is vitally important it is not a strong enough foundation to bear the weight of His [God's] glory that is about to be revealed through true unity. . . . There are major changes in the "wind" right now. For the last several years people have started to gather around *fathers* instead of doctrine. . . . *Apostles are first and foremost fathers by nature . . . In the same way that a father and mother are to bring stability to a home, so the apostles and prophets are the stability of the Church* [Johnson's emphasis].[20]

NAR's APOSTOLIC UNITY COMPARED TO CHRISTIAN UNITY IN THE BIBLE

NAR leaders rightly acknowledge the importance of Christian unity. This is emphasized in Jesus's "High Priestly Prayer" (John 17:20–23). The unity of Jesus's disciples would be a positive witness to the world (John 17:21, 23). Such unity characterized the fledgling church:

> And all who believed were together and had all things in common. And they were selling their possessions and belongings and distributing the proceeds to all, as any had need. And day by day, attending the temple together and breaking bread in their homes, they received their food with glad and generous hearts, praising God and having favor with all the people. And the Lord added to their number day by day those who were being saved. (Acts 2:44–47)

Church unity fostered the salvation of many people, as Jesus said it would.

This wasn't always the case. Serious divisions hindered the church at Corinth, as factions formed around various leaders (1 Cor. 1:11–12). The Corinthians disagreed sharply about church business (vv. 2–16), the Lord's Supper (vv. 17–34), and the exercise of spiritual gifts (12:1–14:40).

The apostle Paul implored churches in Asia Minor to be "eager to main-tain the unity of the Spirit in the bond of peace" (Eph. 4:3), showing humility, gentleness, patience, tolerance, and love (4:2). He didn't admonish them to

---

[20] Bill Johnson, "Apostolic Teams—A Group of People Who Carry the Family Mission," The Elijah List, November 21, 2008; accessed April 24, 2012, http://www.elijahlist.com/words/display_word/7083. Johnson, in the article cited above, does say "there are doctrines that are essential to the Christian faith." He identifies one doctrine as an example: "Jesus is the eternal Son of God."

create unity; they were to "maintain" an already existing unity.[21] What, then, was the foundation of their unity? There's a positional unity grounded in a common faith. Paul says:

> *[being] eager to maintain the unity of the Spirit in the bond of peace. There is one body and one Spirit—just as you were called to the one hope that belongs to your call—one Lord, one faith, one baptism, one God and Father of all, who is over all and through all and in all.* (Eph. 4:3–6)

Clinton Arnold points out that, although Paul is not citing a formal creed and does not attempt to list every essential Christian doctrine, most scholars "think that these three verses contain statements that would have been widely confessed by the early church."[22] It appears then, that Paul saw Christian unity as based, first and foremost, on mutual adherence to the essential doctrines of Christianity, which distinguished true believers sharing in regeneration brought about by the Spirit. This was their "call."

This is a problem for NAR teaching on apostolic unity. Their teaching requires submission to an apostle or group of present-day apostles whom God has appointed to govern a specific city. It doesn't include shared commitment to core Christian beliefs. The unity Paul envisions in Ephesians 4:11–13 is rooted in fundamental beliefs that include the doctrine of the Trinity. Clarity about this passage improves with context. Verses 14 and 15 stress knowledge and "speaking the truth":

> *And he gave the apostles, the prophets, the evangelists, the shepherds and teachers, to equip the saints for the work of ministry, for building up the body of Christ, until we all attain to the unity of the faith and of the knowledge of the Son of God, to mature manhood, to the measure of the stature of the fullness of Christ, so that we may no longer be children, tossed to and fro by the waves and carried about by every wind of doctrine, by human cunning, by craftiness in deceitful schemes. Rather, speaking the truth in love, we are to grow up in every way into him who is the head, into Christ.* (Eph. 4:11–15)

Apostolic unity, in the NAR sense, is not promoted in this or any other passage in the New Testament. In fact, rallying around certain church leaders was the source of division in the church at Corinth. Paul rebuked the

---

[21] Clinton E. Arnold, *Ephesians*, Zondervan Exegetical Commentary on the New Testament (Grand Rapids: Zondervan, 2010), 231.

[22] Ibid., 232.

Corinthians for tying their identity to various Christian leaders: "For when one says, 'I follow Paul,' and another, 'I follow Apollos,' are you not being merely human?" (1 Cor. 3:4).

We do believe that Christians should lay aside relatively minor doctrinal differences and work together to advance God's kingdom. But essential Christian doctrines are nonnegotiable, even when so-called apostolic unity is at stake.

In conclusion, we note an additional problem. Apostolic unity requires concession to teachings that are completely absent from the Bible, teachings peculiar to NAR. It is troubling to witness attempts at unity that trivialize core Christian beliefs while demanding acceptance of doctrines with no Christian pedigree.

We note with genuine disappointment that many Christian leaders today make it a virtual hallmark of their ministries to blast the evangelical church for its many failings (as they would say). Among these is an over-emphasis on classic doctrines of the church, a tendency to make an idol of Scripture, and a concern to root Christian practice in biblically sound principles. In our view, the church could do with a little *more* knowledge of Scripture, a *lot* more emphasis on obedience to the commands of Scripture, and a resolute *refusal* either to accommodate the culture or to advance a triumphalist agenda.

Among true subversives of the church are NAR leaders whose teachings encourage criticism of any church that falls outside the apostolic network and whose tactics facilitate the dissolution of denominations that have been faithful to their doctrinal distinctives in shared commitment to mission in the world. NAR apostles and prophets purport to determine the standards of unity and thereby alienate any who disagree. And in this do they sow discord.

SUMMARY

NAR leaders teach that church unity will be achieved through submission to present-day apostles. They claim such apostolic unity is necessary for the church to transform societies. But the Bible teaches that true Christian unity is based on the regeneration of all believers by the Spirit, enriched by commitment to the truths he has revealed in Scripture (John 14:16–17; 15:26; 16:13).

In the next chapter we explain NAR teachings on miracles.

18

A Miracle-Working Army: NAR Teaching on Miracles

> For years now premier prophets such as Paul Cain and Bob Jones
> have been clearly prophesying, predicting the arising of an end-
> time army identified as Joel's Army. These predictions are long
> standing, and are now in the process of being fulfilled.
>
> —Bobby Connor, *The Elijah List*

Under the leadership of NAR apostles and prophets, the church is to become a miracle-working army that will usher in God's kingdom. This army
goes by various names, including Joel's Army, based on NAR interpretations
of Joel 2,[1] and the Manifest Sons of God, based on a NAR interpretation of
Romans 8:19.[2]

---

[1]   NAR leaders have taught that an end-time church army is prophetically foretold in Joel 2. But they disagree as to which part of Joel 2 depicts this army. Some
believe it is Joel 2:1–11, such as Bob Jones and Bill Hamon. See Bob Jones, "God's
Mercy-Naries," *The Prophetic Ministry and Resources of Bob and Bonnie Jones with
Lyn Kost*, (September 2012), accessed September 2, 2014, http://bobjones.org/in-
dex.cfm?zone=/Docs/Words%20of%202012/2012-09_GodsMercyNaries.htm; and
Hamon, *Apostles, Prophets, and the Coming Moves of God*, 255–56. But this interpretation is foreign to biblical scholarship, and even IHOP disapproves of it. However,
the organization does use the term Joel's Army to refer to godly people who lead a
lifestyle of prayer and fasting. This is based on their interpretation of Joel 2:12–17.
And the IHOP website references with approval a prophecy about Joel's Army given
by the modern prophet Paul Cain. This is known as Cain's "Stadium Vision," which
describes Joel's Army as a miracle-working, end-time army that will usher in God's
kingdom. See Ernest Gruen and Mike Bickle, "Affirmations and Denials: Ernie Gru-
en and Mike Bickle's Joint Statement From 1993," International House of Prayer, May
16, 1993; accessed December 10, 2013, http://www.ihopkc.org/about/affirmations-
and-denials; and Paul Cain, "Stadium Vision," *The Paul Cain Blog*, April 16, 2006;
accessed February 27, 2014, http://paulcain.blogspot.com.

[2]   The name Manifest Sons of God derives from language in the King James
translation of Rom. 8:19.

Belief in miracles as a contemporary phenomenon is not unique to NAR. Most Christians believe that God acts miraculously in the world today. This is true even of many cessationists, as demonstrated in a fascinating book with essays by several cessationists, titled *Who's Afraid of the Holy Spirit?*[3] Their general perspective is that, even though the miraculous gifts have ceased, God still works miracles, including healing people, often in response to prayer. Others, notably those people who identify themselves as Pentecostal or charismatic, go further, believing that God continues to distribute miraculous gifts to his people, including speaking in tongues, prophesying, and divine healing.[4] A ten-country survey of Pentecostals and charismatics conducted by the Pew Forum found that in all ten countries large majorities of Pentecostals and charismatics claim to have personally experienced or witnessed the divine healing of an illness or injury.[5]

Three things set NAR apart from more conventional views about miracles: (1) under the leadership of apostles and prophets, the end-time church will perform miracles that are unprecedented in terms of their grandeur and frequency; (2) new truths revealed by the new apostles and prophets are crucial to "activating" miraculous gifts among individuals; and (3) the followers of apostles and prophets will grow in miraculous gifting until they "loose" God's judgments on earth and become immortal.

We now examine these three teachings.

---

[3]   Daniel B. Wallace and M. James Sawyer, eds., *Who's Afraid of the Holy Spirit? An Investigation into the Ministry of the Spirit of God Today* (Dallas: Biblical Studies Press, 2005).

[4]   An important recent treatment of miracles in the Bible and throughout church history is the two-volume work by Craig Keener, *Miracles: The Credibility of the New Testament Accounts* (Grand Rapids: Baker, 2011). This is the most comprehensive investigation of miracles in print, surpassing all other treatments in scholarly research and exposition. Doug Geivett has, with Gary Habermas, edited a volume of original essays entitled *In Defense of Miracles: A Comprehensive Case for God's Action in Human History* (Downers Grove, IL: InterVarsity Press, 1997).

[5]   Luis Lugo, "Spirit and Power: A 10-Country Survey of Pentecostals," Executive Summary, Pew Forum Survey (2006), accessed May 12, 2014, http://www.pew-forum.org/2006/10/05/spirit-and-power-a-10-country-survey-of-pentecostals3/.

UNPRECEDENTED MIRACLES

NAR teaching is that the miracles performed by the end-time church under the leadership of the new apostles and prophets will be unprecedented, both in terms of their grandeur and their frequency. Mike Bickle, founder of IHOP, pronounces, "The end times is the Church's finest hour, when miracles will occur and supernatural prophetic direction will be released. The miracles of Acts and Exodus will be multiplied and combined on a global level." He grounds this claim in Micah 7:15.[6]

Further, miracles performed by Christians in this generation will be so spectacular they'll make the miracles performed by biblical prophets and apostles seem insubstantial and routine by comparison. Rick Joyner, one of the most influential NAR prophets, declares, "Parting the Red Sea will hardly be remembered as a significant miracle after the things that will be done by those who serve the Lord at the end of this age."[7]

Even the greatness of Jesus's miracles will be trumped by end-time miracles.[8] For this astonishing claim, NAR leaders appeal to Jesus's promise that those who believe in him would do the same works he did *and even "greater works"* (John 14:12; emphasis added).[9]

---

[6] "100 Most Frequently Asked Questions About the End Times," International House of Prayer; accessed December 3, 2013, http://www.ihopkc.org/hispano/files/2011/11/H-100-Most-Frequently-Asked-Questions-about-the-End-Times-2nd-Edit.pdf.

[7] Rick Joyner, *The Apostolic Ministry* (Wilkesboro, NC: MorningStar Publications, 2004), 42.

[8] Rick Joyner, "Abiding in the King Produces Kingdom Authority—The Path of Life, Part 31," MorningStar Ministries, Week 38, 2012; accessed February 23, 2014, http://www.morningstarministries.org/resources/word-week/2012/abiding-king-produces-kingdom-authority-path-life-part-31#.Uwpg0oV6V8o.

[9] Bill Johnson, *When Heaven Invades Earth: A Practical Guide to a Life of Miracles* (Shippensburg, PA: Destiny Image Publishers, 2003), Kindle edition, 185; Mike Bickle, "Session 1: Introduction and Overview of the Book of Revelation," *Studies in the Book of Revelation,* Twelve-part series taught at the International House of Prayer University, Spring Semester 2014, p. 8, MikeBickle.org; accessed May 6, 2014, http://www.mikebickle.org.edgesuite.net/MikeBickleVOD/2014/20140207_Introduction_and_Overview_of_the_Book_of_Revelation_BOR01_study%20notes.pdf.

The "greater" miraculous works to be performed by NAR apostles, prophets, and their followers include:

- healing every patient within entire hospitals and mental institutions through the simple laying of hands on the buildings;[10]
- diverting raging floods with a single word;[11]
- possessing authority over all natural laws, such as gravity, time, space, and mass;[12]
- commanding mountains to be literally cast into the sea and having the mountains obey them;[13]
- routinely multiplying food and resources;[14]
- prophetically revealing simple, natural cures for fatal diseases;[15]
- prophesying with comprehensive knowledge of *everything* that happens before it occurs (nothing will take them by surprise);[16] and,
- participating in regular counsels with angels.[17]

NAR leaders note that miracles won't be an end in themselves. They will contribute to the fulfillment of a popular NAR prophecy known as the Great End-Time Harvest, when more than a billion people will convert to belief in Jesus Christ.[18] Because miracles performed by the apostles will be so impressive, mass conversions are expected:

[10]   Joyner, *The Apostolic Ministry*, 41; Rick Joyner, *The Harvest* (Pineville, NC: MorningStar Publications, 1989), 27.

[11]   Joyner, *The Harvest*, 27.

[12]   Rick Joyner, "The Fullness of Time," *MorningStar Prophetic Bulletin*, no. 73, MorningStar Ministries; accessed November 19, 2011, http://www.morningstarministries.org/resources/prophetic-bulletins/2012/fullness-time#.Uou-EuIoEYB.

[13]   Joyner, "Abiding in the King Produces Kingdom Authority."

[14]   Joyner, "The Fullness of Time."

[15]   Johnny Enlow, *The Seven Mountain Prophecy: Unveiling the Coming Elijah Revolution* (Lake Mary, FL: Creation House, 2008), 109.

[16]   Joyner, *The Apostolic Ministry*, 41–42.

[17]   Joyner, "The Fullness of Time."

[18]   Mike Bickle, *Growing in the Prophetic: A Practical, Biblical Guide to Dreams, Visions, and Spiritual Gifts*, rev. ed. (Lake Mary, FL: Charisma House, 2008); PDF e-book available at Mike Bickle.org, accessed August 14, 2014, http://mikebickle.org/books, 77. This figure, a "billion," is repeated frequently by NAR leaders. It appears

News teams will follow apostles like national leaders, recording great miracles which will be shown with unabashed enthusiasm. Some of these individual broadcasts will result in more conversions than Christian networks have seen during their entire existence. . . .

Miracles which exceed even the most spectacular Biblical marvels will cause whole nations to acknowledge Jesus.[19]

And while the most spectacular miracles are usually attributed to the apostles and prophets, miracles will be performed by all those who receive the new truths revealed by the apostles and prophets.

THE ACTIVATION OF MIRACULOUS GIFTS THROUGH THE RECEPTION OF NEW TRUTHS

To become God's miracle-working army, the church must first be equipped by the apostles and prophets. Believers must receive new truths—that is, teachings and practices—that will endow them with miraculous power. Bill Hamon says, "Saints will not automatically begin manifesting the supernatural works of Jesus by sitting in the pews and doing 'business as usual.'" To operate in supernatural power and miracles, Christians must, to use a biblical metaphor with supernatural overtones, "walk on the water of new truth."[20]

The following "new truths" are practices that allegedly activate miraculous power in individuals.

The laying on of hands

Miraculous gifts, such as those of physical healing or prophesying, can be "transferred" from apostles and prophets to others through a practice known as the laying on of hands.[21] This practice is promoted by countless

---

to have come from a prophecy given by the prophet Bob Jones. See Jennifer LeClaire, "Prophet Bob Jones Passes Away," *Charisma News,* February 14, 2014; accessed June 15, 2014, http://www.charismanews.com/us/42794-prophet-bob-jones-passes-away.

19   Joyner, *The Harvest,* 25–26.

20   Bill Hamon, *The Day of the Saints: Equipping Believers for Their Revolutionary Role in Ministry* (Shippensburg, PA: Destiny Image Publishers, 2002), 45.

21   Bill Hamon, *Apostles, Prophets, and the Coming Moves of God: God's End-Time Plans for His Church and Planet Earth* (Santa Rosa Beach, FL: Destiny Image Publishers, 1997), 192–93, 283.

NAR leaders.[22] Many NAR conferences feature a time for the transference of gifts, when attendees come forward and receive the laying on of hands by an apostle or prophet.

Fasting from food[23]

A breakthrough of unprecedented miraculous power in the church is planned by IHOP, which has instituted a Global Bridegroom Fast, held the first Monday through Wednesday of every month, and seven consecutive days beginning on the first Monday in December, until Christ returns.[24] Bickle teaches that the rewards of fasting include miraculous power in personal ministry and the release of unprecedented prophetic revelation in the end time. This will include God's dispatching angels to some of his end-time prophets to bestow special understanding.[25]

24/7 Prayer

Non-stop, round-the-clock prayer, popularly known as 24/7 prayer, is also key to releasing miraculous power in the church. IHOP operates a 24/7 Prayer Room where continual prayer and worship have been held twenty-four hours a day, seven days a week, since 1999. IHOP-style prayer rooms have opened in cites throughout the United States and the world. More is going on here than the gathering of Christians to pray. These rooms prepare prayer warriors for their end-time role in "loosing" divine judgments against the Antichrist's kingdom.[26]

---

[22] Johnson, *When Heaven Invades Earth*, 79.

[23] Latter Rain leader Franklin Hall's book *Atomic Power with God with Fasting and Prayer* (1946; repr., Phoenix, AZ: Hall Deliverance Foundation, 1992) popularized the teaching that fasting is a key to attaining miraculous gifting. NAR leaders frequently point to this book as influencing their own views on the importance of fasting.

[24] "Global Bridegroom Fast," International House of Prayer, accessed December 3, 2013, http://www.ihopkc.org/about/global-bridegroom-fast.

[25] Mike Bickle and Dana Chandler, *The Rewards of Fasting: Experiencing the Power and Affections of God* (Kansas City, MO: Forerunner Books, 2005); PDF e-book available at Mike Bickle.org, accessed August 14, 2014, http://mikebickle.org/books., 24–27.

[26] For further discussion of Bickle's teaching about how prayer will be used to "loose" God's judgments, see the next section in this chapter.

Soaking

The purpose of this practice is to experience greater intimacy with God by soaking in His presence. Such intimacy will activate miraculous gifts and supernatural experiences. Soaking often involves elements such as finding a place of solitude, praying in one's native language, speaking in tongues, and waiting upon God to manifest his presence. This presence may be mediated by dreams, visions, trances, out-of-body experiences, angelic visitations, or being "transported in the Spirit," rather like Philip, an early Christian convert and evangelist who was miraculously transported between geographical regions (Acts 8:39–40).[27] The production of "soaking music" to aid people in their soaking practices has become an industry within NAR.

Speaking in tongues[28]

Also known as glossolalia, speaking in tongues is seen as a key to activating other miraculous gifts.[29] At so-called prophetic workshops, such as those led by Hamon, participants seek to activate the miraculous gift of prophecy by engaging in an activation exercise that involves finding a partner, starting to speak in tongues, and then saying out loud whatever comes into their minds as a prophetic word for their partner.

Activating miraculous gifts in people—also known as training them to move in the supernatural—is a major emphasis in the movement. It is detailed in numerous books, such as *Developing a Supernatural Lifestyle: A Practical Guide to a Life of Signs, Wonders, and Miracles*[30] by popular NAR

---

[27] Gary Oates, "Soaking: The Key to Intimacy with God," The Elijah List. January 9, 2012; accessed December 5, 2013, http://www.elijahlist.com/words/display_word.html?ID=10620.

[28] Speaking in tongues, or *glossolalia*, is often viewed as a miraculous spiritual gift of communicating in a heavenly language. Some also view it as a gift of communicating in human languages unknown to the speakers, and believe it is given chiefly for evangelistic purposes.

[29] Bill Hamon, *Seventy Reasons for Speaking in Tongues: Your Own Built In Spiritual Dynamo* (Shippensburg, PA: Destiny Image Publishers, 2012), 137.

[30] Kris Vallotton, *Developing a Supernatural Lifestyle: A Practical Guide to a Life of Signs, Wonders, and Miracles* (Shippensburg, PA: Destiny Image Publishers, 2007). Vallotton is the senior associate leader of Bethel Church in Redding, California.

leader Kris Vallotton; and at conferences, such as Supernatural Lifestyle Conferences.[31]

Schools of the supernatural have been formed at apostolic churches, many associated with Bill Johnson's Bethel Church in Redding, California—a sort of NAR version of Lourdes. The churches purchase a DVD curriculum, which, for the first year of 112 classes, costs $6,495. These schools, however, are not found only in NAR churches. Some Vineyard churches also have them. Bethel's own School of Supernatural Ministry was founded in 1998 with only 36 students. It has since grown substantially, training more than 1,800 students during the 2012–2013 school year.[32]

In addition to being activated in the miraculous gifts, students are trained to activate others. During the school's two-year program, students circulate among various churches to provide training in what they call supernatural evangelism. This is sometimes called prophetic evangelism,—a form of evangelism that relies on the use of miraculous gifts, such as prophecy and healing, to share God's love with people.[33]

Students take church members into their local communities to participate in a NAR activity known as Treasure Hunts, which are conducted by teams of three or four people. Before a Treasure Hunt, team members ask God to give them prophetic "words of knowledge"[34]—also called clues— about specific people they will find in the community. The clues they seek include a person's name, descriptions of that person's appearance, and any ailments (such as recurring headaches or a bad knee).[35] Students mark these

---

[31]   These conferences are led by Kevin Dedmon Ministries, an organization based at Bethel Church in Redding, California.

[32]   "Mission," Bethel School of Supernatural Ministry, accessed February 23, 2014, http://bssm.net/about/mission.

[33]   Another term used for "supernatural evangelism" is "power evangelism."

[34]   A "word of knowledge" is often viewed as a miraculous spiritual gift of receiving supernatural knowledge from God, found in 1 Cor. 12:8.

[35]   We obtained these details about the practice of Treasure Hunts from a book written by Kevin Dedmon, who teaches at the Bethel School of Supernatural Ministry and oversees the school's Treasure Hunt outreaches. See Dedmon, *The Ultimate Treasure Hunt: A Guide to Supernatural Evangelism through Supernatural Encounters* (Shippensburg, PA: Destiny Image Publishers, 2007), Kindle edition.

clues on a treasure map, which they then use to guide them to a person—called a treasure—who matches their clues.

Here's an example recounted by a team member. During one Treasure Hunt conducted in a Wal-Mart, the clues included "Starbucks coffee," "hurt right arm," and "frozen foods." The treasure hunters located a woman buying Starbucks coffee-flavored ice cream in the frozen food section. When they approached the woman and told her about their activity, she looked at their list of other clues and revealed that she had an injured right arm. She allowed the team members to pray for her and her arm was immediately healed.[36]

LOOSING JUDGMENTS AND BECOMING IMMORTAL

Some prominent NAR leaders teach that the followers of apostles and prophets will progress in their miraculous gifting until they conquer sickness and cleanse the earth of evil. When this happens, they will finally be manifested as individual sons of God, patterned after the original Son of God, Jesus Christ. As Bill Hamon says, "Jesus was not to be one-of-a-kind but the firstborn among many just like Him."[37] Together, these "manifest sons of God" will become a type of corporate Christ, a literal extension of the incarnation of Christ on earth.[38] This teaching about the arrival of a

---

[36] Dedmon, *The Ultimate Treasure Hunt*, 23.

[37] Bill Hamon, *Prophetic Scriptures Yet To Be Fulfilled: During the Third and Final Church Reformation* (Shippensburg, PA: Destiny Image Publishers, 2010), 39.

[38] Hamon calls the church "the One Universal Many-Membered Corporate Body of Christ" (see *Prophetic Scriptures Yet to Be Fulfilled*, 40), and says it is the "*full* expression of Christ Jesus, as Jesus is the full expression of His heavenly Father" [our emphasis; see his *The Day of the Saints*, 74]. He also says, "While Jesus was on Earth, His natural body was the home and headquarters of God here on Earth. Now the Church, as the corporate Body of Christ, is the home and headquarters for Jesus Christ here on Earth" (*The Day of the Saints*, 73–74). Hamon does not, from what we have seen, ever qualify his statements to indicate that there is anything that sets apart Christ's incarnation from the incarnation of the corporate Body of Christ. The Manifest Sons of God teaching that the church is to be a literal incarnation of Christ was also taught by Earl Paulk, the founder of Cathedral at Chapel Hill, a megachurch in Decatur, Georgia. See Robert M. Bowman Jr., Craig S. Hawkins, and Dan R. Schlesinger, "The Gospel According to Paulk: A Critique of 'Kingdom Theology,'" *Christian Research Journal* 11, no. 1 (Summer 1988).

corporate Christ is often described as the church giving birth to the "many-membered man-child."

Individually, the sons of God will attain Divine Health. This means they can expect to live a thousand years, according to George Warnock (1917–2007), a leader in the Latter Rain movement and a pioneer of this doctrine.[39] NAR disciples who are already elderly will experience a reversed aging process, literally growing physically younger.[40] Rick Joyner also says they will be able to heal every physical condition: "There will be no plague, disease, or physical condition, including lost limbs, AIDS, poison gas, or radiation, which will resist the healing and miracle gifts working in the saints during this time."[41]

Some NAR participants will become immortal, according to one of NAR's most prominent leaders: Bill Hamon. Before we explain Hamon's teaching on immortality, we note that he often uses what can only be viewed as loose and ambiguous language. His teachings are not always clear. This must be kept in mind in any assessment of his teaching on immortality.

If we have understood Hamon's teaching correctly, he believes that those Christians who follow end-time apostles and prophets will become immortal. In other words, they will never die. He finds biblical precedent for this teaching in two Old Testament figures, Enoch, who "walked with God, and he was not, for God took him," and the prophet Elijah, who "went up to heaven by a whirlwind" (Gen. 5:24; 2 Kings 2:1).[42] Hamon also believes this promise of becoming immortal is spoken of in Romans 8:23: "And not only the creation, but we ourselves, who have the firstfruits of the Spirit, groan inwardly as we wait eagerly for adoption as sons, the redemption of our bodies."[43]

How will the followers of apostles and prophets become immortal? In the same way we have described for NAR teaching about activating miraculous gifts, that is, by continuing to receive the new truths revealed by apostles and prophets. This seems to be the key to understanding Hamon's teaching.

---

[39]   George H. Warnock, *Feast of Tabernacles,* (N.p.: The Church in Action, 1951; repr., 1980), Kindle edition, chapter 12.

[40]   Joyner, *The Apostolic Ministry,* 171.

[41]   Joyner, *The Harvest,* 167–68.

[42]   Hamon, *Apostles, Prophets, and the Coming Moves of God,* 265–66.

[43]   Ibid., 263.

One would hope for greater clarity about a matter of such importance, yet the teaching seems to be that by receiving the new truths, individuals will gain more and more miraculous power until they are able to defeat death, humanity's greatest enemy. Hamon writes:

> They are now being equipped with the revelation and powerful authority to go against the most formidable fortress and wall that satan[44] has ever built. Jesus paid the price for the redemption of our bodies and took the keys of death from the devil, taking them to heaven when He arose. Jesus has already provided everything for the full redemption of our spirit, soul and body. Yet there is no Church history account of even one member of the Body of Christ being able to appropriate Christ's victory over death. None of God's saints have gotten out of this world alive in their physical body. All have been taken out by the agent of death. Satan is determined that none will ever leave without dying, but Jesus has other plans (1 Cor. 15:51–54; 2 Cor. 5:4; 1 Thess. 4:13–18; 2 Thess. 1:5–11; Ps. 102:18–20; Rom. 8:23). . . .
>
> This restorational army will not only continue until all truth is restored, but will appropriate the last truth that will enable them to overcome the last enemy.[45]

The notion that the followers of end-times apostles and prophets can become immortal did not originate with Hamon. It was taught by Latter Rain leaders, including Warnock, as early as the 1950s.[46] Warnock taught that immortality could be experienced *before* Christ's return.

Unlike Warnock, Hamon seems to believe that the redemption of believers' bodies will occur *at* Jesus's return, as other Christians also believe. But, contrary to what Christians have historically believed, this event will not be "solely a sovereign act of God apart from divine revelation and faith appropriation of the saints," according to Hamon.[47] In other words, it will only happen when Christians receive the new truths that have been given by apostles and prophets.

---

[44] Destiny Image Publishers intentionally does not capitalize the first letter of Satan's name, for the organization wishes "not to acknowledge him, even to the point of violating grammatical rules." See *Apostles, Prophets, and the Coming Moves of God,* iv.

[45] Ibid., 263, 265.

[46] Warnock, *Feast of Tabernacles,* chapter 14.

[47] Ibid., 265.

Hamon's teaching that Christians can become immortal through the reception of new truths is extreme, even for NAR. We want to stress this point because we do not intend to imply that all other NAR leaders agree with this teaching.

The purpose of receiving immortal bodies is to "enable the army of the Lord to finalize the war against all evil" and to allow the army to have "unlimited abilities."[48] Hamon says, "The army of the Lord will progress on in the war until they have accomplished all they can in their limited mortal bodies."[49]Then, equipped with unlimited miraculous power,[50] they will execute the judgments of God described in the book of Revelation: "The victorious, overcoming last-day army of the Lord saints will fulfill the numerous scriptures declaring the downfall of satan[51] and all evil; the fall and destruction of Babylon; the subduing of all enemies under Christ's feet; etc."[52]

This army of NAR revolutionaries may begin executing judgment before they receive their immortal bodies. Mike Bickle teaches that the endtime church will loose Jesus's judgments on the wicked. He seems to believe this will begin before Christ returns. The judgments to be loosed are the plagues described in the book of Revelation, including hail, falling stars, and an army riding fire-breathing horses; these will destroy one-third of the earth's population.[53] Bickle teaches that these judgments are what Jesus had in mind when he promised his followers that they would do "greater works" than he did while he was on earth. "Jesus never turned the water into

---

[48]   Ibid., 265.

[49]   Ibid., 264, 265.

[50]   In addition to unlimited miraculous power, the immortalized will be equipped with a type of moral perfection or extraordinary holiness. If they did not have moral perfection or extraordinary holiness, then God would not be able to entrust them with such tremendous power. See Hamon, *Apostles, Prophets, and the Coming Moves of God*, 259.

[51]   Again, Destiny Image Publishers intentionally does not capitalize Satan's name.

[52]   Hamon, *Apostles, Prophets, and the Coming Moves of God*, 266.

[53]   See Rev. 9:18. Some Bible scholars believe this army is not an army of humans riding horses, but rather a demonic army. For Bickle's teaching on the church "loosing" the trumpet judgments see Bickle, "Session 1: Introduction and Overview of the Book of Revelation."

blood. He turned it into wine, but never to blood. He never brought down the Roman Empire, the evil leaders of the Roman Empire, but He will bring down the evil leaders of the earth and bring them all down. He will do it in concert with His people."[54]

The idea that Christians will loose God's judgments comes from a totally new NAR interpretation of the book of Revelation. Most Christians who believe that Revelation is about events that will transpire in the end time believe that the Christians alive at that time will be raptured to Christ before he releases his judgments on earth.[55] Those who believe that the church will not be raptured first don't believe that Christians have any part in loosing the judgments. In contrast to the majority of Christians, Bickle believes the church will remain on earth during the judgments *and* that it will be actively involved in loosing those judgments.

SUMMARY

All miracle-working power promised to NAR followers, enabling them as an army of God to loose divine judgments on earth and even overcome death for themselves, depends on adopting the new truths revealed by NAR apostles and prophets. This, however, is out of step with what the majority of Christians have historically believed.

In the next chapter we evaluate NAR teachings about a miracle-working army in light of Scripture.

---

[54]   Bickle, "Session 1: Introduction and Overview of the Book of Revelation," 8.

[55]   The "prewrath" interpretation does not view the seals as God's wrath—only the trumpets and bowls— hence, in the prewrath view the church will experience the first six seals. See Alan Kurschner, *Antichrist Before the Day of the Lord: What Every Christian Needs to Know About the Return of Christ* (Pompton Lakes, NJ: Eschatos Publishing, 2013).

A Biblical Analysis of a NAR Miracle-Working Army

> Are all apostles? Are all prophets? Are all teachers? Do all work miracles? Do all possess gifts of healing? Do all speak with tongues? Do all interpret?
>
> —The Apostle Paul, *1 Corinthians 12:29–30*

We now evaluate and analyze NAR teachings on miracles, specifically, the following three teachings:

- That under the leadership of apostles and prophets, the end-time church will perform miracles unprecedented in terms of their grandeur and frequency.
- That new truths revealed by contemporary apostles and prophets are the keys to activating miraculous spiritual gifts among individuals.
- That the followers of apostles and prophets will grow in miraculous gifting until they loose God's judgments on the earth and become immortal.

UNPRECEDENTED MIRACLES

NAR leaders teach the rise of a glorious end-time church under the leadership of apostles and prophets, a church characterized in part by its unprecedented miraculous power. This belief depends crucially on an interpretation of Jesus's promise made to his disciples in John 14:12: "Truly, truly, I say to you, whoever believes in me will also do the works that I do; and greater works than these will he do, because I am going to the Father."

Conservative New Testament interpreters differ on the correct understanding of this verse, that is, whether or not it's a promise about miracles. Some, such as D. A. Carson, believe that miracles cannot be excluded from

Jesus's promise,[1] while others, such as Andreas J. Köstenberger, doubt that they're included.[2]

For the sake of argument, let's allow that Jesus's promise was about miracles. If that's the case, then the need for present-day apostles and prophets evaporates. Why? Because Jesus's promise has been available to *all* of his followers throughout history—to whomever believes in him, as it says John 14:12. The promise is not just for a spiritual elite who follow end-time apostles and prophets.

But just what are the greater works Jesus spoke of? Some think these deeds would be greater because they would influence more people. Jesus's disciples did spread out after his departure and were not confined to a single geographical region; and their work was remarkably fruitful, even revolutionary (see Acts 16:19–21; 17:6; 19:23–29). But there's more to consider. "Greater" probably also refers to the enlargement of Jesus's works and a fuller understanding of them, following the resurrection and through these men. D. A. Carson writes of this passage:

> Both Jesus' words and his deeds were somewhat veiled during the days of his flesh; even his closest followers . . . grasped only part of what he was saying. But Jesus is about to return to his Father, he is about to be glorified, and in the wake of his glorification his followers will know and make known all that Jesus is and does, and their every deed and word will belong to the new eschatological age that will then have dawned.[3]

We concur. Yet, whatever *greater* means, the consensus is that it cannot refer to the grandeur of the miracles performed by Jesus's followers. What could be more obvious? What miraculous work could possibly outstrip the stunning works of Jesus. Calming storms, giving sight to the blind, and, most impressively, raising the dead, including himself (John 10:17–18)?

Mike Bickle suggests that loosing divine judgments on earth is more spectacular than these other miracles. But we beg to differ. Bringing a person back from death to life is every bit as spectacular—perhaps more

---

[1]   D. A. Carson, *Gospel according to John,* The Pillar New Testament Commentary (Grand Rapids: Eerdmans, 1991), 495.

[2]   Andreas J. Köstenberger, "The 'Greater Works' of the Believer according to John 14:12," *Didaskalia: The Journal of Providence College and Seminary* 6, no. 2 (Spring 1995), 42.

[3]   Carson, *Gospel according to John,* 496.

so—than loosing a plague of hailstones. Furthermore, nothing in the Gospel of John—the larger context of Jesus's promise—indicates that Jesus had end-time judgments in mind when he spoke of "greater works." Bickle's interpretation of John 14:12 is strained to the breaking point.[4] It's a wonder anyone would believe such a thing. This NAR doctrine is certainly not unequivocally supported in this passage.

Finally, John 14:12 gives no basis for interpreting "greater" in terms of frequency, as if working miracles would be more normative, or commonplace, for Jesus's followers than it was for him.

THE ACTIVATION OF MIRACULOUS GIFTS
THROUGH THE RECEPTION OF NEW TRUTHS

A major emphasis of NAR is that miraculous gifts can be activated through receiving new truths revealed by present-day apostles and prophets. In contrast, the apostle Paul wrote that the miraculous gifts of the Holy Spirit are *gifts*. They're not powers that can be activated. And they're distributed directly by the Holy Spirit to individuals as he alone decides (1 Cor. 12:11). They cannot be acquired by individuals at will.

Furthermore, Paul makes it very clear that not all can have each of these gifts. He asks rhetorically, "Are all apostles? Are all prophets? Are all teachers? Do all work miracles? Do all possess gifts of healing? Do all speak with tongues? Do all interpret?" (1 Cor. 12:29–30). The intended answer is no. Not all have the gift of prophesying or the working of miracles or healing. NAR teaching that miraculous gifts can be activated in any who desire them conflicts with Scripture in those places where gifts are addressed most fully.

To each is given the manifestation of the Spirit for the common good. For to
one is given through the Spirit the utterance of wisdom, and to another the

---

[4] Bickle also cites Micah 7:15 to show that the end-time church will perform unprecedented miracles, including loosing divine judgments. But it appears that he has read into the verse his own presuppositions, just as he has done with John 14:12. In order to arrive at his interpretation of Micah 7:15, he would need to demonstrate at least three things about this verse: (1) that the "marvelous things" referred to include divine judgments, (2) that the "marvelous things" will happen in the end time just prior to Christ's return, and (3) that the "marvelous things" are performed by the church. It seems that he will have an especially difficult time demonstrating the third point.

utterance of knowledge according to the same Spirit, to another faith by the same Spirit, to another gifts of healing by the one Spirit, to another the working of miracles, to another prophecy. (1 Cor. 12:7–10)

Whether or not certain of those gifts are still given today, such as the gifts of healing and prophecy, is the subject of much debate in the church. But even among those who believe these gifts are still being given, the NAR teaching that such gifts can be activated through new truths is challenged by leading charismatics and Pentecostals.

For example, the Assemblies of God, the world's largest Pentecostal denomination, has issued an official statement against the teaching that spiritual gifts can be imparted to individuals through the practice known as "the laying on of hands and prophecy." The statement reads: "According to Scripture, however, the Spirit, and only the Spirit imparts gifts to Spirit-filled believers. . . . Only the Holy Spirit can give supernatural gifts. . . . Although we are to be vessels yielded to the prompting of the Spirit, the Holy Spirit does not rely on human announcement to proclaim the gifts He gives as He alone chooses."[5]

And the NAR idea that people can *learn* to prophesy—through the type of training offered in NAR supernatural schools of ministry is questioned by leaders in the Pentecostal and charismatic camps. As Pentecostal-charismatic historian Vinson Synan says, "The practice of learning to prophesy in a classroom setting seems to take a gift of the Spirit, which is given and controlled by the Holy Spirit, and place it in human hands apart from a worshiping community."[6]

What about the schools of the prophets found in the Old Testament? It's true that groups of prophets banded together and formed communities. But there's no indication that these companies of prophets were schools where people learned to prophesy. Rather, they were simply communities made up of people who already were prophets.

NAR teaching on the activation of a gift has more in common with New Age teachings than with biblical Christianity. New Agers believe that everyone is born with supernatural powers they can "activate" or "awaken" or

---

[5] "Imparting of Spiritual Gifts," Assemblies of God, accessed November 12, 2013, http://ag.org/top/Beliefs/topics/sptlissues_imparting_spiritual_gifts.cfm.

[6] Vinson Synan, "2000 Years of Prophecy," in *Understanding the Fivefold Ministry*, ed. Matthew D. Green (Lake Mary, FL: Charisma House, 2005), 55.

"unlock" by engaging in various New Age practices.[7] This concept of activating the gifts is foreign to the New Testament.

Of course, it's also true that many practices promoted by NAR leaders—such the laying on of hands, fasting, and prayer—are found in the Bible. There are instances when an apostle laid his hands on an individual and seemed to impart spiritual gifts (Acts 19:6; 1 Tim. 4:14; 2 Tim. 1:6). Notice, however, that in each of these instances, one of the apostles of Christ played a key role in the impartation.[8] In the case of Timothy, where church elders were involved (1 Tim. 4:14), the apostle Paul was also present (2 Tim. 1:6). As we've shown, there is no scriptural evidence that there still exists an office of apostle. If it takes an apostle to impart a spiritual gift, those lined up today for the gifts they desire will be waiting for quite some time!

Teaching about practices like fasting and prayer are not new truths revealed through present-day apostles and prophets. These practices have characterized the church throughout its history. What is new are specific types of fasts and prayer "revealed" to NAR leaders. The Global Bridegroom Fast and 24/7 prayer rooms promoted by IHOP—these are novelties.

IHOP leaders suggest that participation in the Global Bridegroom Fast is needed for the realization of God's end-time purposes, including the release of unprecedented miraculous power in the church. A statement on the IHOP website declares that the Global Bridegroom Fast was instituted directly by Jesus as a practice to continue until his Second Coming. "In January 2002, the word of the Lord came, saying, 'I am raising up a global bridegroom fast; ask Me to release one hundred million believers worldwide to come before Me in one accord for three days each month until I return.'"[9]

---

[7]   See, for example, these New Age sources: Rebecca Rosen, *Spirited: Unlock Your Psychic Self and Change Your Life* (New York: HarperCollins, 2010); Doreen Virtue, *The Lightworker's Way: Awakening Your Spiritual Power to Know and Heal* (Carlsbad, CA: Hay House, 1997). A Christian source on the New Age movement is Douglas R. Groothuis, *Unmasking the New Age* (Downers Grove, IL: InterVarsity Press,) 1986.

[8]   Recall our definition of "apostles of Christ"—that is, those apostles mentioned in 1 Cor. 15:1–7 who had seen the resurrected Christ and operated with special authority in the first Christian era.

[9]   "Global Bridegroom Fast," International House of Prayer, accessed December 3, 2013, http://www.ihopkc.org/about/global-bridegroom-fast. The statement does not say specifically to whom the word of the Lord came.

The purpose of the fast includes prayer for "spiritual breakthrough in the worldwide Church, with unprecedented unity, purity, and power"; "the great [end-time] harvest [of souls]"; and "fulfillment of all the prophetic promises to national Israel."[10] Thus, the Global Bridegroom Fast is a strategic new practice essential to the church's mission in the world.[11] The boast that a Global Bridegroom Fast is required of millions in the church is staggering. This is quite a revelation, and one that places present-day apostles and prophets on a par with biblical apostles and prophets.

Ditto for the practice of operating 24/7 prayer rooms. To be sure, prayer is a good thing. We commend non-stop, round-the-clock praying by those who are so inclined. But Bickle teaches that this practice is not optional, saying, "Jesus *requires* night-and-day prayer for the full release of justice in the Church and society" [our emphasis].[12] He finds support for this in Luke 18:7–8: "And will not God give justice to his elect, who cry to him day and night? Will he delay long over them? I tell you, he will give justice to them speedily. Nevertheless, when the Son of Man comes, will he find faith on earth?"[13] Typical of NAR hermeneutics, Bickle's interpretation neglects context and ignores alternative, more plausible meanings. This isn't an appeal to erect non-stop, round-the-clock prayer rooms. It simply teaches that God will give justice to those who persist in prayer.

If we apply Bickle's methods of interpretation consistently, we get bizarre results. Joshua 1:8 and Psalm 1:2 would be grounds for establishing 24/7

---

[10] Ibid.

[11] Fasting guidelines on the International House of Prayer website state that fasting is always voluntary and can never be forced or made compulsory. But even though the Global Bridegroom Fast is not forced on particular individuals, it is still presented as a practice that must be embraced by many people in the church for God's end-time purposes to be realized. Thus, it is not a compulsory practice for a particular individual, but it does seem to be compulsory for the corporate church, or at least a large segment of it. See "Fasting Guidelines and Information," International House of Prayer, accessed February 23, 2014, http://www.ihopkc.org/about/fasting-guidelines-and-information.

[12] Mike Bickle, "What the Spirit Is Saying about the Church," Mike Bickle. org; accessed May 6, 2014, http://www.mikebickle.org.edgesuite.net/MikeBickleVOD/2010/20101014_What_the_Holy_Spirit_Is_Emphasizing_in_this_Generation_IPP3.pdf.

[13] Ibid.

Bible-reading rooms. (We hope no one thinks we're promoting a new essential practice for the church! But it might not be a bad idea for people to read the Bible.) While Scripture reading is an essential practice for Christian maturity, establishing special rooms where Scripture is read non-stop around the clock is not essential. The same holds for establishing special 24/7 prayer rooms.

LOOSING JUDGMENTS AND BECOMING IMMORTAL

Some influential NAR leaders teach that their followers will grow in miraculous gifting until they can overcome sickness and death and execute God's judgments described in the book of Revelation. Here again we encounter teachings that cannot be found in Scripture.

The teaching about overcoming sickness and death is based on a faulty interpretation of Romans 8:19–23. This passage does speak of an end-time event when Christians will experience the redemption of their mortal bodies into immortal bodies. But this redemption will not occur piecemeal or progressively as Christians adopt new truths revealed by present-day apostles and prophets. Rather, this redemption will occur all at once and instantaneously (1 Cor. 15:52). And it will be accomplished solely by Christ, without the meddling of apostles or prophets, and quite apart from adopting any new truths taught by newly minted apostles and prophets. How wonderful the truth exclaimed by the apostle Paul: "But our citizenship is in heaven, and from it we await a Savior, the Lord Jesus Christ, who will transform our lowly body to be like his glorious body, by the power that enables him even to subject all things to himself" (Phil. 3:20–21).

Another NAR teaching (that of Hamon) is that the church is a type of corporate Christ. The New Testament does use the term "Christ's body" as a metaphor for the church. This image depicts the reality that Christ indwells believers and works through the church. But it emphatically does not authorize the abhorrent idea that the church literally becomes Christ. Scripture also teaches that Christians become "partakers of the divine nature" (2 Peter 1:4). But this promises that Christians, indwelt by God's Holy Spirit, will be made into the image or likeness of Christ so that they will become holy as well. The idea that human persons, regenerate or not, can somehow attain deity—either individually or corporately—is a manifest heresy. We hope Hamon can demonstrate that this is not his view. We urge other NAR leaders, including those who warmly endorse Hamon's books,[14] to demonstrate their solidarity with classical Christianity on these points. If they do not, then NAR followers may become confused about what they mean and fall into serious error.

Bickle is to be commended for rejecting extreme expressions of the Manifest Sons of God doctrine. A statement on the IHOP website is helpful:

> We affirm that all born-again believers will be "manifest" as sons of God after the second coming of Christ.
>
> We deny that we will experience the fullness of our inheritance as sons of God before Jesus returns.
>
> Explanation: Some uphold the false teaching that in this age believers can have faith that will enable them to attain to qualities of life that are reserved only for believers in the resurrection.[15]

This point of clarification doesn't state which qualities of life are reserved for believers after Christ's return. Perhaps immortality is to be included. Bickle does claim to be forming an end-time movement of people who will develop unprecedented miraculous power and loose God's judgments on earth prior to Christ's return. These capacities are for the here and now and are not postponed until the resurrection of the saints. So there remains some mystery about his perspective on the Manifest Sons of God teaching.

That end-time Christians will loose God's judgments cannot be supported by Scripture. Those scholars who believe the church will join Christ in executing judgments on the nations (Rev. 19:14) also believe that the judgments denoted here concern spiritual warfare, not the passing of literal judgment. Others hold that if these are literal judgments, then they will be loosed after Christ's return, not before. The question of timing matters, since the judgments will be executed under Christ's physically present leadership and direction after he returns. Then, too, Christians will receive their

---

[14]   His books have been endorsed by many well-known NAR leaders, including C. Peter Wagner, Cindy Jacobs, and David Cannistraci—and they are sold by IHOP's Forerunner Bookstore.

[15]   Ernest Gruen and Mike Bickle, "Affirmations and Denials: Ernie Gruen and Mike Bickle's Joint Statement From 1993," International House of Prayer, May 16, 1993; accessed December 10, 2013, http://www.ihopkc.org/about/affirmations-and-denials.

glorified bodies and be completely free of sin. No sinful motivations will interfere with the execution of justice as the true sons of God join Christ in this sobering task.

Apparently, Bickle believes that Christians will loose judgments on unbelievers through their prayers prior to Christ's return and prior to their glorification and complete sanctification. If true, it is a terrible truth, fraught with potential for abuse and the introduction of great injustice. Jesus rebuked James and John when they presumed to call down fire from heaven on people who had rejected Jesus (Luke 9:54–55).

SUMMARY

In summary, there is no biblical support for NAR teachings about the rise of a miracle-working army that will perform greater miracles than those performed by Jesus or the apostles of Christ. Furthermore, Scripture nowhere commends the notion of training miracle-workers. No place in Scripture encourages the conviction that men and women may increase in miraculous power until they overcome sickness and death and execute God's judgments.

Conclusion

Our aim has been to present a biblical response to the New Apostolic Reformation. We have made every effort to describe the movement fully and accurately, and have sought to evaluate it fairly, with careful attention to the logic of the NAR proponents' position and their appeals to Scripture.

We have argued that the Bible does not support the NAR teaching that present-day apostles and prophets must govern the church. Nor does it support the teaching that they are revealing new truths the church needs for it to advance God's kingdom, including new teachings and practices that will enable the church to become an end-time, miracle-working army.

This extremist view of contemporary apostles and prophets is best seen in the details of NAR teachings. While there are more traditional expressions of conviction about the gifts of apostle and prophet today, the New Apostolic Reformation clearly demarcates a new development within today's religious milieu. It should not be confused with mainstream teachings among noncessationists, including mainstream Pentecostals and charismatics. Confusing the two, however, places those with more conventional convictions about these things at risk. Discernment is needed if believers are to understand the actual dynamics of the New Apostolic Reformation and identify where it departs from traditional teachings.

If the details of our exposition and our assessment are correct, then it's incumbent on Christians to resist association with this extremist movement and to be wary of its infiltration of our churches. We believe it is more dangerous to claim authority as a NAR apostle or prophet if he or she is mistaken, than it is to challenge the movement if its claims should turn out to be right. God will honor the determination of every believer to be as discerning as possible in consideration of these things. The discernment God desires from us is available to us quite apart from dependence on the word of a supposed prophet or apostle. That's how it always has been. Our chief means of discernment is responsible study of the Bible and common sense in obedience to the express commands of God and in partnership with the Holy Spirit (John 7:17; 16:13; Acts 17:11).

Appendix A

The Great Chain of Prophets

We have argued against present-day prophets who govern the church, prophesy to nations, or reveal new truths that are binding on all Christians. One reason for doing so is, we suggest, that biblical prophets were linked in a continuous chain of divine revelation, stretching across many centuries, going back to Moses right on through to the ministry of Jesus. While there were intervals when no new revelation was given, there were no gaps in the chain of prophets itself. A natural progression in the chain was ensured by major overlapping themes in their prophecies and important indicators of new revelation to come.

This challenges NAR claims that God intended for a great company of present-day prophets to reveal new truths to the universal church. If he did intend this, then why is there not greater overlap with earlier links in the chain of revelation? Why is the new revelation of NAR prophets not anticipated earlier in the chain?

LINKS IN THE CHAIN

Most Jews of the Second Temple period (516 BC to AD 70) believed that prophets who gave universally authoritative revelation—that is, revelation that is binding on all God's people—ceased after Malachi. That is not to say they believed that all types of prophecy ceased. The popular notion that all types of prophecy ceased in Israel has been challenged by a number of scholars, who have argued that many Jews during the intertestamental period were seen as having the gift of prophecy or certain types of prophetic abilities.[1] But these prophetically gifted Jews were not, generally, regarded as giving revelation on an authoritative par with Old Testament canonical revelation.

---

[1] See, for example, David E. Aune, *Prophecy in Early Christianity and the Ancient Mediterranean World* (Grand Rapids: Eerdmans, 1983; repr., Eugene, OR: Wipf and Stock, 2003), 103–6.

Moses had predicted a series of prophets—successive links in the chain—who would come on the scene after his own death (Deut. 18:15–19). These prophets would be like Moses, they would provide revelation for the nation of Israel, and they would come from among the Israelites' own countrymen, that is, from Israel.

Malachi, the last prophet of the Old Testament, had predicted a reintroduction of prophets into the stream of Israel's history with the coming of another prophet like Elijah. Thus, Malachi foretold a new link in the chain of revelation, a chain originating with Moses.

Malachi was the last link in this chain of prophets in the Hebrew Bible (i.e., the Old Testament). His prediction of a prophet like Elijah (Mal. 4:5) was fulfilled by John the Baptist. John, in turn, predicted the rise of a prophet greater than himself, and considered himself the forerunner to this prophet named Jesus (Matt. 3:11–12; Luke 3:16–17; John 1:8; 1:26–27). Jesus eventually foretold the prophetic roles that the apostles would play in producing Scripture when he spoke of their receiving the word, from the Holy Spirit, that Jesus had received from the Father and taking it to others (John 16:13–16). Jesus said, in effect, that anyone who believed his message should believe the apostles, for they were his messengers, delivering the message they had received from Jesus, who had received it from the Father (John 16:15). The apostles formed a community of authoritative messengers whose word was received because of their immediate connection with Jesus. We should acknowledge and anticipate any prophecy that they might in turn anticipate.

As it happens, the apostles did point to the next event on God's revelatory calendar. This is spoken of by the apostle John in the book of Revelation.

> *The revelation of Jesus Christ, which God gave him to show to his servants the things that must soon take place. He made it known by sending his angel to his servant John, who bore witness to the word of God and to the testimony of Jesus Christ, even to all that he saw. Blessed is the one who reads aloud the words of this prophecy, and blessed are those who hear, and who keep what is written in it, for the time is near.* (Rev 1:1–3)

This Revelation concludes:

> *And he said to me, "Do not seal up the words of the prophecy of this book, for the time is near . . .*

Behold, I am coming soon, bringing my recompense with me, to repay everyone for what he has done. . . .

The Spirit and the Bride say, "Come." And let the one who hears say, "Come." . . . He who testifies to these things says, "Surely I am coming soon." Amen. Come, Lord Jesus!

The grace of the Lord Jesus be with all. Amen. (Rev 22:10, 12, 17, 20–21)

The return of Christ is the next great event on God's revelatory calendar. We note that, in association with Christ's return, Revelation also predicts the rise of "two witnesses"—two prophets whose words will have authority over people of all nations (Rev. 11:5–6, 9–10). Perhaps they, too, are links in the chain.

So we see that the pattern continues. Every new link in the chain of universally authoritative revelation is anticipated, and then fulfilled. Every step in the progression of revelation follows a peculiar pattern: prophecy as to what will come next, its purpose, and how it will be recognized, a hiatus, then fulfillment, consistent with what was predicted.

WAITING FOR THE NEXT LINK

What does this mean for Christians today? It means that we are presently living during a cessation of universally authoritative revelation. But what should Christians do as they await Christ's return? We can look to the Israelites to see what they did during the approximately four hundred years after the Old Testament period while awaiting the next expected event in God's prophetic calendar, the arrival of a new Elijah (Mal. 4:4–6). The last words in the prophecy of Malachi are instructive.

Remember the law of my servant Moses, the statutes and rules that I commanded him at Horeb for all Israel.

Behold, I will send you Elijah the prophet before the great and awesome day of the LORD comes. And he will turn the hearts of fathers to their children and the hearts of children to their fathers, lest I come and strike the land with a decree of utter destruction. (Mal. 4:4–6)

That is quite an ending—or the beginning of an interlude, if you will. Notice two significant features of these final words of the Old Testament.

First, the people of Israel are hereby put on notice that they are to listen to the word of the Lord through the law of Moses and they are to obey his commands. Second, they are to anticipate another prophet, one like Elijah, who will appear prior to "the great and awesome day of the LORD."

Malachi's listeners are told, in effect, that the next great event in the chain of revelation would come at the arrival of this Elijah, and that the people of Israel are to study and obey the law of Moses in the meantime. What ensued was not meant to be a period of four hundred silent years, but a period of close listening to the God of Hebrew Scripture through the writings the people had received over the centuries. During the cessation of universal revelation following Malachi, the Israelites had the law and the prophets for their continued exhortation and guidance.

We see Malachi's instructions put into practice by Ezra, who ministered after Malachi and, thus, after the (temporary) cessation of universally authoritative prophecy. What did this leader of Israel—who was not a prophet and who, apparently, had no contact with prophets—do during this time? He devoted himself to the study of Scripture: "For Ezra had set his heart to study the Law of the LORD, and to do it and to teach his statutes and rules in Israel" (Ezra 7:10).

Christians today should follow suit. Though universally authoritative revelation has ceased, believers are not left with silence but with God's Word in both the Old and New Testaments. As we await the next great event on God's revelatory calendar—the return of Christ—we do well if we give ourselves to the careful study of Scripture, and look not to so-called new truths from present-day prophets.

Appendix B

Todd Bentley's Commissioning and Apostolic Decrees

Apostolic decrees are among the most powerful tools for transforming society, according to leaders in the New Apostolic Reformation. What is an apostolic decree? An apostolic decree irreversibly settles some aspect of the future with authoritative proclamations that release God's power. Or, as C. Peter Wagner puts it: "In proclamation, we are not asking God to do something. We are declaring, with the authority of God, that such-and-such a thing that we know to be the will of God will happen."[1]

Wagner says that both petition and proclamation are taught in Scripture. He writes: "The two forms of tapping into divine authority are described in Job 22. The petition form is in verse 27: 'You will make your *prayer* to Him, He will hear you, and you will pay your vows.' The proclamation form is in verse 28: 'You will also *declare* a thing, and it will be established for you; so light will shine on your ways [Wagner's emphasis]."[2]

God wants apostles to go beyond making petitions to issuing decrees, says Wagner. He points to a well-known event in the Old Testament to illustrate an apostolic decree.

> A case in point is Moses on the banks of the Red Sea. "And the Lord said to Moses, 'Why do you cry to me? Tell the children of Israel to go forward. But lift up your rod and stretch out your hand over the sea and divide it. And the children of Israel shall go on dry ground through the midst of the sea'" (Exod. 14:15–16). God told Moses specifically that intercession "crying to me" would not do it in this case; an apostolic decree was necessary.[3]

Wagner also says that proclamation, not petition, was used in every instance of raising the dead in the New Testament. He concludes that "this

---

[1] C. Peter Wagner, *Dominion!: How Kingdom Action Can Change the World* (Grand Rapids: Chosen Books, 2008), 134.

[2] C. Peter Wagner, *Apostles Today: Biblical Government for Biblical Power* (Ventura, CA: Regal Books, 2006), 82.

[3] Ibid.

may indicate that the higher the level of prayer, the more that proclamation rather than petition is called for."[4]

A controversial and highly publicized apostolic decree was made on June 23, 2008, when Todd Bentley was formally commissioned as an evangelist to lead the Lakeland Revival in Florida. Under Wagner's leadership, prominent apostles gathered for the ceremony, which was broadcast worldwide by GOD TV. The purpose of the ceremony was to decree the apostolic alignment of Bentley with three apostles—Ché Ahn of Pasadena, California; Bill Johnson of Redding, California; and John Arnott of Toronto, Canada.[5] By becoming apostolically aligned with these three apostles, who represent an apostolic network called Revival Alliance, Bentley was agreeing to come under their authority. This is in line with the NAR teaching that all offices of the church, including the office of evangelist, must submit to apostles.

During the ceremony, Wagner referred to Ahn, Johnson, and Arnott as "apostolic pillars of today's church."[6] He also compared their commissioning of Bentley to similar events in the book of Acts, when three apostles—James,[7] Cephas, and John—extended the right hand of fellowship to Paul and Barnabas. Wagner stated that the "commissioning represents a powerful transaction taking place in the invisible world," then said: "I take the apostolic authority that God has given me, and I decree to Todd Bentley: your power will increase. Your authority will increase. Your favor will increase. Your influence will increase. Your revelation will increase. I also decree that a new supernatural strength will flow through this ministry [the Lakeland Revival]."[8]

---

[4]   Wagner, *Dominion!*, 135.

[5]   Chuck Pierce and C. Peter Wagner, "Florida Outpouring Receives Endorsements and Oversight—Includes Chuck Pierce, C. Peter Wagner, and More," The Elijah List, July 2, 2008; accessed February 20, 2014, http://www.elijahlist.com/words/display_word/6611.

[6]   "Todd Bentley's Apostolic and Prophetic Commissioning, Part 1 of 4," YouTube video, 10:01, posted by "Dominic Muir," June 24, 2008; accessed February 25, 2014, http://www.youtube.com/watch?v=nVdY9ufJmz8.

[7]   There is debate as to whether James, Jesus's half-brother and a leader of the church in Jerusalem, was an apostle or merely an influential leader who worked closely with the apostles.

[8]   "Todd Bentley's Apostolic and Prophetic Commissioning."

But less than two months after this apostolic decree was issued, Bentley announced that he and his wife were separating, and he abruptly abandoned the revival. Following on the heels of his announcement were reports that he had been drinking excessively during the revival and that he had become inappropriately involved with one of his female staff members.[9] Bentley later married this woman. Soon after he stepped down, the revival fizzled out completely.

The apparent failure of this particular apostolic decree—issued by Wagner, one of today's most prominent apostles, along with three other "apostolic pillars"—raises serious doubt about the validity of apostolic decrees.

---

[9]   Adrienne S. Gaines, "Todd Bentley Remarries, Begins Restoration Process, *Charisma*, March 10, 2009; accessed February 20, 2014, http://www.charismamag. com/site-archives/570-news/featured-news/3974-todd-bentley-remarries-begins-restoration-process.

Appendix C

Prominent NAR Networks

We include this detailed list of prominent NAR networks to assist readers in identifying initiatives, organizations, ministries, and leaders associated with the movement. We've critically evaluated many of the tenets promoted within these networks. This list brings together many of the agents at work within the New Apostolic Reformation.

INTERNATIONAL COALITION OF APOSTOLIC LEADERS (ICAL), FORMERLY THE INTERNATIONAL COALITION OF APOSTLES (ICA)[1]

This coalition, based in Fort Worth, Texas, was founded in 1999. It is the largest network of apostles in the world, made up of approximately four hundred apostles from forty-five nations.[2] Its stated purpose is "to connect each member's wisdom and resources in order to function more strategically, combine their efforts globally, and effectively accelerate the advancement of the Kingdom of God on earth."[3] The coalition holds annual meetings and regional and international summits. Membership is restricted to those who receive a formal invitation from the convening apostle, after nomination by two members. The annual membership fee for a US apostle, as of December

---

[1]   Under John P. Kelly's leadership, in 2013 the International Coalition of Apostles was renamed the International Coalition of Apostolic Leaders. A reason given for the name change is that the council members had "a sense that many apostles around the world don't feel comfortable with calling themselves 'apostle,' for instance within the worlds of evangelicalism and Pentecostalism." See "Why the Name Change?," European Coalition of Apostolic Leaders, November 16, 2013; accessed December 27, 2013, http://ecaleaders.eu/maler/convenors-blog/article/329181.

[2]   "Connecting Apostles for Kingdom Advancement," Oslokirken, November 17, 2012; accessed February 20, 2014, http://www.oslochurch.org/maler/article/article/131282.

[3]   "A Word from John P. Kelly, Convening Apostle," International Coalition of Apostolic Leaders, accessed February 20, 2014, http://www.coalitionofapostles.com.

2013, was $450. The coalition stopped making its membership list available to the public in 2010. In the years prior to that, influential people who were named as apostles in the coalition included, among others:[4]

- E. H. Jim Ammerman of Chaplaincy Full Gospel Churches
- Harold Caballeros, former minister of foreign affairs of Guatemala
- Dick Eastman of Every Home for Christ
- J. Lee Grady of *Charisma* magazine
- Ted Haggard, former president of the National Association of Evangelicals
- Jane Hansen Hoyt of Aglow International
- Chris Hayward of Cleansing Streams Ministries
- Cal Pierce of Healing Rooms Ministries
- Samuel Rodriguez of National Hispanic Christian Leadership Conference
- David Shibley of Global Advance
- Ed Silvoso of Harvest Evangelism
- Brian Simmons of Stairway Ministries
- Stephen Strang of Charisma Media
- J. Doug Stringer of Somebody Cares International
- Héctor Torres of Hispanic International Ministries

Though the general membership list is no longer made public, the members of the coalition's leadership council—called the Apostolic Council—are publicly identified.[5] As of November 2013, they included:

- Joseph Adewale Adefasarin from Lagos, Nigeria (organization unknown)
- Naomi Dowdy of Naomi Dowdy Ministries in Singapore
- Paul Gitwaza of Zion Temple Celebration Center and Authentic Word Ministry in Rwanda
- Carlos Gordillo from Mexico (organization unknown)
- Bill Hamon of Christian International Ministries Network in Santa Rosa Beach, Florida

---

[4]   The website *Talk to Action* has compiled a collection of membership lists from previous years. See "International Coalition of Apostles Membership Lists," *Talk to Action*, September 3, 2011, accessed December 19, 2013, http://www.talk2action.org/story/2011/9/3/9571/00192.

[5]   "Why the Name Change?," ECAL.

- Joseph Mattera of Mattera Ministries International in Brooklyn, New York
- John McNamara of Parkway Church in Canberra, Australia
- Mel Mullen of Word of Life Centre in Red Deer, Alberta, Canada
- Rene Terra Nova of International Restoration Ministries in Manaus, Brazil
- Mark W. Pfeifer of Open Door Ministries in Chillicothe, Ohio
- Jan-Aage Torp of Oslochurch in Oslo, Norway
- C. Peter Wagner of Global Spheres in Corinth, Texas
- Lance Wallnau of Lance Learning in Keller, Texas
- Barbara Wentroble of International Breakthrough Ministries In Argyle, Texas

In association with ICAL, the European Coalition of Apostolic Leaders has been formed, along with forty-five national coalitions, including:

- Australian Coalition of Apostles
- Canadian Coalition of Apostles
- Coalition of Apostles in the Solomon Islands
- Coalition of Nigerian Apostles
- Ecuadorian Coalition of Apostles
- Honduran Coalition of Apostles
- Mexican Coalition of Apostles
- Papua New Guinea Coalition of Apostles
- Puerto Rican Coalition of Apostles
- South African Coalition of Apostles
- Zimbabwean Coalition of Apostles[6]

APOSTOLIC COUNCIL OF PROPHETIC ELDERS (ACPE)

This council of prophets, formed in 1999, meets together before the start of each year to pray and receive revelation from God. They compile the revelations they receive and release an annual "Word of the Lord," which is published by many organizations, including *Charisma* magazine. Membership is by invitation only and includes approximately 20 to 25 persons at any

---

[6] "2014 National Coalitions," International Coalition of Apostolic Leaders, accessed December 19, 2013, http://www.coalitionofapostles.com/membership/national-coalitions/.

given time. The full membership list is no longer made public, but individuals who have been identified as either present or former members include:[7]

- Elizabeth Alves, an author and former long-time board member of Aglow International
- Mike Bickle of the International House of Prayer
- Paul Cain, honorary member, of Paul Cain Ministries
- Wesley and Stacey Campbell of Revival Now Ministries
- Kim Clement of Kim Clement Center
- Paul Keith Davis of White Dove Ministries
- Lou Engle of The Call
- Joseph Garlington of Covenant Church of Pittsburgh in Pennsylvania
- Ernest Gentile of Christian Community Church in San Jose, California
- Mary Glazier of Windwalkers International
- James Goll of Encounters Network
- Bill Hamon of Christian International
- Harry Jackson of Hope Christian Church in Beltsville, Maryland
- Cindy Jacobs, the convening apostle, and Mike Jacobs, both of Generals International
- Jim Laffoon of King's Park International Church in Durham, North Carolina
- Ong Sek Leang of Metro Tabernacle in Malaysia
- David McCracken of David MacCracken Ministries
- Bart Pierce of Rock City Church in Baltimore, Maryland

---

[7] These names are listed in prefaces to the Apostolic Council of Prophetic Elders "Word of the Lord" documents that have been published by the Elijah List through the years. See Steve Shultz, "2003 Word of the Lord—Apostolic Council of Prophetic Elders," The Elijah List, February 24, 2003; accessed February 25, 2014, https://www.elijahlist.com/words/display_word.html?ID=1409; C. Peter Wagner, Cindy Jacobs, et al., "Word of the Lord for 2007—Released through the Apostolic Council of Prophetic Elders," The Elijah List, November 1, 2006; accessed February 25, 2014, http://www.elijahlist.com/words/display_word/4655. We note that past involvement by individuals with this council, or any other NAR group, need not indicate that they are NAR themselves. They may not have known at the time of their initial involvement what the council's purposes and objectives are; the council also may have evolved and become more easily identifiable as NAR later on.

- Chuck Pierce of Global Spheres
- Rick Ridings of Succat Hallel in Jerusalem
- John and Paula Sandford of Elijah House
- Michael Schiffman of Chevra USA
- Gwen Shaw of End-Time Handmaidens and Servants International
- Dutch Sheets of Dutch Sheets Ministries
- Steve Shultz of the Elijah List
- Jean Steffenson of Native American Resource Network
- Sharon Stone of Christian International Europe
- Tommy Tenny of GodChasers Network
- Héctor Torres of Hispanic International Ministries
- C. Peter Wagner of Global Spheres, with his wife, Doris Wagner
- Barbara Wentroble of International Breakthrough Ministries
- Dominic Yeo of Trinity Christian Centre in Singapore
- Barbara Yoder of Shekinah Regional Apostolic Center in Ann Arbor, Michigan

REVIVAL ALLIANCE

This alliance is made up of six major organizations:[8]

- Bethel Church in Redding, California (Bill and Beni Johnson)
- Catch the Fire Ministries in Ontario, Canada (John and Carol Arnott)
- Global Awakening in Mechanicsburg, Pennsylvania (Randy and DeAnne Clark)
- Global Celebration in Valrico, Florida (Georgian and Winnie Banov)
- HRock Church in Pasadena, California (Ché and Sue Ahn)
- Iris Ministries in Redding, California (Rolland and Heidi Baker)

A Revival Alliance Conference, held January 21–24, 2014, in Toronto, Canada, celebrated the twenty-year anniversary of the Toronto Blessing revival.

UNITED STATES REFORMATION PRAYER NETWORK

This fifty-state network was founded by Cindy Jacobs of Generals International in Red Oak, Texas. It seeks to mobilize 500,000 intercessors—10,000

---

[8]   Revival Alliance website, accessed June 6, 2014, http://revivalalliance.com.

in each US state—to targeted prayer and action for the purpose of reforming the United States back to its biblical roots. The type of prayer—or "reformation intercession"—advocated by Jacobs involves NAR practices of strategic-level spiritual warfare, including spiritual mapping and the binding of evil territorial spirits.[9]

HEARTLAND APOSTOLIC PRAYER NETWORK

This apostolic network, founded in 2006 under the apostle John Benefiel in Oklahoma City, Oklahoma, seeks to "change the heart of America and the Nations." One of the initiatives promoted by the Heartland Apostolic Prayer Network is known as Divorcing Baal, which involves leading individuals and corporate groups of Christians in making an official prophetic "decree of divorce" from an evil demonic principality identified as Baal. This network claims to have a leader and network in all fifty US states and to be represented in fifty nations.

OTHER APOSTOLIC PRAYER NETWORKS IN THE UNITED STATES

Numerous apostolic prayer networks have formed in US states, many affiliated with the United States Reformation Prayer Network and the Heartland Apostolic Prayer Network. These apostolic networks include:

- Arkansas Apostolic Prayer Network
- Colorado Concert of Prayer
- Florida Apostolic Prayer Network
- Illinois Apostolic Prayer Network
- Indiana Apostolic Prayer Network
- Louisiana Apostolic Prayer Network
- Minnesota Apostolic Prayer Network
- Missouri Prayer Global Mission
- New England Apostolic Prayer Network
- Ohio Reformation Prayer Network
- Oklahoma Apostolic Prayer Network
- Power Grid Apostolic Network (Kansas)
- Pray New York
- Texas Apostolic Prayer Network

---

[9] Cindy Jacobs, *Reformation Manifesto: Your Part in God's Plan to Change Nations Today* (Minneapolis: Bethany House, 2008), 180–96.

Bibliography

"About ICAL." International Coalition of Apostolic Leaders. Accessed December 26, 2013. http://www.coalitionofapostles.com/about-ica.

"About the Freedom Federation." Freedom Federation. Accessed February 25, 2014. http://freedomfederation.org/content/about.

"ACPE Word of the Lord for 2014." *Generals News*, January 29, 2014. Accessed February 1, 2014. Generals International. http://www.generals.org/news/single-view/article/acpe-word-of-the-lord-for-2014.

"AD2000 United Prayer Track Launches Praying Through the Window II: 'The 100 Gateway Cities.'" *Mission Frontiers*, March 1, 1995. Accessed August 11, 2011. http://www.missionfrontiers.org/issue/article/ad2000-united-prayer-track-launches-praying-through-the-window-ii-the-100-g.

Alec, Wendy. *Journal of the Unknown Prophet: Legacy to a Renegade Generation.* N.p.: UK: Warboys Media, 2002.

"Apostles and Prophets." General Presbytery of the Assemblies of God, August 6, 2001. Accessed September 29, 2010. http://ag.org/top/Beliefs/Position_Papers/pp_downloads/pp_4195_apostles_prophets.pdf.

Arnold, Clinton E., *Ephesians*. Zondervan Exegetical Commentary on the New Testament. Grand Rapids: Zondervan, 2010.

———. *3 Crucial Questions about Spiritual Warfare*. 3 Crucial Questions. Grand Rapids: Baker, 1997.

Assemblies of God. *Minutes of the Twenty-third General Council of the Assemblies of God, Convened at Seattle, Washington, September 9–14, 1949: With Constitution and Bylaws, Revised*. Springfield, MO: General Council of the Assemblies of God, 1949. Flower Pentecostal Heritage Center. http://ifphc.org/DigitalPublications/USA/Assemblies%20of%20God%20USA/Minutes%20General%20Council/Unregistered/1949/FPHC/1949.pdf. PDF e-book.

Aune, David E. *Prophecy in Early Christianity and the Ancient Mediterranean World*. Grand Rapids: Eerdmans, 1983. Reprint, Eugene, OR: Wipf and Stock, 2003.

Austin, Michael W., and R. Douglas Geivett, eds. *Being Good: Christian Virtues for Everyday Life*. Grand Rapids: Eerdmans, 2012.

"The Awakening 2012 Speakers." Freedom Federation. Accessed June 6, 2014. http://freedomfederation.org/content/awakening_2012_speakers.

"The Awakening 2012 Speakers, Page 2." Freedom Federation. Accessed June 6, 2014. http://freedomfederation.org//content/awakening_2012_speakers2.

"The Awakening Schedule: April 15–16, 2010." Freedom Federation. Accessed June 6, 2014. http://freedomfederation.org/content/schedule.

Barnett, P. W. "Apostle." In *Dictionary of Paul and His Letters*, edited by Gerald F. Hawthorne and Ralph P. Martin. Downers Grove, IL: InterVarsity Press, 1993.

Barron, Bruce. *Heaven on Earth? The Social and Political Agendas of Dominion Theology*. Grand Rapids: Zondervan, 1992.

Bauer, Walter. *A Greek-English Lexicon of the New Testament and other Early Christian Literature* (BDAG). 3rd ed. Revised and edited by Frederick William Danker. Chicago: University of Chicago Press, 2000.

Berding, Kenneth. *What Are Spiritual Gifts? Rethinking the Conventional View*. Grand Rapids: Kregel Publications, 2006.

Bevere, John. *Under Cover: The Promise of Protection Under His Authority*. Nashville, TN: Thomas Nelson, 2001.

Bickle, Mike. "Bob Jones' Discipline." Undated transcript of a recording on audiocassette [November 1991?]. In the authors' possession.

———. "Encountering Jesus Disc 1." Audio recording, 57:32. The Internet Archive. N.d. Accessed September 2, 2014. https://archive.org/details/EncounteringJesus.

———. *Growing in the Prophetic: A Practical, Biblical Guide to Dreams, Visions, and Spiritual Gifts*. Rev. ed. Lake Mary, FL: Charisma House, 2008. Mike Bickle. org. Accessed August 14, 2014. http://mikebickle.org/books. PDF e-book.

———. "IHOP TV Podcast 3." YouTube video, 10:59. Posted by "onething TV." December 3, 2008. Accessed September 2, 2014. http://www.youtube.com/watch?v=K5FMsDrNyn4.

———. "A Message from Mike Bickle." Video. International House of Prayer. November 29, 2012. http://www.ihopkc.org/prayerroom/#asset/zj9i9b37/auto/true.

———. "Session 1: Introduction and Overview of the Book of Revelation." *Studies in the Book of Revelation*. Twelve-part series taught at the International House of Prayer University. Spring Semester 2014. MikeBickle.org. Accessed May 6, 2014. http://www.mikebickle.org.edgesuite.net/MikeBickleVOD/2014/20140207_Introduction_and_Overview_of_the_Book_of_Revelation_BOR01_study%20notes.pdf.

———. "Session 2: Explosion of Light, the White Horse, and the Chariots." *Encountering Jesus: Visions, Revelations, and Angelic Activity from IHOP-KC's Prophetic History*. Transcript, April 25, 2011. MikeBickle.org. Accessed September 2, 2014. http://www.mikebickle.org.edgesuite.net/MikeBickleVOD/2011/20110425_T_Explosion_of_Light_the_White_Horse_and_the_Chariots_IPH02.pdf.

———. "Session 2: Great Light, White Horse, Chariot, and Sands of Time." *Prophetic History*. International House of Prayer. [September 18, 2009?] Accessed September 28, 2009. http://www.ihopkc.org/resources/files/2011/09/PH02-_Friday_AM_Great_Light_White_Horse_Chariot_and_Sands_of_TimeMS.pdf.

———. "Session 8: The Blueprint Prophecy and the Black Horse." *Encountering Jesus: Visions, Revelations, Angelic Visitations from IHOP-KC's Prophetic History*. Transcript, September 19, 2009. MikeBickle.org. Accessed August 15, 2014. http://www.mikebickle.org.edgesuite.net/MikeBickleVOD/2009/20090919C-T-The_Blueprint_Prophecy_and_the_Black_Horse_IPH08.pdf.

———. *The Seven Longings of the Human Heart*. Kansas City, MO: Forerunner Books, 2006. Mike Bickle.org. Accessed August 15, 2014. http://mikebickle.org/books. PDF e-book.

———. *Studies in the Book of Revelation*. Twelve-part series taught at the International House of Prayer University. Spring Semester 2014. MikeBickle.org. Accessed May 6, 2014. http://mikebickle.org/resources/series/studies-in-the-book-of-revelation.

———. "What the Spirit is Saying about the Church." Mike Bickle.org. Accessed May 6, 2014. http://www.mikebickle.org.edgesuite.net/MikeBickleVOD/2010/20101014_What_the_Holy_Spirit_Is_Emphasizing_in_this_Generation_IPP3.pdf.

Bickle, Mike, and Dana Candler. *The Rewards of Fasting: Experiencing the Power and Affections of God*. Kansas City, MO: Forerunner Books, 2005. Mike Bickle.org. Accessed August 14, 2014. http://mikebickle.org/books. PDF e-book.

Bickle, Mike, Jack Deere, and Rick Joyner. "Update on Paul Cain, Part 5." MorningStar Ministries. 2007. Accessed February 19, 2014. http://www.morningstarministries.org/resources/special-bulletins/2007/update-paul-cain-part-5#.UwRurYV6V8o.

"Bill Hamon Prophecy." Kids in Ministry International. Accessed February 20, 2014. http://kidsinministry.org/bill-hamon-prophecy.

"Biography [of Rory and Wendy Alec]." GOD TV. Accessed February 19, 2014. http://www.god.tv/rory_and_wendy/biography.

Blomberg, Craig L., and Jennifer Foutz. *A Handbook of New Testament Exegesis.* Grand Rapids: Baker Academic, 2010.

"Bob Jones Memorial Service." GOD TV video, 88:07, February 21, 2014. Accessed June 13, 2014. http://www.god.tv/bob-jones-ministries/video/bob-jones-memorial-service/bob-jones-memorial-service.

Bowman, Robert M., Jr., Craig S. Hawkins, and Dan R. Schlesinger. "The Gospel According to Paulk: A Critique of 'Kingdom Theology.'" *Christian Research Journal* 11, no. 1 (Summer 1988): 15.

"'Breakthrough' Kingdom Outpouring Conference and Miracle Impartation Nights, Nashville, TN; September 24–27." The Elijah List. August 3, 2008. Accessed August 15, 2014. http://www.elijahlist.com/words/display_word/6710.

Burer, Michael H., and Daniel B. Wallace. "Was Junia Really an Apostle? A Re-examination of Rom 16.7." *New Testament Studies* 47 (2001): 76–91.

Cain, Paul. "Stadium Vision." *The Paul Cain Blog.* April 16, 2006. Accessed February 27, 2014. http://paulcain.blogspot.com.

"California Root 52 Report." Generals International. August 13–20, 2010. Accessed May 6, 2014. http://www.generals.org/prayer/root-52/prayer-reports/california-report/.

"The Call California—November 1, 2008." TheCall. Accessed August 15, 2014. http://www.thecall.com/Groups/1000016919/TheCall/Gatherings/TheCall_Cali-forCal_Fall/TheCall_California_Fall.aspx.

"The Call Nashville: Senator Brownback." YouTube video, 7:58. Posted by "XSTATIC-MOM." July 18, 2007. Accessed February 24, 2014. http://www.youtube.com/watch?v=isOKfyriSfA.

"The Call San Diego: Dr. James Dobson." YouTube video, 4:37. Posted by "kdar-pa." November 3, 2008. Accessed June 6, 2014. https://www.youtube.com/watch?v=7NuwK18b6KI.

Calvin, John. *The Epistles of Paul the Apostle to the Galatians, Ephesians, Philippians and Colossians.* Calvin's New Testament Commentaries 11. Translated by T. H. L. Parker. Edited by David W. Torrance and Thomas F. Torrance. Grand Rapids: Eerdmans, 1996.

Cannistraci, David. *Apostles and the Emerging Apostolic Movement: A Biblical Look at Apostleship and How God is Using it to Bless His Church Today.* Ventura, CA: Renew Books, 1996.

Carson, D. A. *The Gospel according to John*. The Pillar New Testament Commentary. Grand Rapids: Eerdmans, 1991.

"Catherine Brown Prophecy." Kids in Ministry International. December 30, 2004. Accessed February 20, 2014. http://kidsinministry.org/catherine-brown-prophecy.

Chan, Francis. "Francis Chan Speaking at IHOP-KC's Onething 2013." YouTube video, 1:02:26. Posted by "BeautyforAshes 613." December 31, 2013. Accessed September 2, 2014. https://www.youtube.com/watch?v=yMy4hDMOMj4.

"Children's Ministry." Bethel Redding. Accessed February 20, 2014. http://bethelredding.com/ministries/children.

Clement, Kim. "Kim Clement Expounds On the Controversial 35-day Prophecy: 'Osama bin Laden Will be Uncovered.'" The Elijah List. March 5, 2004. Accessed August 15, 2014. https://www.elijahlist.com/words/display_word/1978.

Clement, Kim, Steve Shultz, and Bob Jones. "Kim Clement and Bob Jones 'Weigh In' on the March 11, 2004 Prophecy." The Elijah List. April 16, 2004. Accessed August 15, 2014. http://www.elijahlist.com/words/display_word/2095.

"Connecting Apostles for Kingdom Advancement." Oslokirken. November 17, 2012. Accessed February 20, 2014. http://www.oslochurch.org/maler/article/article/131282.

Dawson, John. *Taking Our Cities for God*. Lake Mary, FL: Charisma House, 1989.

Dedmon, Kevin. *The Ultimate Treasure Hunt: A Guide to Supernatural Evangelism through Supernatural Encounters*. Shippensburg, PA: Destiny Image Publishers, 2007. Kindle edition.

Devenish, David. *Fathering Leaders, Motivating Mission: Restoring the Role of the Apostle in Today's Church*. Milton Keynes, UK: Authentic Media Limited, 2011. Kindle edition.

DeWaay, Bob. "John the Baptist and Prophets to Nations." *Critical Issues Commentary* 67. November/December 2001. Accessed September 2, 2014. http://www.cicministry.org/commentary/issue67.htm.

"Dr. Bill Hamon's Story." Christian International Ministries Network. Accessed February 7, 2014. http://christianinternational.com/dr-bill-hamon.

Eberle, Harold, and Martin Trench. *Victorious Eschatology: A Partial Preterist View*. Yakima, WA: Worldcast Publishing, 2006.

Eckhardt, John. *Moving in the Apostolic: God's Plan to Lead His Church to the Final Victory*. Ventura, CA: Regal Books, 1999.

Elijah Streams Facebook page. Facebook. Accessed February 20, 2014. https://www.facebook.com/ElijahStreams/info.

"End-Time Revival—Spirit-Led and Spirit-Controlled: A Response Paper to Resolution 16." General Presbytery of the Assemblies of God. August 11, 2000. Accessed September 30, 2010. http://ag.org/top/Beliefs/Position_Papers/pp_downloads/pp_endtime_revival.pdf.

Enlow, Johnny. *The Seven Mountain Mantle: Receiving the Joseph Anointing to Reform Nations*. Lake Mary, FL: Creation House, 2009.

———. *The Seven Mountain Prophecy: Unveiling the Coming Elijah Revolution*. Lake Mary, FL: Creation House, 2008.

"Fasting Guidelines and Information." International House of Prayer. Accessed February 23, 2014. http://www.ihopkc.org/about/fasting-guidelines-and-information.

Fawcett, William. "Mike Bickle: The White Horse Prophecy." *Beyond Grace*. August 24, 2011. Accessed September 2, 2014. http://beyondgrace.blogspot.com/2011/08/mike-bickle-white-horse-prophecy.html.

"Final Day to Register for Our 'What Is God Saying for 2014?' Conference." The Elijah List. January 8, 2014. Accessed January 28, 2014. http://www.elijahlist.com/words/display_word.html?ID=12976.

Flinchbaugh, C. Hope. "Ignite the Fire." *Charisma*, February 28, 2007. Accessed February 20, 2014. http://www.charismamag.com/site-archives/146-covers/cover-story/2172-ignite-the-fire.

Freedom Federation website. http://freedomfederation.org.

Gaines, Adrienne S. "Todd Bentley Remarries, Begins Restoration Process." *Charisma*, March 10, 2009. Accessed February 20, 2014. http://www.charismamag:com/site-archives/570-news/featured-news/3974-todd-bentley-remarries-begins-restoration-process.

Geivett, R. Douglas, and Gary R. Habermas, eds. *In Defense of Miracles: A Comprehensive Case for God's Action in History*. Downers Grove, IL: IVP Academic, 1997.

Geivett, R. Douglas, and Paul K. Moser, eds., *The Testimony of the Spirit: New Essays* (forthcoming, Oxford University Press).

"Global Bridegroom Fast." International House of Prayer. Accessed December 3, 2013. http://www.ihopkc.org/about/global-bridegroom-fast.

Grady, J. Lee. "Prophetic Minister Paul Cain Issues Public Apology for Immoral Lifestyle." *Charisma*, February 28, 2005. Accessed February 4, 2014. http://www.charismamag.com/site-archives/154-peopleevents/people-

and-events/1514-prophetic-minister-paul-cain-issues-public-apology-for-immoral-lifestyle-.

Green, Matt. "Leaders Tackle Tough Integrity Issues." *Charisma*, n.d. Accessed June 6, 2014. http://www.charismamag.com/spirit/devotionals/daily-breakthroughs?view=article&id=1180:leaders-tackle-tough-integrity-issues&catid=154.

Green, Matthew, Jennifer LeClaire, Jackson Eckwugum, and J. Lee Grady. "Apostles Among Us." *Ministry Today* (Nov.-Dec. 2004). Accessed February 20, 2014. http://ministrytodaymag.com/index.php/ministry-today-archives/163-fivefold-ministries-focus/9982-apostles-among-us.

Groothuis, Douglas R. *Unmasking the New Age*. Downers Grove, IL: InterVarsity Press, 1986.

Grudem, Wayne A., ed. *Are Miraculous Gifts for Today? Four Views*. Grand Rapids: Zondervan, 1996.

———. *The Gift of Prophecy in the New Testament and Today*. Rev. ed. Wheaton, IL: Crossway, 1988; rev., 2000.

———. *Systematic Theology: An Introduction to Biblical Doctrine*. Grand Rapids: Zondervan, 1994.

Gruen, Ernest. *Documentation of the Aberrant Practices and Teachings of Kansas City Fellowship (Grace Ministries)*. Shawnee, KS: Full Faith Church of Love, 1990. Available online from Banner Ministries. Accessed June 29, 2014. http://www.banner.org.uk/kcp/Abberent%20Practises.pdf. PDF e-book.

———. *Thoughts and Ponderings*. Blog post, February 2, 2008. http://apollos.wordpress.com/2008/02/02/ernie-gruen/.

Gruen, Ernest, and Mike Bickle. "Affirmations and Denials: Ernie Gruen and Mike Bickle's Joint Statement From 1993." International House of Prayer. May 16, 1993. Accessed December 10, 2013. http://www.ihopkc.org/about/affirmations-and-denials.

Hall, Franklin. *Atomic Power with God with Fasting and Prayer*. 5th ed. Printed by author, 1946. Reprint, Phoenix, AZ: Hall Deliverance Foundation, 1992.

Hamon, Bill. *Apostles, Prophets, and the Coming Moves of God: God's End-Time Plans for His Church and Planet Earth*. Santa Rosa Beach, FL: Destiny Image Publishers, 1997.

———. *The Day of the Saints: Equipping Believers for Their Revolutionary Role in Ministry*. Shippensburg, PA: Destiny Image Publishers, 2002.

———. *The Eternal Church*. Santa Rosa Beach, FL: Christian International, 1981.

———. *Prophetic Scriptures Yet to Be Fulfilled: During the Third and Final Church Reformation*. Shippensburg, PA: Destiny Image Publishers, 2010.

———. *Prophets and Personal Prophecy: God's Prophetic Voice Today.* Shippensburg, PA: Destiny Image Publishers, 2001.

———. *Prophets and the Prophetic Movement: God's Prophetic Move Today.* Shippensburg, PA: Destiny Image Publishers, 2001.

———. *Prophets, Pitfalls and Principles: God's Prophetic People Today.* Shippensburg, PA: Destiny Image Publishers, 2001.

———. *Seventy Reasons for Speaking in Tongues: Your Own Built In Spiritual Dynamo.* Shippensburg, PA: Destiny Image Publishers, 2012.

Harmon, Cedric. "God's Lightning Rod." *Charisma,* March 31, 2001. http://www.charismamag.com/life/156-j15/features/issues-in-the-church/303-gods-lightning-rod.

Hayford, Jack. "A Watershed Moment." *Ministry Today,* n.d.; originally published in *Ministries Today* (March/April 2004). Accessed February 20, 2014. http://ministrytodaymag.com/index.php/ministry-today-archives/155-special-report/8629-a-watershed-moment#sthash.GYsTEGTT.dpuf.

Hilber, John W. "Diversity of OT Prophetic Phenomena and NT Prophecy." *Westminster Theological Journal* 56, no. 2 (1994): 243–58.

Hill, David. *New Testament Prophecy.* New Foundations Theological Library. Atlanta: John Knox Press, 1979.

"HIM Annual International Leadership Conference" Facebook page. Facebook. Accessed June 6, 2014. https://m2.facebook.com/events/118728981474114?_rdr.

Hirsch, Alan. Letter to the editor. *Books and Culture* (Sept.-Oct. 2012). Accessed December 20, 2013. http://www.booksandculture.com/articles/2012/sepoct/letters-so12.html.

Holvast, René. "Spiritual Mapping: The Turbulent Career of a Contested American Missionary Paradigm, 1989–2005." PhD Dissertation, Utrecht University, 2008. http://dspace.library.uu.nl/handle/1874/29340. PDF e-book.

"How It All Began." Destiny Image. Accessed February 25, 2014. http://www.destiny-image.com/about-us.

Hudson, Waymon. "American Evangelical Lou Engle Promotes 'Kill the Gays' Bill at Sunday's Rally in Uganda." *The Huffington Post.* May 4, 2010. Accessed December 11, 2012. http://www.huffingtonpost.com/waymon-hudson/american-evangelical-lou_b_560819.html.

"Imparting of Spiritual Gifts." Assemblies of God. Accessed November 12, 2013. http://ag.org/top/Beliefs/topics/sptlissues_imparting_spiritual_gifts.cfm.

"International Coalition of Apostles Membership Lists." *Talk to Action.* September 3, 2011. Accessed December 19, 2013. http://www.talk2action.org/story/2011/9/3/9571/00192.

"International House of Prayer (IHOP or IHOP-KC)." Apologetics Index. Accessed August 15, 2014. http://www.apologeticsindex.org/1212-international-house-of-prayer-ihop.

"The International Transformation Network." Harvest Evangelism. Accessed August 15, 2014. http://www.harvestevan.org/international-transformation-network1.html.

Jackson, Andrew. "Forerunner Eschatology: Mike Bickle's End-Time Teaching and the International House of Prayer." *Christian Research Journal* 32, no. 4 (2009). Accessed August 15, 2014. http://www.equip.org/PDF/JAF2324.pdf.

Jackson, Bill. *The Quest for the Radical Middle: A History of the Vineyard.* Cape Town, South Africa: Vineyard International Publishing, 1999. Kindle edition. Jacobs, Cindy. "Cindy Jacobs: 2011 ACPE Word of the Lord." The Elijah List. January 24, 2011. Accessed August 15, 2014. http://www.elijahlist.com/words/display_word/9526.

———. "Cindy's Mexico Report." *Generals News*, Generals International. May 2011. Accessed January 28, 2014. http://www.generals.org/news/single-view/article/cindys-mexico-report.

———. *The Power of Persistent Prayer: Praying With Greater Purpose and Passion.* Minneapolis: Bethany House, 2010.

———. *The Reformation Manifesto: Your Part in God's Plan to Change Nations Today.* Minneapolis: Bethany House, 2008.

Johnson, Bill. "Apostolic Teams—A Group of People Who Carry the Family Mission." The Elijah List. November 21, 2008. Accessed April 24, 2012. http://www.elijahlist.com/words/display_word/7083.

———. *When Heaven Invades Earth: A Practical Guide to a Life of Miracles.* Shippensburg, PA: Destiny Image Publishers, 2003. Kindle edition.

Johnson, Todd M., ed. *World Christian Database.* Leiden/Boston: Brill, 2013. www.worldchristiandatabase.org.

Johnson, Todd M., and Kenneth R. Ross, eds. *Atlas of Global Christianity.* Edinburgh: Edinburgh University Press, 2009.

Johnston, Philip S., ed. *The IVP Introduction to the Bible.* Downers Grove, IL: InterVarsity Press, 2006.

"Jones, Bob." Apologetics Index. Accessed February 22, 2014. http://www.apologeticsindex.org/j00.html#jones.

Jones, Bob. "God's Mercy-Naries." *The Prophetic Ministry and Resources of Bob and Bonnie Jones with Lyn Kost*. September 2012. Accessed September 2, 2014. http://bobjones.org/index.cfm?zone=/Docs/Words%20of%202012/2012--09_GodsMercyNaries.htm.

———. "Hold On to Your Dreams." The Prophetic Ministry of Bob and Bonnie Jones. September 7, 2012. Accessed February 22, 2014. http://www.bobjones.org/Docs/Words%20of%202012/2012_HoldOnToYourDreams.htm.

Jones, Peter R. "1 Corinthians 15:8: Paul the Last Apostle." *Tyndale Bulletin* 36, no. 1 (1985): 5–34.

Joyner, Rick. "Abiding in the King Produces Kingdom Authority—The Path of Life, Part 31." MorningStar Ministries. Week 38, 2012. Accessed February 23, 2014. http://www.morningstarministries.org/resources/word-week/2012/abiding-king-produces-kingdom-authority-path-life-part-31#.Uwpg0oV-6V8o.

———. *The Apostolic Ministry*. Wilkesboro, NC: MorningStar Publications, 2004.

———. *The Final Quest*. Charlotte, NC: MorningStar Publications, 1996.

———. "The Fullness of Time." *MorningStar Prophetic Bulletin, no. 73*. MorningStar Ministries. Accessed November 19, 2011. http://www.morningstarministries.org/resources/prophetic-bulletins/2012/fullness-time#.Uou-EuIoEYB.

———. *The Harvest*. Pineville, NC: MorningStar Publications, 1989.

———. "Lessons Learned from the Recent Elections—The Path of Life, Part 44." MorningStar Ministries. Week 51, 2012. Accessed February 4, 2014. http://www.morningstarministries.org/resources/word-week/2012/lessons-learned-recent-elections-path-life-part-44#.UvGRFbSmR8o.

———. "On Women and Children." Kids in Ministry International. http://kidsinministry.org/rick-joyner. Excerpt taken from *The Harvest*, by Rick Joyner. New Kensington, PA: Whitaker House, 1997.

———. "Response to *Charisma*'s Article." MorningStar Ministries. May 8, 2007. Accessed February 4, 2014. http://www.morningstarministries.org/about/questions-and-answers/response-charismas-article-rick-joyner#.UvGMJb-SmR8o.

Keener, Craig S. *Miracles: The Credibility of the New Testament Accounts*. 2 vols. Grand Rapids: Baker, 2011.

Kelly, John, and Paul Costa. *End-Time Warriors*. Ventura, CA: Regal Books, 1999.

Kids in Ministry International Facebook page. Facebook. Accessed June 6, 2014. https://www.facebook.com/kidsinministry/info.

King, Patricia. "Heavenly Oil and Gemstones in Puerto Rico!" YouTube video, 10:19. Posted by "Ftureman." January 11, 2012. Accessed February 6, 2014. http://www.youtube.com/watch?v=tpqBYpo9WkA.

Köstenberger, Andreas J. "The 'Greater Works' of the Believer according to John 14:12." *Didaskalia: The Journal of Providence College and Seminary* 6, no. 2 (Spring 1995): 36–45.

Kurschner, Alan. *Antichrist Before the Day of the Lord: What Every Christian Needs to Know About the Return of Christ.* Pompton Lakes, NJ: Eschatos Publishing, 2013.

LeClaire, Jennifer. "Prophet Bob Jones Passes Away." *Charisma News,* February 14, 2014. Accessed June 15, 2014. http://www.charismanews.com/us/42794-prophet-bob-jones-passes-away.

Lenski, R. C. H. *The Interpretation of St. Paul's Epistles to the Galatians, to the Ephesians and to the Philippians.* Minneapolis: Augsburg Publishing House, 1961.

Lugo, Luis. "Spirit and Power: A 10-Country Survey of Pentecostals." Executive Summary. Pew Forum Survey (2006). Accessed May 12, 2014. http://www.pewforum.org/2006/10/05/spirit-and-power-a-10-country-survey-of-pentecostals3/.

MacArthur, John. *Strange Fire: The Danger of Offending the Holy Spirit with Counterfeit Worship.* Nashville: Thomas Nelson, 2013. Kindle edition.

Marshall, I. Howard. "Apostle." In *New Dictionary of Theology,* edited by Sinclair B. Ferguson and David F. Wright. Master Reference Collection. Downers Grove, IL: InterVarsity Press, 1988.

Mathonnet-VanderWell, Steve. "The RCA and the NAR." *Perspectives: A Journal of Reformed Thought.* August/September 2012. Accessed February 20, 2014. http://www.rca.org/perspectives-as-we-see-it-the-rca-and-nar.

McMullen, Carey. "Florida Outpouring: Internet Draws Thousands to Lakeland Revival." *The Ledger.com.* May 18, 2008. Accessed February 20, 2014. http://www.theledger.com/article/20080518/NEWS/805180341.

"Members." Freedom Federation. Accessed February 25, 2014. http://freedomfederation.org/content/members.

Metzger, Bruce M. *The Canon of the New Testament: Its Origin, Development and Significance.* Oxford: Oxford University Press, 1987. Reprint, 2009.

Miller, Lisa. "The Newsweek 50: E. A. Adeboye." *Newsweek,* December 19, 2008. http://www.newsweek.com/newsweek-50-e-adeboye-83039.

"Minister Removed After Confession of Sexual Misconduct." *The Olathe Daily News,* November 13, 1991. Posted on *Religion News Blog.* Accessed February 4,

2014. http://www.religionnewsblog.com/16929/minister-removed-after-confession-of-sexual-misconduct.

"Ministry Assumptions." Harvest International Ministry. Accessed February 20, 2014. http://harvestim.org/index.php?a=about&s=membership&ss=ministry-assumptions.

"Mission." Bethel School of Supernatural Ministry. Accessed February 23, 2014. http://bssm.net/about/mission.

Morris, Leon. *The Gospel according to John: The English Text with Introduction, Exposition and Notes.* The New International Commentary on the New Testament. Grand Rapids: Eerdmans, 1971.

Oates, Gary. "Soaking: The Key to Intimacy with God." The Elijah List. January 9, 2012. Accessed December 5, 2013. http://www.elijahlist.com/words/display_word.html?ID=10620.

"100 Most Frequently Asked Questions About the End Times." International House of Prayer. Accessed December 3, 2013. http://www.ihopkc.org/hispano/files/2011/11/H-100-Most-Frequently-Asked-Questions-about-the-End-Times-2nd-Edit.pdf.

"Orlando Statement." *Ministries Today* (March/April 2004): 63.

Ortiz, Kelle, and Os Hillman. "Transcript of Interview of Loren Cunningham on Original 7 Mountains Vision." 7 Cultural Mountains. November 19, 2007. Accessed August 11, 2011. http://www.reclaim7mountains.com/apps/articles/default.asp?articleid=40087&columnid=4347.

Otis Jr., George, Lisa Knorr, and Michael Lienau. *Transformations: A Documentary.* Transformations Media, 1999. DVD.

"Our Purpose." The Oak Initiative. Accessed February 25, 2014. http://www.theoakinitiative.org/our-purpose#.UwzvqoV6V8o.

Pierce, Chuck, Cindy Jacobs, and Kim Clement. "Chuck Pierce, Cindy Jacobs and Kim Clement: Highways Are Buckling! His Glory and Unity Will Come!" The Elijah List. January 19, 2010. Accessed February 28, 2011. http://www.elijahlist.com/words/display_word/8407.

Pierce, Chuck, and C. Peter Wagner. "Florida Outpouring Receives Endorsements and Oversight—Includes Chuck Pierce, C. Peter Wagner, and More." The Elijah List. July 2, 2008. Accessed February 20, 2014. http://www.elijahlist.com/words/display_word/6611.

Pierce, Chuck D., and Rebecca Wagner Sytsema. *The Future War of the Church: How We Can Defeat Lawlessness and Bring God's Order to the Earth.* Ventura, CA: Regal Books, 2001.

"Premillennialism Reigns in Evangelical Theology: Evangelical Leaders Survey." National Association of Evangelicals. March 7, 2011. Accessed November 29, 2013. http://www.nae.net/resources/news/539-premillennialism-reigns-in-evangelical-theology.

"Prophetic Evangelism: Radical Faith for Miracles, Salvations, Daytime." Class taught by Virginia Stehlik at New Life Church, Colorado Springs, Colorado, May 22, 2013–August 27, 2014. Accessed June 6, 2014. http://www.newlifechurch.org/group.jsp?ID=550.

"Prophets and Personal Prophecies." Assemblies of God. Accessed August 9, 2014. http://ag.org/top/Beliefs/topics/sptlissues_prophets_prophecies.cfm.

"Purpose/Vision Statement for the Summit." Kingdom Economic Summit. Accessed February 24, 2014. http://www.kingdomeconomicsummit.com.

Rajah, Abraham S. *Apostolic and Prophetic Dictionary: Language of the End-Time Church.* Bloomington, IN: WestBow Press, 2013.

Revival Alliance website. Accessed June 6, 2014. http://revivalalliance.com.

Robertson, Josh. "Hundreds Attend Faith Healing Schools Linked to Fundamentalist Bethal [sic] Church." *Courier-Mail,* May 28, 2011. Accessed August 15, 2014. http://www.couriermail.com.au/news/queensland/hundreds-attend-faith-healing-schools-linked-to-fundamentalist-bethal-church/story-e6freoof-1226064378133.

Rosen, Rebecca. *Spirited: Unlock Your Psychic Self and Change Your Life.* New York: HarperCollins, 2010.

Salisbury, Richard, and Elizabeth Hawley. *The Himalaya by the Numbers: A Statistical Analysis of Mountaineering in the Nepal Himalaya.* Seattle, WA: Mountaineers Books, 2012.

Shorter, Kevin. "Call to Pray and Act by Chuck Colson and Jim Garlow." Prayer Couch, September 20, 2010. Accessed June 6, 2014. http://prayer-coach.com/2010/09/20/call-to-pray-and-act-by-chuck-colson-and-jim-garlow/.

Shultz, Steve. "2003 Word of the Lord—Apostolic Council of Prophetic Elders." The Elijah List. February 24, 2003. Accessed February 25, 2014. https://www.elijahlist.com/words/display_word.html?ID=1409.

Shulz, Cara. "Christian Group Directs 'Spiritual Warfare' Against Pagan Goddess." Pagan Newswire Collective-Minnesota Bureau. July 25, 2011. Accessed December 27, 2012. http://pncminnesota.com/2011/07/25/christian-group-directs-spiritual-warfare-against-pagan-goddess.

"Signs and Wonders Camp 1." International House of Prayer. Accessed February 20, 2014. http://www.ihopkc.org/signsandwonders1.

Simmons, Brian. "Song of Solomon, Part 1." *Passion for Jesus Conference.* YouTube video, 51:29. Posted by "HealingWaters." February 19, 2012. Accessed June 18, 2014. https://www.youtube.com/watch?v=H8pmNZnlzIA.

"Special Message from IHOP-KC." International House of Prayer Northwest. October 12, 2010. Accessed February 20, 2014. http://internationalhouseofpray-ernorthwest.org/special-message-from-ihop-kc.

"Spheres." Call2All. Accessed February 24, 2014. http://www.call2all.org/Groups/1000090335/call2all/About/Spheres/Spheres.aspx#.UwvdoIV6V8o.

"Stand for Right: An RPN Update." E-mail from United States Reformation Prayer Network to USRPN mailing list. June 2, 2014. http://us2.campaign-archive1.com/?u=2c8533b164a12dac690d3544f&id=0bb9d077bf&e=02548e3d54.

Stone, Sharon, and Cindy Jacobs. "Sharon Stone and Cindy Jacobs: 'Prophetic Words about the Current Economic System and Political Crisis.'" The Elijah List. September 24, 2008. Accessed January 28, 2014. https://www.elijahlist.com/words/display_word/6884.

Synan, Vinson. "2000 Years of Prophecy." In *Understanding the Fivefold Ministry*, edited by Matthew D. Green. Lake Mary, FL: Charisma House, 2005.

Tabachnick, Rachel. "Lou Engle Only One of Many of Sen. Brownback's NAR Apostle Problems." *Talk to Action.* October 17, 2010. Accessed August 15, 2014. http://www.talk2action.org/story/2010/10/17/11135/471.

———. "NAR Apostles' Brand of 'Transformation' to be Promoted at Conference at Harvard," *Talk to Action.* March 24, 2011. Accessed January 28, 2014. http://www.talk2action.org/story/2011/3/24/142629/678.

———. "New Apostolic Prayer Guide Attacks California Labor Unions, Prepares for Election 2012." *Talk to Action.* March 2012. Accessed December 17, 2013. http://www.talk2action.org/story/2012/3/1/13944/32151.

———. "Oak Initiative Confirms Resignation of Co-Founder and Vice President Samuel Rodriguez." *Talk to Action.* September 21, 2011. Accessed December 17, 2013. http://www.talk2action.org/story/2011/9/21/01935/7353.

Tashman, Brian. "Bakker and Jacobs Claim to Have Prophesied September 11th Attacks." *Right Wing Watch.* August 23, 2001. Accessed February 21, 2014. http://www.rightwingwatch.org/content/bakker-and-jacobs-claim-have-prophesied-september-11th-attacks.

———. "Newt Gingrich Names 'Apostle' Dutch Sheets to His Faith Leaders Coalition." Right Wing Watch. January 26, 2012. Accessed December 17, 2013. http://www.rightwingwatch.org/content/newt-gingrich-names-apostle-dutch-sheets-his-faith-leaders-coalition.

Thiselton, Anthony C. *The First Epistle to the Corinthians.* The New International Greek Testament Commentary. Grand Rapids: Eerdmans, 2000.

"Todd Bentley's Apostolic and Prophetic Commissioning, Part 1 of 4." YouTube video, 10:01. Posted by "Dominic Muir." June 24, 2008. Accessed February 25, 2014. http://www.youtube.com/watch?v=nVdY9ufJmz8.

Tompkins, Scott. "California Event Mobilizes New Missions Partners." *Resonate News*, November 12, 2011. Accessed June 6, 2014. http://www.resonatenews.com/home/newsheadlines/331.

Torres, Héctor. *The Restoration of the Apostles and Prophets: How It Will Revolutionize Ministry in the 21st Century.* Nashville: Thomas Nelson, 2001.

"Transform World Vision 2020." *Transform World Newsletter,* February 4, 2013. Transform-world.net. Accessed June 6, 2014. www.transform-world.net/newsletters/2013/PrayerHost.docx.

"Transformations: When God Comes to Town." YouTube video, 8:26. Posted by "Yustos Anthony." May 21, 2011. Accessed September 1, 2014. https://www.youtube.com/watch?v=nDqY29Fbu8M.

"2014 National Coalitions." International Coalition of Apostolic Leaders. Accessed December 19, 2013. http://www.coalitionofapostles.com/membership/national-coalitions/.

Vallotton, Kris. *Developing a Supernatural Lifestyle: A Practical Guide to a Life of Signs, Wonders, and Miracles.* Shippensburg, PA: Destiny Image Publishers, 2007).

———. "Your Identity as Sons of God." YouTube video, 23:52. Posted by "Whizzpopping." January 27, 2011. Accessed August 15, 2014. http://www.youtube.com/watch?v=GZtTSY889rA.

Van Horn, Charisse. "IHOP Revival Stirs Controversy, Cult or Genuine Move of God (Videos)." *Examiner.com.* April 20, 2011. Accessed February 17, 2014. http://www.examiner.com/article/ihop-revival-stirs-controversy-cult-or-genuine-move-of-god-videos.

"Video: Steve Douglas [*sic*], 'Join the Movement.'" Call2All. May 1, 2011. Accessed June 6, 2014. http://www.call2all.org/Articles/1000103667/call2all/About/E_zine_Archive/2011_Archive/0501_Video_Steve.aspx#.U5IpHSghXNt.

Virtue, Doreen. *The Lightworker's Way: Awakening Your Spiritual Power to Know and Heal.* Carlsbad, CA: Hay House, 1997.

"Voice of the Apostles 2013: Third Day." Sched. Accessed June 6, 2014. http://voiceoftheapostles2013.sched.org/artist/thirdday#.U5JJzCghXNs.

"Voice of the Apostles Conference – Orlando, Florida, August 12–16, 2013." Global Celebration. Accessed June 6, 2014. http://www.globalcelebration.com/news/370/16/Voice-of-Apostles-Conference.

von Buseck, Craig. "Revival Breaks Out at Kansas City IHOP: Spreads Via Web." *Church Watch*. Christian Broadcasting Network. November 25, 2009. Accessed August 15, 2014. http://blogs.cbn.com/ChurchWatch/archive/2009/11/25/revival-breaks-out-at-kansas-city-ihop-spreads-via-web.aspx.

Wagner, C. Peter. *Apostles Today: Biblical Government for Biblical Power*. Ventura, CA: Regal Books, 2006.

———. "Are Seminaries Making the Grade?" *Ministry Today*. Posted August 31, 2000. Accessed June 6 2014. http://ministrytodaymag.com/index.php/ministry-leadership/higher-education/536-are-seminaries-making-the-grade.

———. *Changing Church*. Ventura, CA: Regal Books, 2004.

———. *The Church in the Workplace: How God's People Can Transform Society*. Ventura, CA: Regal Books, 2006.

———. *Churchquake! How the New Apostolic Reformation Is Shaking Up the Church as We Know It*. Ventura, CA: Regal Books, 1999.

———. "The Doc Responds." *Ministry Today* (n.d.). Accessed December 19, 2013. http://ministrytodaymag.com/index.php/ministry-today-archives/152-fivefold-ministries/10011-the-doc-responds#sthash.WuwTabNB.dpuf.

———. *Dominion! How Kingdom Action Can Change the World*. Grand Rapids: Chosen Books, 2008.

———. "The New Apostolic Reformation." *Renewal Journal* 15 (April 12, 2012). Accessed August 15, 2014. https://renewaljournal.wordpress.com/2012/04/12/the-new-apostolic-reformation-byc-peter-wagner/. Originally published as chapter 14 of *The Transforming Power of Revival: Prophetic Strategies into the Twenty-first Century*, edited by Harold Caballeros and Mel Winger. N.p.: Peniel, 1998.

———. "The New Apostolic Reformation Is Not a Cult." *Charisma News*, August 24, 2011. Accessed June 6, 2014. http://www.charismanews.com/opinion/31851-the-new-apostolic-reformation-is-not-a-cult.

———. "The Power to Heal the Past." *Renewal Journal*, July 28, 2011. Accessed February 24, 2014. http://renewaljournal.wordpress.com/2011/07/18/the-power-to-heal-the-past-by-c-peter-wagner.

———. *Spheres of Authority: Apostles in Today's Church*. Colorado Springs, CO: Wagner Publications, 2002.

———. *Your Spiritual Gifts Can Help Your Church Grow.* 15th Anniversary Edition. Ventura, CA: Regal, 1994, c1979.

———. *Warfare Prayer: What the Bible Says about Spiritual Warfare.* Shippensburg, PA: Destiny Image Publishers, 2009.

———. *What the Bible Says about Spiritual Warfare.* Ventura, CA: Regal Books, 2001.

———. *Wrestling with Alligators, Prophets and Theologians: Lessons from a Lifetime in the Church—A Memoir.* Ventura, CA: Regal Books, 2010.

Wagner, C. Peter, Cindy Jacobs, et al. "Word of the Lord for 2007—Released through the Apostolic Council of Prophetic Elders." The Elijah List. November 1, 2006. Accessed February 25, 2014. http://www.elijahlist.com/words/display_word/4655.

Wallace, Daniel B., and M. James Sawyer, eds. *Who's Afraid of the Holy Spirit? An Investigation into the Ministry of the Spirit of God Today.* Dallas: Biblical Studies Press, 2005.

Waltke, Bruce K., and Charles Yu. *An Old Testament Theology: An Exegetical, Canonical, and Thematic Approach.* Grand Rapids: Zondervan, 2007.

Warfield, B. B. *Counterfeit Miracles.* New York: Charles Scribner's Sons, 1918. Reprint, Edinburgh, Scotland: Banner of Truth, 1982.

Warnock, George H. *The Feast of Tabernacles.* N.p.: The Church in Action, 1951. Reprint, 1980. Kindle edition.

"What is a PowerClub?" Kids in Ministry International. Accessed February 25, 2014. http://kidsinministry.org/what-is-a-powerclub.

"What Is the Prayer Room?" International House of Prayer. Accessed August 15, 2014. http://www.ihopkc.org/prayerroom.

"What the Prophets Are Saying about Kids." Kids in Ministry International. Accessed February 20, 2014. https://kidsinministry.org/what-the-prophets-are-saying-about-kids.

"Why the Name Change?" European Coalition of Apostolic Leaders. November 16, 2013. Accessed December 27, 2013. http://ecaleaders.eu/maler/convenors-blog/article/329181.

Willard, Dallas. *Knowing Christ Today: Why We Can Trust Spiritual Knowledge.* New York: HarperCollins, 2009.

"William Branham (1909–1965)." Apologetics Index. Accessed August 15, 2014. http://www.apologeticsindex.org/b05.html#note1.

Wilson, Bruce. "YouTube Censors Viral Video Documentary on Palin's Churches." *Talk to Action.* September 13, 2008. Accessed February 24, 2014. http://www.talk2action.org/story/2008/9/13/1538/09770.

Wilson, D. J. "William Marion Branham." In *The New International Dictionary of Pentecostal and Charismatic Movements,* edited by Stanley M. Burgess. Grand Rapids: Zondervan, 2002.

Wimber, John. Letter to Vineyard Church Pastors. November 7, 1991. In the authors' possession.

"A Word from John P. Kelly, Convening Apostle." International Coalition of Apostolic Leaders. Accessed February 20, 2014. http://www.coalitionofapostles.com.

Wyler, Grace. "Meet the Radical Evangelical Army Behind Rick Perry." *Business Insider,* July 21, 2011. Accessed December 17, 2013. http://www.businessinsider.com/rick-perry-the-evangelicals-behind-the-response-2011-7-21?op=1#ixzz2nlgGO600.

Name Index

Subject Index

abortion, *27, 98*

abusive leadership, *82*

academia, NAR in, *23–24*

accountability, for apostles, *82*

accuracy, of prophets, *114–15*

AD2000 and Beyond, *157*

African Independent Churches
movement, *3*

Agabus, *124, 125, 126*

Ahijah the Shilonite, *121*

Almolonga, Guatemala, *174–75*

ambassadorial apostles, *44*

American Association of Christian
Counselors, *17*

amillennialism, *151*

Anna, *124*

ancestry test (prophets), 147

Andronicus, *67–68*

Apollyon, *162*

apostles

  accountability of, *40*

  authority of, *36–42, 47–50*

  casting out territorial spirits, *153*

  categories of, *42–44*

  definition of, *31–32*

  flexible range of meaning, *68, 78*

  formal vs. functional, *71–72*

  as limited, temporal office, *51–55*

  as missionaries and church
    planters, *31*

  New Testament definition of, *56*

  as present-day office, *3, 8, 31–32,
    34–44, 53–54, 118*

apostles of Christ, *33–34, 72–73, 78,
  83, 85, 87, 124n12, 147n21. See also
  formal apostles*

apostles of the churches, *34, 72–73,
  74, 75, 79. See also functional
  apostles*

Apostolic Church (early 1900s), 3

Apostolic Council of Prophetic Elders
  (ACPE), 44, 96n1, 97, 214–16

apostolic covering, *39*

apostolic decrees, *209–11*

Apostolic movement, *112*

Apostolic Network of Global
  Awakening, *11*

apostolic networks, *39–40, 82,
  175–76*

"apostolic overlap", *84*

apostolic-prophetic movement, *1n1*

apostolic succession, *2n4, 47n7*

apostolic team members, *43*

apostolic unity, *173–80*

Arkansas Apostolic Prayer
  Network, *217*

Arminianism, *177*

Army of the Lord Movement, *112*

ascension gifts, *51*

Asherah, prophets of, *127*

Assemblies of God, *11, 100–101, 197*

Australian Coalition of Apostles, *214*

authority, abuse of, *40*

Scripture Index

New Testament